A REVEALING HISTORY
of the WORLD'S
OLDEST PROFESSION

WHORE STORIES

TYLER STODDARD SMITH

AVON, MASSACHUSETTS

DEDICATION

To Mom and Dad, for everything

Published by
Adams Media, a division of F+W Media, Inc.
57 Littlefield Street, Avon, MA 02322. U.S.A.
www.adamsmedia.com

ISBN 10: 1-4405-3605-8
ISBN 13: 978-1-4405-3605-2
eISBN 10: 1-4405-3853-0
eISBN 13: 978-1-4405-3853-7

Printed in the United States of America.

10 9 8 7 6 5 4 3 2 1

All information in this book is based upon extensive research of print and online resources, news interviews and reports, and (in some cases) existing published biographies. The author has taken great care in making every effort to corroborate the information and facts herein with primary source material and has provided extensive bibliographical information. The author and publisher hereby disclaim any liability or responsibility of any nature whatsoever for any erroneous information contained within such primary source materials.

Many of the designations used by manufacturers and sellers to distinguish their product are claimed as trademarks. Where those designations appear in this book and Adams Media was aware of a trademark claim, the designations have been printed with initial capital letters.

Interior illustration 123rf © Anja Kaiser

This book is available at quantity discounts for bulk purchases.
For information, please call 1-800-289-0963.

CONTENTS

"Morals are too often diagnostic of prostatitis and stomach ulcers."
—John Steinbeck, *The Log from the Sea of Cortez*

INTRODUCTION

When I was a small child, I was prone to insomnia and fits of the night terrors. To get me to fall asleep, my mother and father would fasten me into our family's 1971 Toyota Carina, throw in an eight-track cassette of Anne Murray's *Greatest Hits* and drive up and down South Main Street in Houston, Texas, to look at the prostitutes. The blinking neon signs of the no-tell motels, the bling of streetwalkers working their finery, and the day-glo hues of their billowing lingerie were too much stimulation even for a toddler; I would finally shut my eyes and stop struggling against the seat belt while "Shadows in the Moonlight" and the South Main ho stroll played on. I nodded off to sleep not only with visions of sugar plum fairies, but also of leather-clad fairies, common harlots, desperate dope fiends, glamorous go-girls, and rowdy rent-boys all gyrating in my little head.

It wasn't *my* idea to expose me to a life on the street like that, but back in the 1980s, you had to get out of your house to experience life and love and also to look at prostitutes. Today you can just go to some live-stream dung dungeon and e-jaculate along with the rest of the blundering online nymphos to stuff you're not even creative enough to imagine, or ask for.

Since then, I've visited prostitutes from Nuevo Laredo to Amsterdam, Hamburg to Tokyo, and Las Vegas to Havana, and one thing never changes: People are too quick to make assumptions about what "visiting" means. Where I'm from, "visiting" can mean anything from "talking and catching up with folk" to "setting fire to a miniature pony," although

I haven't heard it used that way in ages. The point is, I miss the calming effect provided by those idealized streetwalkers of my youth.

What? You're not buying the nostalgic "visiting whores put me to sleep as a child" excuse for writing a hooker book? The lecherous lullaby ride not convincing enough? That was a 100 percent true story, but here's a more recent and possibly more accurate illustration of why I came to write *Whore Stories*, documented in an IM exchange last year between me and my agent, Jon Sternfeld. At the time, I was working on some leading-edge inventions, which is something I do when I am lonely and unemployed.

TSS: what's the worst thing about europe?
JS: I don't know. France?
TSS: making love in small cars.
JS: so?
TSS: kids keep having sex in those little "Smart" cars—I've seen it myself—and I think it spells future spinal trouble.
TSS: you there?
JS: yes.
TSS: So i've invented a car wash where you rent a limo with your manfriend or ladyfriend and it's in a big limo—plenty of room. and palliative oils. it'll be cheap. good tunes, too.
JS: A car-wash whorehouse?
TSS: a drive-thru love station with rain.
JS: hey, that's something—you should write something about whores.

And so I did.

If you are offended that the politically correct term "sex worker" is not used to describe the characters in this book, I apologize. But then *you* try to write a book called *Sex Worker Stories!* See, even with the exclamation point, *Sex Worker Stories!* sounds more like a serialized bodice-ripper involving one nurse tech's search for true love in a haunted sperm bank. Aside from the common term used in the title, the words slut, harlot, trick, chickenhawk, rent-boy, trollop, prossy, hooker, gigolo, etc. are used liberally within. What can I say? The lexicon of love is a bountiful trove.

Selective word choice aside, the biographical material in *Whore Stories* is essentially accurate, providing you, dear reader, with an informative, entertaining, and revealing look at the men and women who have blazed the bawdy trail of prostitution since the dawn of time. Some of these people have become legends for turning tricks, like Xaviera "The Happy Hooker" Hollander, La Belle Otero, and the self-proclaimed "Rosa Parks" of male prostitution, Markus Bestin. Others have traded sex for money at some point in their lives, and then became famous for other reasons, like Al Pacino, Malcolm X, Former First Lady Nancy Reagan, and Valerie Solanas (she shot Andy Warhol). Still others have turned into man-eating spiders, like the Japanese whore-deity Jorogumo. And finally there are people who have no real claim to Fame: They are just intriguing individuals who happen to have been hookers.

The aim of this book, then, is a simple one: to look into some of the shadier corners of human history, and to shed a little light on an eternally compelling figure: the prostitute. And if you're thinking of asking me any more questions about my "field research," then making the international sign for "doing it," I'll tell you the same thing I told my agent: Cut it out, pervert. This is a historical document.

TSS

Chapter I

BORN TO WHORE

Do you believe in destiny? I don't, especially when good things happen to people I hate. Then again, when good things happen to people I love, I usually end up hating them for their success in the long run anyway. So maybe *that's* destiny.

It is perhaps a stretch to say that someone or another was truly "born to whore." And while I believe that my neighbor Sarah was born to be wild (you can tell by the way she throws knives at the mailman), it's probably selling many of these born whores short to say all they have to offer is their bodies. In fact, Madame de Pompadour, one of the most renowned prostitutes of all time, was known more for the brilliance that came out of her mouth than the unmentionables that went into it. The men and women that follow probably did (or will do) some other interesting things with their lives. But in the end, we're going to remember these naturals for how they played on the field of prostitution. Either way, these prominent prossies deserve a chapter of their own, and here it is.

LAO AI

PROFILE

DAY JOB: Fraudulent eunuch

CLAIM TO FAME: Personal ho-go stick to the Empress Dowager

THEATER OF OPERATIONS: China in the Third Century B.C.

In imperial China's most famous history book, *Records of the Grand Historian* (or *Shiji*), we're told of a man named Lao Ai who had an enormous penis. The Grand Historian, an academic named Sima Qian, has the following story on good authority. As the *Shiji* tells it, Lü Buwei, a chancellor and regent for the Qin government (and illegitimate father to the boy who would become China's notorious First Emperor), needs to find an impressive set of sex organs that he can keep on retainer and offer up to the Empress Dowager to keep her happy in his absence. He finds this "prodigious penis" in the person of Lao Ai, whom Lü presumably ran into at a hot springs or a truck stop. The *Shiji* goes on to explain:

> At times [Lü Buwei] would indulge in song and music, making Lao
> Ai dance around with his penis stuck through a wheel of tong wood.
> He arranged for the Empress Dowager to hear about this, in order to
> entice her. When the Empress Dowager heard, as expected, she . . .
> covertly gave a generous bribe to the officer charged with castrations
> to falsely sentence him and to pluck out his eyebrows and beard to
> make him appear a eunuch. As a result, he was made a servant of the
> queen dowager.

We're not sure how Lao Ai felt about this career change, but he was most likely a member of the peasantry, so almost anything was better than rice farming and slaving around with a slop bucket while festooned in manure. He was also "rewarded with very rich gifts" and eventually, "all the affairs [in the royal house] were decided by Lao Ai."

Unfortunately, all this attention and fame went to Lao Ai's head and his lack of humility angered the emperor.

Once the emperor-to-be heard that Lao Ai was an obnoxious talking penis and not really a eunuch, and that he was banging his own mom, he lost patience with Lao and the Dowager, exiling the Empress, executing Lao by having him torn apart with horse-drawn carriages, throwing Lao's two children into sacks and beating them to gore, and exterminating three generations of Lao's relatives. But, the name "Lao Ai" has lived on for centuries, synonymous in China for anything to do with fornication and penises—and the actual Lao Ai, I suppose, whenever his name comes up in bar trivia.

VALERIA MESSALINA

PROFILE

DAY JOB: Roman empress

CLAIM TO FAME: Threw some of Rome's most off-the-hook orgies; insatiable sex-hen

THEATER OF OPERATIONS: First-century Rome

The problem with royal inbreeding is that, with a long enough timeline, you're going to have an increase in poor decision making and a decrease in your regal comeliness. But that doesn't mean you can't still party your jugs off. And that's exactly what Valeria Messalina, third wife and second cousin of the Roman Emperor Claudius (of *I, Claudius* fame) did.

The year was 38 B.C. There was lots going on in the world, but a girl gets bored just farting around the building site for a new "Colosseum," where, according to the press releases, nude dudes will be chased around and around by tigers. Yawn. If you're Valeria Messalina, however, you hook up with Caligula and enjoy his legendary orgies until the civil engineers can get their act together. Time passes and life is good.

But then, by some labyrinthine turn of events that included political posturing, elaborate bloodline calculations, and arcane Roman pro-
tocols, Messalina and Claudius were married. They were a budding
power couple, even though Claudius was kind of gimpy and given to
drooling. Messalina quickly produced two children, both of whom bore
an uncanny resemblance to Caligula. Claudius remained clueless, but
after Caligula's murder, the historically well-lubricated gears of the
Roman orgy scene ground to a halt. Claudius was a new and different
kind of emperor.

But this is not some PBS special, so let's get back to the orgies and
the toga parties. Have a look at Juvenal's poem about Valeria's clandes-
tine easy riding while her spazzed-out husband snores and slobbers in
his sleep:

> Having concealed her raven locks under a light-colored peruke, she
> took her place in a brothel . . . under the feigned name of Lycisca, her
> nipples bare and gilded . . . she graciously received all comers, asking
> from each his fee. . . Then . . . she took back to the imperial pillow all
> the odors of the stews.

This kind of thing would be tantamount to ex-Italian Premier Silvio
Berlusconi's wife, actress Veronica Lario, creeping out of the Palazzo
Grazioli master bedroom in a blonde wig with Goldschläger bottle caps
affixed to her nipples, and hitting the street using the provocative moniker, "She-Wolf." Back in Claudius's time, you didn't have the *politi-
razzi* snapping photos of your night moves, so Valeria did all she could
to make her sexcapades common knowledge. At one point she even
engaged in a public sex battle (like a rap battle, but with less rhyming
and more pubic hair) with a prostitute to see who could service the most
men in one day. Winner: Valeria.

It was, alas, her insatiable sexual appetite that got her killed. When
Claudius learned that Valeria had not only married his political rival,
Silius, but also consummated their union before a large live crowd of
sex-show enthusiasts, he had no choice but to have her head removed.
Silius's, too, because *c'mon*, man.

SHAI SHAHAR

PROFILE

DAY JOBS: U.S. Armed Services; struggling actor; amateur psychologist

CLAIM TO FAME: Live sex show trailblazer

THEATER OF OPERATIONS: Israel, Amsterdam

Before Shai Shahar became one of the modern era's most famous gigolos, he was visited by the specter of his rabbi. "Never complain about your destiny until you know what it is," said the rabbi, leading Mr. Shahar headlong into whoring himself.

Indeed, Shai Shahar has the distinction of being the first male ever to exhibit himself in one of the flesh-market window displays of Amsterdam's famous red-light district. Innovation is the key to success, but it doesn't hurt to keep an ear open for prescient rabbis speaking from the grave.

Born in Washington, D.C., in 1954, Shai Shahar joined the United States Army for a tour of duty, then emigrated to Israel in 1980, where he found a wife, had a daughter, and did some more soldiering in the Israeli Defense Forces (IDF) until the aforementioned magic rabbi entreated with him to move to Holland, where his dreary destiny might float away, like panties in the wind. And, sure enough, it did.

Shahar's career lasted over a decade, an eternity in whore years, and his clientele included royalty, housewives, politicians, starlets, and pretty much everyone in between. His fee was an impressive $1,000+ per night. In an interview with *Heeb* magazine, Shahar explained the secrets behind his amorous expertise:

> I learned everything I know from reading sex magazines when I was young. I later graduated into watching porn films and practicing with girlfriends. I was 35 when I started, so I came to the job with a fair degree of life and love experience.

Sex magazines? You don't get the strongest gigolo gig around look-ing at *Swank* all day. So what *was* Shahar's trick, so to speak? How did the man have so much game? As he told it:

> The game is a simple thumbnail psychology ditty that has one describe her favorite color, favorite animal, how it feels to be in water, lots of water . . . and how it feels to be in a white-room with no doors.

It seems a fool's errand to try and recommend this technique to anyone not looking to get about-faced by a petrified "customer." And what exactly is a psychological ditty? *Only the Good Die Jung*? We can only speculate.

A one-of-a-kind creature in the world of whoredom, Shahar got out of the gigolo game after amassing a small fortune. He reached the ne plus ultra of high-profile sex vocations when he starred as half of a live-sex duo at Amsterdam's noted Casa Rosso and Moulin Rouge Theaters—a cushy gig, almost like a Siegfried and Roy extravaganza of sex. Shahar hung up his he-whore act a number of years ago, but it seems the rabbi may be urging him on to greater things, as he explains that his fantasy is to appear on Broadway in *Guys and Dolls*.

BLANCHE DUMAS

PROFILE

DAY JOB: Sideshow attraction

CLAIM TO FAME: "The Three-Legged Courtesan"

THEATER OF OPERATIONS: Martinique; Paris

Here's a variation on the Riddle of the Sphinx: What has three legs, four breasts, two vaginas, and a voracious sexual appetite that can only be satisfied by a Portuguese man with three legs, twenty-eight toes, three

testicles, two penises, and is so randy that, according to the photographer C. D. Fredericks, the mere "sight of a female is sufficient to excite
his amorous propensities," a man who "functionates with both of the
penes, finishing with one, then continu[ing] with the other"?

Answer You Probably Thought: A newspaper

Correct Answer: Blanche Dumas, the "Three-Legged Courtesan"

Blanche Dumas was born in the French colony of Martinique in
1860 to parents of "normal" physical appearance. Examined by doctors and documented in the Anomalies and Curiosities of Medicine, a
twenty-five-year-old Blanche is described as having:

> a modified duplication of the lower body. There was a third leg attached
> to a continuation of the processus coccygeus of the sacrum. . . . There
> were two vaginæ and two well-developed vulvæ, both having equally
> developed sensations. The sexual appetite was markedly developed,
> and coitus was practised in both vaginæ.

There comes a time in a person's life when he or she must evaluate
his or her assets, take stock of what really matters, and make a move. For
Blanche, that move was to Paris, where she made a handsome living as a
courtesan and served as a refreshing novelty for the more curious-minded
sex-seeker. Unfortunately, Blanche's sexual desires were still left unful-
filled. It was a dark and disappointing time for a three-legged, multivagi-
naed working girl from the colonies. But wait! Here comes Juan Baptista
dos Santos, the only man on the planet capable of satisfying her rabid
lust, and vice-versa. Baptista dos Santos was not as profligate with his talent (two penises, both locked, loaded, and ready to party), often turning
down great sums of money to display his double trouble.

But upon hearing dos Santos was passing through Paris, Blanche
made contact and the two developed a special connection, their post-
coital triage no doubt resembling a garage sale of helixed genitalia and
assorted anatomical oddities. In the end, Dumas and dos Santos appear
to have lived happily ever after, with Dumas saying goodbye to the courtesan life and dos Santos saying hello to the kind of gnarly and bone-
breaking sex life I once imagined when I ate the bad acid.

XAVIERA HOLLANDER

PROFILE

DAY JOB: Secretary, Dutch Consulate

CLAIM TO FAME: Authoring one of the most successful memoirs in history, *The Happy Hooker;* legendary NYC madam; gave new meaning to the expression "doggy-style."

THEATER OF OPERATIONS: Manhattan

It's a rare thing for the sex industry to produce a "fairy tale" scenario that doesn't involve a trick towel and a hefty credit card bill. So let's get acquainted with Xaviera Hollander, otherwise known as "The Happy Hooker." Unlike so many unfortunate souls who've sold their bodies to the night, Ms. Hollander has come out of the whole affair unscathed. Rather, the ex-prostitute and madam is now a millionaire memoirist and business tycoon whose musings and advice have appeared in the *Penthouse* column "Call Me Madam" for more than thirty years.

Born Vera de Vries in 1943 in what is now Indonesia, Hollander once held the dubious distinction of being selected "Miss Tick" (better known as "Holland's Greatest Secretary") before moving to New York and starting one of the most successful brothels the city has ever known, "The Vertical Whorehouse."

The "Vertical Whorehouse," which Hollander operated from 1969 to 1971, was located in a high-rise at Seventy-Third Street and York Avenue in Manhattan, and advertised un-ironically in the *New York Times* real estate section as having "the ultimate in services and conveniences," canine companions notwithstanding.

In a Pygmalionian career arc that took her from serving as a lowly secretary at the Dutch consulate to reigning as the Big Apple's most sought-after madam in a matter of a few years, Hollander raised a few eyebrows, along with other assorted body parts, even among FBI agents and local law enforcement charged with bringing her down. This kind of thing doesn't look good, so authorities came and shut down the Vertical Whorehouse for good. The Happy Hooker was promptly booted out of the country to relocate in Toronto.

But, not all Hollander's brilliance proved to be along the x-axis. Her landmark 1972 memoir, *The Happy Hooker: My Own Story*, launched this prostitute into the cultural stratosphere. With a genital warts-and-all attitude toward discussing her experiences in the sex trade, *The Happy Hooker* went on to become an international bestseller and the only memoir on the list where the protagonist copulates with a German shepherd during a sojourn in South Africa. "I'd be a moral fraud if I ignored it," she noted with no apparent sense of irony.

Today, with numerous bestsellers to her name, a client list for the ages, and a couple of quaint B&Bs in Amsterdam and Marbella, the Happy Hooker is still living the high life. . . . HEY! You still there? It's okay—nobody blames you—we're all still thinking about the German shepherd, too.

MADAME DE POMPADOUR

PROFILE

DAY JOB: Bourgeois loafer

CLAIM TO FAME: Mistress of Louis XV

THEATER OF OPERATIONS: Versailles, France (eighteenth century)

Jeanne Antoinette-Poisson was born in 1721 in Paris and died forty-two years later as Madame de Pompadour, the most-favored mistress of King Louis XV and European trend-setter/courtesan extraordinaire. Upon her death, the Enlightenment bigwig, Voltaire, mourned her loss, writing, "I was indebted to her and I mourn her out of gratitude." I'm so sure, Voltaire. Your "gratitude" no doubt comes from not having to shell out for that last fellatio fête, which must have been a frustrating disappointment since the literature indicates Madame de Pompadour wasn't particularly adept or interesting in the sack. Novelist and public intellectual, Robertson Davies, writes:

> Pompadour was not a physically ardent woman, and love-making tired her. After about eight years of their association Louis XV did not sleep with her. . . . But it was to Pompadour that he talked, and it was to Pompadour that he listened.

Even though some French snoots were disgusted with the king for taking a commoner with a new-wave hair do for his mistress, Madame de Pompadour, an intrepid self-promoter and working girl, eventually won the country over, and then she helped plunge France into the Seven Years' War and bankruptcy.

While Louis XV was a handsome chap before smallpox transformed him into an oozing black scab in tights, it only takes a few genetic missteps before you wind up with alarming mutants like Louis's grandson, Louis XVI, whom Lillian C. Smythe, the editor of the letters written by Comte de Mercy, Austrian ambassador to the court of Versailles, describes as a *"waddling, blinking, corpulent, bungling, incapable imbecile."*

Join us next week for "Dueling Banjos, Dueling Bourbons: A Homely History of the French Monarchy."

When young Jeanne was only nine, her mother took her to a fortune teller, who in a moment of uncharacteristic prescience for a soothsayer told the young Jeanne and her mother that someday Jeanne would serve as mistress to the king. Maybe you're like me: The last time I went to a tarot reader, she told me I smelled like too much wine and gave me "predictions" about the best way to get back on the uptown express. Sure enough, I found my way back uptown, and Madame de Pompadour became a king's mistress, but I sense that we were the lucky ones.

After the obligatory stop at a nunnery, the gorgeous Jeanne was married off at the age of nineteen to a financier named Charles-Guillame d'Étiolles. She produced a few children, but showed no signs of settling down. She hung out with royalty, networked—*owned* it. And finally, after finagling an invitation to one of the many costume balls at the Palace of Versailles (where King Louis XV came dressed as some shrubs), Jeanne and the king got to talking, and before you know it the two were appearing together frequently. I should mention that during this scandalous courtship, France was at war with Austria. It's just like the French to embrace a leader dressed up like a red-tipped photinia and carrying on with a prostitute when there's a war on.

Madame de Pompadour eventually became heavily involved with domestic and foreign affairs—any kind of affair one could imagine, really. She even managed to befriend that pesky nuisance, the queen. The French people seemed to have a love-hate relationship with Pompadour: They loved her fashion sense, which set the bar for many ladies of the Enlightenment era. However, as is so often the case with celebrity, fame also inspired haters. In a dirty little ditty composed by one Comte de Maurepas, the newly minted Madame de Pompadour (Louis XV procured the title for her) was said to be afflicted with *"fleurs blanches,"* or white flowers:

By your noble and free manner,
Iris, you enchant our hearts.
On our path you strew flowers.
But they are white flowers.

It doesn't sound very vile, but if you were an even remotely tapped-in and rococo Frenchman back then, you'd have grasped the significance of the white flowers. No, the Comte is not talking about daises, but a vaginal discharge with a bouquet common to courtesans. They exiled the Comte for being an idiot and Madame de Pompadour deflected the blow, as she always did. In fact, she went on to become one of the world's most recognized names in the fine arts of seduction, solipsism, and sex work.

THE SPANISH BARBARA

PROFILE

DAY JOB: Fantasy fit rent-boy

CLAIM TO FAME: Proudly enduring a humiliating execution under the Borgias

THEATER OF OPERATIONS: Fifteenth-century Rome

Nobody knows from when or where the Spanish Barbara hailed. One can assume that "Spain" would be a safe guess, but in Borgia Rome, things were ass backward. With a regime that bore more resemblance to a donkey show than a papacy, the Borgias spent many afternoons having enemies of the church burned at the stake all over town, in between sundry orgies and flesh buffets. Luckily for us, a social climbing Alsatian named Johann Burchard was a first-rate chronicler of the era, and provides whorestorians with a trove of haunting anecdotes that illustrate the unspeakable cruelty committed by the papacy. In 1498, Burchard records a harrowing tale of one pioneering transvestite prostitute who stood excruciatingly nude before the draconian Borgia despots.

The whore in question was indeed "The Spanish Barbara," and his hellish fate is one Abraham Lincoln might have attributed to something he never called, "the shittier angels of our nature." The following is from Burchard's *Liber Notarum*, his exhaustive diary recounting the Borgias's daily debaucheries:

An honest prostitute, named Cursetta, had been thrown into prison because she had a Moor as a friend who went around in women's

clothing under the name of the Spanish Barbara. . . . As a punishment
for this outrage, [they] were led around together through the city . . .
the Moor in a woman's dress . . . in order that everybody might see his
private parts and recognize the fraud he had perpetrated.

Can you imagine the daring, the unbridled nerve it would take to be
a black tranny prostitute in Borgia Rome? Neither can I. And I also can't
believe that the Spanish Barbara's client list wasn't already aware of the
"fraud" he had perpetrated. You can just see it:

"Hey, Vito! Do you remember Barbara, that smoking hot Spanish
prostitute? Yeah, the one with the penis. Well, you're never going to
believe this—I saw him/her burned at the stake today and guess what?
She's actually a black African *man*. What do you mean 'how didn't I
know?'"

In another tremendous entry to his *Liber Notarum*, Burchard describes an
orgy that's referred to affectionately as "The Dance of the Chestnuts,"
and reveals the scope of indulgences (of all variety) going down on a
typical Sunday night at the Borgia's apostolic palace: "Chestnuts [were]
strewn about, which the prostitutes, naked and on their hands and
knees, had to pick up as they crawled in and out amongst the lamp-
stands. Finally, prizes were offered—silken doublets, pairs of shoes, hats
and other garments—for those men who were most successful with the
prostitutes."

Damn. Some popes have all the fun.

It's awfully curious how one can become inured to violence and torture. Take Guantanamo Bay, Torquemada, and Houston Astros baseball.
People come to expect the lowest common denominator, and Burchard
was no different. His depiction of the following horrors committed
against the Spanish Barbara and his fellows is almost clinical:

The Moor was put in prison, and finally led . . . together with two other brigands with a Sbirre [a Roman policeman] riding before them on an ass carrying on the point of a stick two testicles, which had been cut out from a Jew because he had had intercourse with a Christian woman. . . . The Moor was placed on a pile of wood, and was killed on the pole of the gallows. . . . Then the pile was lighted, but on account of a downpour of rain it did not burn well and only his legs were charred.

Are you fucking kidding me? Somewhere, there should be a monument to the memory of the Spanish Barbara, an enduring reminder of the suffering and revolutionary spirit exhibited by one of history's great iconoclasts. Well, that somewhere is my kitchen, and that monument is gradually emerging from these mashed potatoes in front of me, which I am sculpting to create an effigy of the Moorish transvestite prostitute at the gallows.

I apologize. I hadn't anticipated that my inurement to violence and torture would kick in so soon. If it makes you feel any better, I've eaten mashed potato Spanish Barbara and will strongly consider writing a letter to Rome to see about a real statue, assuming I'm not too inured to sloth to do so.

MILLY COOPER

PROFILE

DAY JOBS: Prostitution, *éminence grise*

CLAIM TO FAME: The oldest whore alive

THEATER OF OPERATIONS: London; Las Vegas

"Life," wrote William Butler Yeats, "moves out of a red flare of dreams into a common light of common hours, until old age bring the red flare again." And sometimes, old age bring not only the red flare again, but the red *light* again. In 2011, the *Daily Mail* reported that ninety-six-year-old Milly Cooper was still making around $80,000 a year working as a prostitute.

Well, go ahead and laugh, but Ms. Cooper's slow thighs still command top dollar for those of us slouching toward Bethlehem heavy into old-school, or just kind of curious about what it would be like to have sex with a person born prior to Prohibition. But Cooper's tale is far from over and one that begins on the other side of the Atlantic.

> *"In America you can get away with murder, but not with sex."*
> —Xaviera Hollander

A scrappy woman from London's East End, Milly Cooper met a wealthy American man who soon translated her to Las Vegas, where she found work as a showgirl. The happy couple had a child together, but then in 1945, her beau was killed in action during World War II, leaving Cooper destitute and stuck in Vegas. There are a frustratingly finite number of activities one can do to scrape by in Vegas, and the easiest is probably rolling drunks or selling dope. After that, the allure and convenience of call-girling probably seemed like the next logical step for an Englishwoman in the sexual slot machine that was postwar Sin City.

What makes Cooper's career so remarkable is the fact that it has endured for so unbelievably long. Despite what must have been a stultifying whoring hiatus while married to an accountant from 1955 to 1979, Cooper eased back into the game and has been going strong ever since. Today, Cooper meets with her clients twice a week (sessions run around $1,250), a robust business for any nonagenarian, especially one who opts for boingo over bingo. Cooper claims to have serviced over 3,500 satisfied customers whose ages run the generational gamut, with Johns ranging from 29 to 92. Of course, Cooper does have some harsh venom to spit about the direction the business has taken over the past century. In particular, the competition today disgusts her. According to Ms. Cooper:

Nowadays, the girls have vast boobs and skinny bodies and parade around half-naked. In my day, we would call those girls "trollops." The industry's become mucky. At least I am maintaining standards. I always dress elegantly and my clients are gentlemen.

Prostitutes today! There was once a time when America had some dignity.

THE PAINTED WOMEN

PROFILE

DAY JOBS: Prostitution, mostly

CLAIM TO FAME: Models and muses to some of the great art and artists of all time

THEATER OF OPERATIONS: Spain; France; most of Europe

If it weren't for prostitutes, we'd be deprived of some of our most cherished artwork. Perhaps it is the prostitutes' willingness to appear nude for long periods of time that make them such popular canvas characters for artists. Whatever the reason, our art history illustrates a long-standing affair between many of our most celebrated painters and their sultry, street-jiving subjects. It's high time we meet some:

Rosa La Rouge

The ginger-headed Rosa was the favorite model of Toulouse-Lautrec. Rosa is the prostitute who is pictured in Toulouse-Lautrec's haunting *À Montrouge* (1886–87). She stands in a doorway with a menacing countenance of curiosity—or is it disgust? It could be disgust over the fact that she was asked to keep her clothes on for *À Montrouge*. Or, she could be curious as to whether or not she'd given Toulouse-Lautrec syphilis, which she had.

Victorine Meurent

There remains great debate as to whether or not the model for many of impressionist painter Edouard Manet's masterworks was a prostitute. For many years, the subject of Manet's universally known *Olympia* and *Le déjeuner sur l'herbe* was said to have ended up shit-faced in a brothel, dying young of the syphilis that would afflict Manet. In the end, it was discovered that Victorine was an accomplished painter in her own right—her work was accepted to the Paris salon in 1876, a year when Manet failed to make the cut. How do we account for this sin of omission? Sexism, mostly. God forbid a *coquette* knows her way around anything more artful than a cock. I'd like to see *you* try and make a living as an eighteen-year-old female painter in Paris in the 1860s without pawning your parts. Trust me, it's near to impossible, no matter what knowledge and equipment you've brought from the future.

The Young Ladies of Avignon

While it's disconcerting how one young lady's vagina is creeping up and seems to be eating her belly button, not to mention the rhombus nose located on another demoiselle's knee and the ominous googley eyes of them all, staring at us like a Euclidian train wreck, this piece remains a masterpiece of modern whore art. In Picasso's legendary *Les Demoiselles d'Avignon* the ladies of the night are actually pretty sexy, although the *racoleuses* do carry eyes too wise for young women, and one in particular appears to have a hair weave. Sometimes considered the seminal work that pushed the art world into "modernism," according to noted art critic John Berger, *Les Demoiselles d'Avignon* continues to endure because of its "shock" value. Berger writes in *The Success and Failure of Picasso* that:

> A brothel may not in itself be shocking. But women painted without charm or sadness, without irony or social comment, women painted like the palings of a stockade through eyes that look out as if at death—that is shocking.

I disagree. What is shocking is not the creepy memento mori aspect of the piece. What is shocking is the figure squatting in the lower-right corner of the canvas that appears to be a naked man with a sunburned crotch wearing an African tribal mask. One assumes the actual young ladies of Avignon were better represented in person, as one look at this masterpiece makes one wonder how Avignon ever got *any* revenue from horny revelers on holiday.

ASPASIA

PROFILE

DAY JOB: *Hetaira*

CLAIM TO FAME: "First Lady of Athens"

THEATER OF OPERATIONS: Classical Athens

Born in Ionia around 469 B.C., Aspasia, "The First Lady of Athens," lover of Pericles, the only woman invited to the tailgate at the death of Socrates, member of the fabled *hetaira* (a kind of Greek sorority of nympho call girls) and ardent feminist, has been described alternately as (1) one of the most beautiful and educated women of her era, a gifted diplomat, speech writer, rhetorician, and real boogie-down in the bedroom; and (2) a gold-digging whore who was responsible for the Peloponnesian War, God bless her. What is it with the Greeks blaming women for their wars?

Read from Aristophanes's play, *The Archarnians*:

> Some young drunkards go to Megara and carry off the courtesan Simaetha; the Megarians, hurt to the quick, run off in turn with two harlots of the house of Aspasia; and so for three whores Greece is set ablaze. Then Pericles, aflame with ire on his Olympian height, let loose the lightning, caused the thunder to roll, upset Greece and

passed an edict, which ran like the song, "That the Megarians be banished both from our land and from our markets and from the sea and from the continent.

Nice going, *Aspasia*. You've ruined Christmas—again. The truth is, Aspasia was a well-bred girl from neighboring Miletus, but she was beset by that enduring confederacy of audible feces: *player haters*.

"It's easy to fool the eye but it's hard to fool the heart."
—Al Pacino

Soon after her arrival in Athens, Aspasia became initiated into the *hetaira*, that sexy sorority of courtesans. Hearing rumors around town of a free-loving, liberated female with a nice, fat fanny, none other than Pericles, the leader of democratic Athens, stopped over to see Aspasia for himself. Pericles's and Aspasia's ensuing relationship provoked the scandal du jour in Athens, not because Pericles ditched his wife and two kids to shack up with Aspasia, which he did, but more because Aspasia assumed equal rights as a citizen of Athens. You can image the backlash.

Aspasia was no milksop. She gave the finger to the bigotry and hatred directed her way, and like an ancient Greek whore Wonder Woman, Aspasia used her magic bracelets and/or perseverance to deflect criticism and emerge as one of the most celebrated figures of Classical Greece, blowing the minds and members of an elite group of philosophers and politicos, ranging from Plato and Socrates to Xenophon and Cyrus (the Younger, of Persia). After Pericles's death from plague, Aspasia eventually remarried and settled down, managing to die at a relatively old age of something other than the plague— no small achievement back then.

FEBO DI POGGIO

PROFILE

DAY JOB: High school

CLAIM TO FAME: Michelangelo's boy toy

THEATER OF OPERATIONS: Sixteenth-century Italy

The painter Raphael claimed that Michelangelo was "lonely as a hang-man." Well, Michelangelo may have had some of the tortured artist in him, and he was certainly ugly as sin, but he was hardly lonely when it came to matters of the flesh. Michelangelo made sure that he always surrounded himself with young men of questionable account, but he took to one in particular: Febo Di Poggio.

Knowing the company Michelangelo kept, it should come as little surprise that the figures portrayed in *The Last Judgment* may have been inspired by his frequent jaunts to gay bordellos and Turkish baths. In fact, Elena Lazzarini, an art historian from Pisa University, asserts that the Sistine Chapel's soaring fresco is just one giant celestial orgy. Author of the book, *Nudity, Art and Decorum: Aesthetic Changes in the Art of the 16th Century*, Lazzarini notes, "One of the damned is dragged down to Hell by his testicles, and amongst those who are blessed there are kisses and embraces, undoubtedly homosexual in nature." Judge not, lest ye be judged, art lovers.

Febo was a wily young man-whore who served as Michelangelo's model, mount, and muse for over a decade. "Up from the earth I rose with his wings, and death itself I could have found sweet," Michelangelo writes of his "little blackmailer." But Febo was a bit of a shit. After a spat, Michelangelo panicked and broke into verse in an attempt to win back his boy toy:

Naught comforts you, I see, unless I die;
Earth weeps, the heavens for me are moved to woe;
You feel of grief the less, the more grieve I.
O sun that warms the world where'er you go,
O Febo, light eterne for mortal eyes!
Why dark to me alone, elsewhere not so?

In response, Febo moved back in, "adopted" Michelangelo as his own father, and then proceeded to hook his daddy for money to buy all the new haute Medici styles and new-wave imports from Sicily. It makes you feel kind of bad for Michelangelo until you realize that he was one of the most famous artists and sculptors the world has ever known, so cry me a *Pieta*, Mike. In the end, Febo's expensive habits and unspecified "betrayal" proved too much for Michelangelo, who ended the relationship by kicking Febo to the curb, then painting the altar wall of the Sistine Chapel with *The Last Judgment*. In a particularly ironic turn, a few equally boy-friendly (and typically intolerant) cardinals were outraged that Michelangelo included genitalia fit only for a "public-bath or tavern" in his masterful depictions of both the beautiful and the damned.

BAGOAS

PROFILE
DAY JOB: Slave
CLAIM TO FAME: Alexander the Great's backdoor man
THEATER OF OPERATIONS: Persia, around the fourth century B.C.

There's nothing funny about a child being forced into slavery and prostitution, or being castrated, or having to endure getting raped repeatedly by a snot-slinging drunk Alexander the "Great." In fact, it's all extraordinarily nauseating. But despite enduring these horrors, Bagoas (the word *bagoas* means "eunuch" in Old Persian), the catamite slave of King Darius III of Persia and then Alexander, managed to make quite the impression on history.

> *"I took the oldest profession on Earth*
> *and I did it better than anyone on Earth. Alexander the Great*
> *conquered the world at 32. I conquered it at 22."*
> —Heidi Fleiss

As told by Plutarch, Alexander fell for Bagoas (one wonders how Alexander's wife, Roxane, took the news) upon watching a dance contest in the desert, in which the young boy was the hands-down winner, using that winning combination of *duende* and *pasodoble*. Alexander's soldiers then dared Alexander to kiss the boy, which he did to great fanfare from the troops. Right in the middle of the desert the greatest army ever assembled was holding dance competitions and playing spin-the-scabbard games. If historical texts are to be believed, Bagoas and Alexander eventually grew to share a "mutual" love for one another—although you have to ask yourself, what choice did the poor kid have? Even Diogenes wrote Alexander to tell him what a degenerate he thought the young emperor was. All of Alexander's officers went along with the addition of Bagoas to this desert disco, except for one man named Orsines, who, according to the historian Curtius in his *History of Alexander*, foolishly barked that he'd come "to honor the friends of Alexander, not his whores." He went on to argue, "It was not the custom of the Persians to take males in marriage who had been turned into women for the sake of being fucked."

Bagoas suffered much, but by this time he was done suffering fools. Upon hearing Orsines's insults, the emasculated young man entreated with Alexander to hang Orsines from the highest tree, and Alexander took care of that somewhere on the way to conquering the known world. What's more, Bagoas was appointed a member of the vaunted *trierarchs,* advisors who above all others had the ear (among other body parts), of Alexander in matters of politics, war, and civics. A political post seems small consolation for a life of castrated servitude, but one can hope Bagoas found happiness knowing he could always support himself by dirty dancing in the desert.

CAROL "THE SCARLOT HARLOT" LEIGH

PROFILE

DAY JOB: Poet; pioneer in women's rights

CLAIM TO FAME: Coined the term "sex worker"

THEATER OF OPERATIONS: San Francisco

Carol Leigh was born in New York City in 1954 to Trotskyite parents, whose subversive work in the garment business kept the family afloat. In her autobiographical collection *Unrepentant Whore*, Carol writes that from an early age, her parents taught her that "nonconformity was the loftiest state," although her mother, also a pragmatist, advised, "Think for yourself and marry a doctor," then promptly disowned her fifteen-year-old daughter for dating a *goyim*.

Leigh took the first part of her mother's life coaching to heart, and seems to have thought to herself, "I think it's time to start getting laid a lot." It was 1967, and the sexual revolution was in full swing, offering Leigh the chance to realize her dreams of nonconformity and nudity. In another passage from *Unrepentant Whore*, she writes:

> Prostitution came to me at the intersection of my needs and proclivi-
> ties—my radical political bent, my feminism, my sexual curiosity, and
> a response to the stigma I already felt for engaging in premarital sex.

This doesn't give us a particularly illuminating look into anything juicy, except the literary technique of stringing together overwrought pronouncements like John Cheever when they let him write while shit-faced. Indeed, Leigh studied under Cheever in Boston University's graduate program in creative writing.

After a few false starts, like charging $5 for palm-jobs to creeps at a nude modeling studio and $25 for fellatio while "leaning on some-one's old Ford station wagon" outside of the Golden Banana Strip Club on amateur night, the Scarlot Harlot packed up her things and headed West. Perhaps she was heeding the legendary advice of Horace Greeley, or maybe she was just paying attention to less legendary advice from the local weatherman. "The blizzard of '78 was the last straw," she writes.

In September of 1978, the Scarlot Harlot burst onto the San Francisco massage parlor scene. Okay, fair; nobody has ever "burst" onto a massage parlor scene, but for this good little Jewish girl, the move was a sea change.

> I took a job at a very seedy massage parlor. I figured they must be sell-ing sex, because they certainly weren't selling ambiance. I was imme-diately enamored of my friendly, beautiful co-workers, and my first trick was handsome and sweet. After work, I rushed home to look in the mirror. Now there's a prostitute, I told myself. I hadn't changed. I looked back across that line that had separated me from the old me, the good girl. The line had disappeared.

At the same time the Scarlot Harlot was hooking for all she was worth, she was also a fervent political activist. At a conference orga-nized by Women Against Violence in Pornography and Media, she even coined the term "sex work," and she was tireless in her efforts to pro-mote various feminist causes. Today, Ms. Leigh, who still gives readings and "performances" as Scarlot Harlot, is a prominent spokeswoman for COYOTE, a sex workers' rights organization; she also curates and directs the San Francisco Sex Worker Film and Video Festival, which sounds a lot like Cannes, but more nude.

JEFF GANNON

PROFILE

DAY JOBS: White House Press Corps reporter

CLAIM TO FAME: "Spanorcing" himself from reality

THEATER OF OPERATIONS: Washington, D.C.

It's probably safe to assume that former White House press reporter Jeff Gannon had to maintain separate curriculum vitae. That is, of course, unless the following description/personal statement was the kind of thing the Dubya Bush White House was looking for from its press corps:

- Ex-USMC Jock: Available for hourly, overnight, weekend or longer travel—OUT ONLY!
- Personal Trainer: Safe-Sane-Strenuous-Satisfying workouts, Sports training, and competition, especially wrestling. . . .
- Big SPORTS Fan: Will go to the game with you, then take you home and. . . .
- AGGRESIVE, VERBAL, DOMINANT TOP
- I DON'T LEAVE MARKS. . . . ONLY IMPRESSIONS

That was Gannon as his alter ego, "Bulldog," on USMCPT.com, one of the many gay escort sites featuring Gannon's services when he was busy hammering home another, decidedly more conservative agenda, at 1600 Pennsylvania Ave. in the mid-aughts, or 2000s, or whatever the hell we decided to call that decade.

Why is it that so often the most vehement critics of homosexuals are other homosexuals pretending not to be homosexuals? It's confusing to the public, rooted in self-loathing, and it makes you look like a perfect vermin. It also embarrasses the rest of us who are perfectly fine with you being all-gay, sometimes-gay, or just a little gay. And what's really frustrating is when the hate-monger actually has a platform, like say a White House reporter.

Meet Jeff Gannon (real name James Guckert, which, he claims, is "too hard to pronounce"), hard-hitting gay male prostitute disguised as straight White House news reporter whose daily "questions" for the George W. Bush "administration" were so soft and odious they served as the journalistic equivalent of anal leakage. In 2006, Gannon, the White House shill, dropped this greaser to then-President Bush during a presidential press conference:

> How are you going to work—you've said you are going to reach out
> to these people—how are you going to work with [Senate Democratic
> leaders] who seem to have spanorced themselves from reality?

That's what we call quintessential softball journalism, folks. Luckily, Gannon does have *some* bona fides—otherwise we might have mistaken him for a White House plant. It turns out Gannon once worked as a journalist for Talon News, a website consisting of himself and Bobby Eberle, President of GOPUSA, a conservative action group. Now, Jeff Gannon knows all about two (or more) dudes in a room, but sorry—two dudes in a room does not a newsroom make. And still, day after day, Gannon was allowed into the White House to ask probing questions, and to spit out idiocies that may have included, "Would you like to have sex for $200/hr?"

Well, we're sure that at least one such question was answered in the affirmative, as "The Bulldog," offered more than reasonable rates for X-rated pics and sex services on numerous websites, including: *hotmilitarystud.com*, *militaryescorts.com*, and *militaryescortsm4m.com*. Just to be clear, neither Jeff Gannon, nor James Guckert, was ever in the military. In addition, records show that—even in a post 9/11 environment in which every booger that came and went from the White House was assuredly accounted for—Gannon was allowed free access with a fabricated name on his press credentials, often showing up even when there were *no* press conferences on the schedule.

Are we implying that Gannon actually serviced members of the White House staff? Well, why the hell not? It would be suspect if you found out that a reporter visited the White House more than 200 times in two years, eluding even the Secret Service, who often lost track of him (they have dozens of records of him exiting without entering and vice-versa), so there is speculation that, in addition to his job playing journalist, his little side biz may also have enjoyed some success in the ~~Whore House~~ White House.

"People criticize me for being a Christian and having some of these questionable things in my past," says Gannon/Guckert. Look, "Bulldog," we don't criticize you for being a Christian and having some of these questionable things in your past. We criticize you for being an asshole and having some of these questionable things in your past.

LIU RUSHI

PROFILE

DAY JOBS: Painter, poet, politico

CLAIM TO FAME: Ming dynasty must-have for the discriminating john

THEATER OF OPERATIONS: China

Liu Rushi (1618–1664) was patient, and to a degree, lucky. During the Ming dynasty China was a place where, despite being a hooker, you could rise through the ranks in the art world without buttinsky gallery owners talking about how featuring a solo show by a local whore might compromise the integrity of their establishment. Sort of. You were also a slave, and you had to sit still while someone wrapped your rotting, infected feet up so tightly that the bones cracked, rendering you virtually immobile: Foot binding was/is one of the more sinister and nauseating fashion trends perpetrated against women since the advent of behaving like a dick.

But Liu Rushi was also a gifted poet, not just some prostitute with a flair for iambic pentameter, a peculiar rhythm, indeed, to anyone accustomed to the beat of traditional Chinese poetry. In fact, Liu Rushi became the most famous prostitute China has ever known and one of its more revered poets and artists to boot. She possessed great beauty and a talent with the quill and scroll, and the girl knew how to party. This is the kind of crossover appeal people like Gore Vidal, Ke$ha, and Dog the Bounty Hunter would kill for. But Liu was different.

Not much is known of her early life, though it's sometimes hypothesized that a scholarly family educated her before selling her into slavery. After countless business "transactions," Liu finally found herself with enough money to buy her freedom, and having a prodigious talent for art, poetry, and sex, she took on the role of courtesan to members of the *Jishe*, a kind of literary group. The *Jishe* was full of talented men, the Chinese intelligentsia, but Liu Rushi shamed those sorry bitches. She became a de facto member of the *Jishe* herself, then moved on to higher art and higher artists.

Enamored of the poet Qian Qianyi's verse, Liu went to his place dressed as a man. Qian was a married man, so you can understand the courtesan's need for discretion. It never looks good when your country's most famous prostitute comes knocking at the door looking foxy and holding in her hot little hand a bag of the most erotic poetry anyone's seen in years.

Qian Qianyi was so moved by the poetry of this "man," that he thought, "What the hell? Nobody's perfect," and brought Liu on as sort of a second "wife" *before* she even revealed herself to be a woman. Mrs. Qianyi must have been *steamed*. It couldn't have helped the family dynamics that Qian was fifty-nine and Liu a fecund twenty-four.

Liu continued with her art and her poetry, and she became extraordinarily skilled at calligraphy, as well. She also delved into politics, becoming an expert on military matters. When the Manchus took control in 1645, Liu advised her now-husband Qian, a Ming minister of the court, to kill himself by jumping in the river as a form of protest. In response her husband offered the compelling arguments that the water was too cold and he couldn't swim, so Liu went back to scheming how best to restore glory to the Ming dynasty. She refused to accompany her husband to the new Qing court in Beijing, and spent the rest of her life dedicated to the Ming loyalist movement and creating timeless poetry and prose.

Unfortunately, the rest of her life ended with Liu Rushi taking her own advice, but being a strong swimmer, she opted to hang herself for the "cause," one of the more loathsome political strategies ever and a significant loss for art no matter the meter of your verse.

SALLY SALISBURY

PROFILE

DAY JOB: Eighteenth-century streetwalker

CLAIM TO FAME: B-list celebrity; tabloid darling

THEATER OF OPERATIONS: London

There wasn't a whole lot of opportunity for upward mobility in London during the early eighteenth century, especially for women. One did what one could to make ends meet, including occasionally schtupping prominent politicians and statesmen. A young woman growing up in "The Square Mile," as London City was once called, had it particularly hard. Apprenticed to a seamstress, Sally Salisbury (born Sarah Pridden around 1690) fell out of favor with her employer and turned to selling raunchy brochures on the streets of London. These proved quite the draw about town. One assumes the real appeal of the pamphlets lay not in the articles, but in the illicit sexual arrangement implied by paying way too much for a crumpled piece of paper.

Sally managed to parlay her pamphlet business into a chance to consort with some of the biggest names in England, including the Duke of Richmond and, purportedly, a young King George II. She soon made a small fortune as a courtesan/prostitute and was living the relatively lavish lifestyle of a B-list celebrity, until a funny thing happened on the way to the opera.

John Finch, the brother of Lord Finch and son of the Countess of Winchelsea promised to bestow upon Sally some excellent opera tickets in exchange for a romp at the Three Tuns Tavern on Chandos Street in Covent Garden. Sally agreed, though wary that once you start accepting vouchers and coupons for sex, you've compromised your operation. Unfortunately, Sally was later humiliated by Finch, who decided the classy thing to do would be to give the tickets to Sally's sister. Well, hell hath no fury like a whore cheated out of her opera tickets, and in the ensuing melee, Sally Salisbury pulled a knife, used it, and was charged with murder.

A letter from Lady Mary Wortley Montagu to the Countess of Mar describes the event with a flourish:

> In a jealous pique [Salisbury] stabbed him to the heart with a knife. He fell down dead immediately, but a surgeon being called for, and the knife drawn out of his body, he opened his eyes, and his first words were to beg her to be friends with him, and kissed her.

That's right, he kissed her. Sally was tried for murder and acquitted, but ultimately convicted of assault, fined 100 pounds, and sentenced to a year in prison. Sadly for Sally, and legions of randy London swells, shortly after arriving to serve out her sentence, she fell victim to a "brain fever brought on by debauch," which sounds like a badass way to go out, but was probably just syphilis.

MARKUS BESTIN

PROFILE

DAY JOB: U.S. Marine

CLAIM TO FAME: First legal male prostitute to work in a brothel

THEATER OF OPERATIONS: Nevada; online

Markus Bestin is a strapping former marine who once commanded $300 an hour at the Shady Lady Ranch brothel, thus laying claim to the title of first legally working male prostitute in America. Born in Alabama in 1984, Markus (his real name is Patrick) was keenly aware of the prejudice and bigotry embedded in the darkest reaches of the Southern psyche. And, like the civil rights warriors who came before him, Markus felt a need to pop the clutch and push through a penile paradigm shift. His quest was to make the world show some respect for the rent boys.

When Markus opened for business he did make one thing clear: "My sphincter is not for sale." He also made the lame announcement that he would prefer to be called a "surrogate lover" rather than a "prostitute." Markus faced daunting resistance, but he persevered. When asked on ABC's *Nightline* about the significance of his groundbreaking new job, Markus responded:

> Basically this is the first time in the economy of the United States that a male has actually stood up and said, "I want to do this for a living." And be protected under law to do it. It's just the same as when Rosa Parks decided to sit at the front instead of the back. She was proclaiming her rights as a disadvantaged, African-American older woman . . . or what Gandhi did when he had a sit-down protest against the British Embassy. And I'm doing the same.

Rosa Parks? Gandhi? Really? Those comparisons are about as monstrously inaccurate as an analogy can get. Markus Bestin was many things to many people—but his paltry, self-serving efforts required nowhere near the courage, and they had nowhere near the significance of Rosa Parks's or Gandhi's, although presumably he's better in the sack.

However, the maverick man-ho is showing a measure of perseverance. While his tenancy at the Shady Lady was short lived, he's now found a home on the Internet—where else? You can find him listed under "Bahamute," or Model #1679 on *www.xxxfilmjobs.com*, which is a kind of myspace.com for desperate porn stars and would-be trailblazing civil rights advocates who think their mistranslated tattoos are life-affirming Chinese maxims but are usually just Szechuan lunch menu specials.

MINEKO IWASAKI

PROFILE

DAY JOBS: Plaintiff; memoirist

CLAIM TO FAME: Basis for the main character in critically acclaimed novel, *Memoirs of a Geisha*

THEATER OF OPERATIONS: Kyoto

Every year in Japan, a select few women go through the *misedashi* (literally, "open for business"), which is a kind of debutante ball for whores. But in Japan, they're not called whores. They're called *geisha*. Geisha, mind you, are not common prosties—think of them as Eastern courtesans, sexual samurais, really. Geisha have been a source of Japanese entertainment for centuries. These alabaster-faced beauties have their origin in the *saburuko*, or "serving girls," who emerged around the seventh century. They were typically wandering girls displaced by war and strife. The popularity of these young women grew until members of the nobility were offering them a home in exchange for performing sexual and sometimes intellectual favors. Some geisha even went on to serve emperors as concubines, occupying important positions of wealth, power, and reverse-cowgirl. And it was on February 15, 1965, that Ms. Iwasaki and dozens of other girls emerged from their "training" to step into the curious world of glorified prostitution.

While you may think of former secretary of state and Nobel Peace Prize winner Henry Kissinger as a devious troll and architect of countless atrocities in Southeast Asia and Latin America, you may be surprised to learn that in his prime, the man was a libidinous lothario. In fact, in a 1972 poll of *Playboy* bunnies, the rascally rabbits selected Kissinger as the man with whom they'd most like to go out on a date.

The sixties ushered in a period of great strides in both civil and women's rights in Japan and the rest of the world. Incurable STDs were virtually nonexistent, birth control pills hit the market, and folks the world over went around fornicating with fierce abandon. It was a good time for Mineko. Shortly after her debut, Iwasaki was earning over $500,000 a year. Her likeness was featured on posters, shopping bags, and billboards. If there had been a rookie-of-the-year award, Mineko Iwasaki would have been the uncontested winner. But again, we're not dealing here with simple copulation. A geisha must have intense training in the arts, including conversation, poetry, dance, music, and blowjob—all sacred pillars of their traditional and storied business plan.

"Hey, you occidental shit-for-brains—we're not prostitutes—what's with the blowjob gag?" an angry geisha or nitpicking historian might ask, and then hiss, "All you did was read *Memoirs of a Geisha* and make presumptions." First of all, that's a lie. *Memoirs of a Geisha* has almost 450 pages in hardcover—way more than I'm willing to tackle, and in addition, I don't even know what "presumptions" means. But Ms. Iwasaki did sue the author of *Memoirs of a Geisha*, Arthur Golden, who outed her as his primary "source," the one who was willing to break the geisha's code of silence and imply that geisha commonly exchange sex for money. The scandal prompted Iwasaki's retirement from geisha-ing at age twenty-nine to begin her second career as memoirist and plaintiff in lawsuits against Golden. The issue of whether or not geisha actually exchange sex for money is something best dealt with on a case-by-case basis, but come the hell *on*. It's tough to earn half a million dollars a year reciting haiku in whiteface—sexy kimono notwithstanding.

In her own memoir, the meandering *I, Geisha*, we learn that Iwasaki faced degradation on a scale previously unthinkable: She was obliged to dance and entertain former president Gerald Ford and his henchman, Secretary of State Henry Kissinger. She describes a lurid affair:

> President *Ford* was at an ozashiki [a geisha party] in a banquet room downstairs while Dr. Kissinger was in one on the floor above. I was asked to entertain at both. I found the contrast most revealing. President Ford was pleasant and engaging. . . . Kissinger, on the other hand, was curious about everything and kept asking questions. He was very amusing, even mildly risqué. The party became quite boisterous and we all ended up dancing around the room together and singing.

Henry Kissinger? Risqué? Boisterous? Dancing? No human being should have to look at that. Clearly, the indignities witnessed by geisha are significantly more heinous than we ever could have imagined.

ETTA (ETHEL) PLACE

PROFILE

DAY JOB: Prostitute at Fanny Porter's bordello in Ft. Worth, TX

CLAIM TO FAME: Mistress of both Butch Cassidy and the Sundance Kid

THEATER OF OPERATIONS: Nevada, Texas, Argentina . . . and parts unknown

For such a famous woman, very little is known about Etta Place. Nobody knows where she came from or when and how she died. The only real evidence we have that she existed at all is a cheesy Old West photo taken with famed outlaw the Sundance Kid around 1901, when those sepia prints and overwrought "Wanted" posters were all the rage. What we do know about Place is that she was the female companion of not only the Sundance Kid but also his partner in crime, Butch Cassidy. And she was a prostitute.

When Butch Cassidy was convicted in Wyoming for stealing horses in 1894, he convinced his captors to permit him one last night on the town, "out on his own recognizance," before beginning a two-year sentence. Inexplicably, his wish was granted, and Butch tied one on, visiting some ladies not-quite-illustrious enough to be mentioned in this milieu, but you can't win 'em all. Even more inexplicably, Cassidy returned to serve his sentence the next day, brass-eyed and bush-tired. He was released after serving three-fourths of his sentence, promising the governor that he'd never thieve livestock or banks in Wyoming ever again. Naturally, Butch then took to robbing trains, as choo-choos weren't covered under their agreement.

Remember that pivotal moment in the 1969 Newman/Redford classic *Butch Cassidy and The Sundance Kid* when it looks like Butch and Etta are about to ditch Sundance and engage in some tawdry sexcapade on a bike? Everything is right in the world, and it appears we're finally going to see penetration in a big Hollywood feature, when BAM! B. J. Thomas starts to sing "Raindrops Keep Fallin' on My Head," Butch and Etta just pedal around like half-wits, and at the end of the movie, the film stock breaks right at the good part and they never tell you if Butch and Sundance escape. Well, Etta's life is similarly frustrating to pin down. I can't even say with any kind of assurance that she knew how to ride a bike.

The prevailing literature indicates that around the turn of the twentieth century, Butch and Sundance came into Fanny Porter's famous San Antonio brothel and legendary "Wild Bunch" hangout, catching the eye (and perhaps the crabs) of the gorgeous Etta (or Ethel, by some accounts) Place. You can just see it: All three of them, staring at each other, twitching; it's like some sexy Mexican stand-off. In the end, Butch and Sundance (who, let's be honest, sound like they should be peeping the rent-boys next door) decided they'd share Etta and take her along on a multihemispheric crime spree, which seems to have actually worked out quite well for everyone involved until they were or weren't tracked down and killed in Bolivia.

While on the run from the law, the triumvirate visited secret remote locations, such as New York City, where Etta and Sundance had that Old West photo taken before they picked up Butch Cassidy and sailed off to Chile for raunchy three-ways and more crime. Some sources claim the three may have tried to make a go of legitimate farming; my guess would be goats, but that's always my guess.

The photo of Place and Sundance, discovered by Pinkerton detectives hot on the gang's trail, gives us a haunting description: A woman who was "27 or 28 years old, 5'4" to 5'5" in height, weighing between 110 lb and 115 lb, with a medium build and brown hair." Well, that narrows it down some. It may appear that the famed Pinkerton Detective Agency was perhaps looking for *you*. Or your friend. Or cousin, even. It's okay, though. I thought the same thing, but there's my cousin Phoebe like she always is, safe and sound in the kitchen—stoned on oven cleaner, watching the toaster for hydras.

Speculation continues to this day as to the real identity of Etta Place. Some say she ditched Butch and Sundance and became a successful rancher, while others maintain she was blown to bits with her boys in Bolivia. But in the end, one thing remains patently clear: If Etta Place is alive today, she's like 130 years old, and could probably make a good living offering tips on healthy living and avoiding the authorities.

PORFIRIO "RUBI" RUBIROSA

PROFILE

DAY JOB: International playboy; diplomat

CLAIM TO FAME: "The Ding Dong Daddy"; sleeping with almost everyone

THEATER OF OPERATIONS: Dominican Republic; Hollywood; your bedroom if you weren't careful

According to the writer Truman Capote, Porfirio "Rubi" Rubirosa had a penis that resembled "an eleven inches café au lait sinker, as thick as a man's wrist." That should be enough to get your attention. But, in addition to his pronounced appendage, Rubi had the uncanny ability to marry rich women, divorce them, then take lots of money and cool stuff from the devastated dupes in the ensuing settlement. But Rubirosa was no ordinary Latin lover—he found time to dabble in both Hollywood and international politics, serving as right-hand man to a bloodthirsty Caribbean American dictator.

"The women who take husbands not out of love but out of greed,
to get their bills paid, to get a fine house and clothes and jewels;
the women who marry to get out of a tiresome job, or to get away from
disagreeable relatives, or to avoid being called an old maid—
these are whores in everything but name. The only difference between
them and my girls is that my girls gave a man his money's worth."
—Polly Adler

Rubi, or "The Ding Dong Daddy," as he was also known, was born in 1909 in the Dominican Republic. His father was a diplomat, and young Rubi enjoyed an idyllic upbringing, mostly in Paris. At seventeen, Rubi left Paris to study law back in the Dominic Republic. However, upon his return to the homeland, Rubi found that his talents were best manifested when he lay prostrate. Upon his arrival, Porfirio was introduced to Rafael Trujillo, the fierce dictator who ruled the Dominican Republic with an iron fist and a jelly belly for thirty years. Trujillo saw in Rubirosa a charismatic figure, a gorgeous piece of ass who could win over the youth of the country. Trujillo once explained, "[Rubi] is good at his job, because women like him and he is a wonderful liar." As a foolproof backup plan, Trujillo ordered his secret police to summarily shoot any youth not won over to the side of the *Trujillistas*.

All Rubi had to do was go around banging the rich and famous while putting in a kind word for a dictator who resembled a prolapsed anus in full military regalia. Trujillo was clearly prepared to assassinate people for crimes as insignificant as farting in the wrong direction, though he never actually did that. But essentially, seducing women and taking their fortunes to fill his and Trujillo's war chest was the Ding-Dong Daddy's *job*.

Let's just do a quick roll call of Rubi's sham marriages, because to catalog every one of his conquests would make a too-lengthy list:

1. Flor de Oro Trujillo—the daughter of the dictator, Rafael Trujillo. Despite Rubi's torrid extramarital affairs, Trujillo never had him killed, which is odd. In fact, he kept his son-in-law and then his ex-son-in-law in cushy diplomatic appointments for most of Rubi's life.
2. Danielle Darrieux—one of the most famous French actresses. She and Rubi married in 1942 and made passionate love in some nice Swiss accommodations until the war was over and everyone was free to leave/cheat/ get divorced.
3. Doris Duke—at the time of their marriage, the richest woman in the world. Even after their short-lived marriage, Rubi would receive $25,000 per year (until remarriage), an armada of fishing boats, a fleet of sports cars, a converted B-25 bomber, and a seventeenth-century mansion in Paris.
4. Barbara Hutton—at the time of their marriage, the *second*-richest woman in the world. From his divorce

with Hutton (seventy-five days later), Rubi wrangled a coffee plantation in his native Dominican Republic, another bomber (you can never have enough), polo horses, enough bling to blind people living as far away as the planet Mars, and a $2.5 million cash payout.

5. Odile Rodin—almost thirty years his junior, this French actress was Rubi's last wife. This marriage lasted until Rubi ran his Ferrari into a tree after staying up all night drinking. He had been celebrating after winning a polo match.

Rubi is dead, but the legend of his flagpole phallus lives on.

XUE SUSU

PROFILE

DAY JOB: Artist/Performer

CLAIM TO FAME: One of the "Eight Great Courtesans" of the Ming Dynasty

THEATER OF OPERATIONS: Late Ming Dynasty China

Gather round you sinful old goats and regard Xue Susu: She was an artist, a poet, and a scholar. Xue Susu was also a knight-errant, which means that she was the kind of gal to lay you down and then slay your enemies—or help you cross a puddle—a paragon of feminine chivalry at a time when the boys, as usual, were sitting around with their dicks in her hands.

During China's late Ming Dynasty period, around the turn of the seventeenth century, the country faced serious problems at home and abroad. In no particular order, an economic crisis involving the price of silver, Japanese pirates, and an imperial court full of unruly and power-hungry eunuchs threatened to plunge the country into chaos.

An earthquake killed almost a million people, and that didn't help much either.

"Christ on a bike, can we get some something *decent* in our crappy lives!" shouted frustrated peasants. Nobody cares about a peasant, so they were up shit creek as usual, but the emperor readily granted requests from wealthy Ming scholars who wanted access to rock-star courtesans like Susu. According to Fan Yunlin, the secretary in the Ministry of War and an admirer of Ms. Susu:

> [Xue Susu's] other feats of shooting birds with pellets and generously parting with one thousand pieces of gold to save somebody from poverty truly make her a female knight-errant for all time.

In Ming China, courtesans had the "luxury" of living outside the traditional strictures of domesticity. Thus Xue Susu and her fellow courtesans were able to enjoy a lifestyle previously afforded only to men. Xue Susu studied archery and travelled freely in Beijing and other more "barbarian regions," honing her sultry skills. In the 1590s Susu secured her celebrity in the literary and artsy salons of Beijing where she played the flute (both jade and skin) and horizontal host for her clients, in addition to reciting poetry and displaying her considerable talents as an archer. Members of the elite were often in attendance, but Susu's services were particularly popular in military circles. Basically, she was a free agent—a kind of sexual Albert Pujols—who could pick and choose her clients with discrimination not typically available to your average street-corner sex-slanger.

In this environment Xue Susu thrived, even though it must have been quite a shock when a Chinese john showed up for a hot and steamy session and found his prostitute decked out in full body armor. In fact, the literature indicates that Susu may have been more adept with iron weaponry than with the fleshy arsenal wielded by your average courtesan. One story tells of how Susu, riled up and ready to rumble with the Japanese, who were always invading China's coast, beseeched one of her lovers—a military man—to organize a punishing attack on the foreign marauders. When he turned out to be all talk, Susu scoffed, spurned him as a lover, and "rode off on her quick steed." You just got your nuts took, Mr. Bigmouth.

A Ming Dynasty eunuch knew never to lose track of his cock and balls, or his "precious," as they were euphemistically called back then. A designated "knifer" lopped off his junk and dropped it in a jar filled with alcohol (giving the expression, "whiskey-dick," a whole new meaning). Why? With every promotion, eunuchs were required to present their jar of genitals to a court official, who would then document the satisfactory completion of the operation. Furthermore, every eunuch was buried with his "precious," as religious norms dictated a man be "complete" when leaving this cruel, cruel world.

Curiously, "loyalty" and "fidelity" were indispensible traits among Ming courtesans, and despite Xue Susu's singular popularity, in 1605 she disappeared, causing mass confusion and sperm retention headaches nationwide. Why? Loyalty. When the scholar/dramatist Shen Defu offered her a career-style gig as his concubine, and then as his wife, the knight-errant courtesan with a penchant for archery and a booty fit to make a Mongol blush finally settled down to the life of the mind, leaving only her art, her poetry, and the memories of her behind behind.

NELL GWYN

PROFILE

DAY JOB: Actress

CLAIM TO FAME: Mistress of King Charles II of England

THEATER OF OPERATIONS: Seventeenth-century London

Eleanor "Nell" Gwynn would be a frontrunner in any contest to choose who best personifies Restoration England. Born to an alcoholic prostitute in the steaming shitbox that was London in 1650, Nell evidently started her career in the prostitutional arts as a youngster, one of the many hazards of growing up in a brothel. Even the *Encyclopedia Britannica*'s entry for Gwyn asserts that she was the "living antithesis of Puritanism," and yet, this once destitute oyster wench from the hood managed, through cunning, wit, humor, and stunning sexual brazenness to beguile the bejesus out of poets, writers, royalty—pretty much everyone who had the good fortune to cross her path.

In her teens, Nell went from hawking fruit, seafood, and sex in front of a theater to strutting her stuff as an actress in her own right. In the latter half of the seventeenth century, she was one of London's main attractions, on stage—and off. The poet John Dryden wrote plays especially for her; Samuel Pepys, the famous diarist, referred to her as "pretty, witty Nell. . . . I kissed her, and so did my wife; and a mighty pretty soul she is."

By 1668 Nell had accumulated a menagerie of lovers including the usual demented British noblemen, and then, in order, she caught the eye, the privates, and the heart of none other than King Charles II of England. Nell and the king made each other's acquaintance during a performance of the oft-forgotten play, *She Wou'd If She Cou'd* at the Duke's House Theater. A court "memorialist" wrote the following account of the meeting:

Upon this occasion he [the king] came to the play incog. and sat in the box next to Nell and her lover [a Mr. Villiers, cousin to the Duke of Buckingham]. As soon as the play was finished, his Majesty, with the Duke of York, the young nobleman [Mr. Villiers], and Nell, retired to a tavern together, where they regaled themselves over a bottle, and the King shewed such civilities to Nell that she began to understand the meaning of his gallantry. . . . When the reckoning came to be paid, his Majesty, upon searching his pockets, found that he had not money enough about him to discharge it . . . upon which Nell observed, that she had got into the poorest company that ever she was in at a tavern. The reckoning was paid by the young nobleman.

And from then on, Little Nell would remain the king's favorite mistress for the next two decades, bearing him two children, and eventually taking up residence at the Burford House in Windsor, a perfect rags-to-riches scenario fit for a fairy tale. And yes, it sucks that Mr. Villiers had to pay for all the shots and the bar food, but sometimes one should just duck dive under the swelling wave of history and let the tide come on in. In fact, today the House of Windsor would give its inbred third gonad for a PR machine like Nell. She charmed a nation; she was a Cinderella figure who personified the people, their dreams, and the dreams of a country. Vilified in some circles as "the indiscreetest and wildest creature that ever was in a Court," Nell Gwyn was alternately revered as "The Whore Who Saved London," presumably because she gave the Brits someone to root for and something to cheer about (Manchester United wasn't invented yet) after 20 percent of the population was wiped out in the great plague of 1665.

LA BELLE OTERO

PROFILE

DAY JOBS: Actress; man-eater

CLAIM TO FAME: Courtesan extraordinaire

THEATER OF OPERATIONS: Spain; France; most of Europe

Caroline Otero was born into poverty in 1868, in Galicia, Spain. Her prospects were bleak, although, in what some would consider a felicitous twist of fate, the young Caroline scored a job working as a maid in Santiago de Compostela. Now, instead of facing starvation and the plague, she was ensured a life of chaste mediocrity. But wait! Caroline had a secret; she could *dance*.

Taking advantage of her gifts, Otero ditched the maid gig and wiggled her poonanny to Portugal with a dance partner called "Paco." There, she found "sponsors" in sundry sugar daddies and/or nobleman. She married one of them, but her groom of approximately 10 minutes lost her in a craps game. It's true; Otero could, and did, do a lot more than just dance. This was especially true after she discovered her preternatural ability to drive her *soupirants* bat-shit crazy with lust.

In 1888, another one of Otero's many sponsors paid her way from Barcelona to Marseilles, France, and one step closer to that elusive dream: Gay Paree. Otero's wild success on stage and in between the sheets in Marseilles convinced her she could go it alone, in the big city, so she ditched her sponsor and strolled onto the scene like a new, luscious, and morally flexible sexual sheriff in town. Upon her arrival, Otero adopted the identity of the sultry Andalusian "gypsy," La Belle Otero, and from there on out all bets were off. Otero became the main attraction, dancing at Paris's legendary *Folies Bergère*, and it was on.

According to a 1965 article published in *Time* magazine shortly after her death, things could get deadly:

Admirers gave her gilded carriages and chateaux, buckets of jewels, and a mansion on the Champs-Elysées. A U.S. millionaire invited Otero to a simple supper of caviar and oysters—in each oyster lay a pearl. By 1894 she was so rich that she spurned an offer of 10,000 francs for one night, and the luckless man killed himself in humiliation.

La Belle Otero was a class act. She had a stripper brassiere encrusted with diamonds, and they claim her voluptuous breasts inspired the perky domed cupolas that stand today atop the Carleton Hotel in Cannes. But 10,000 *francs*? One story holds that during a single evening at the Café de Paris, five of Europe's kings descended on her table, looking for love: Nicholas II of Russia, Britain's Edward VII, Wilhelm II of Prussia, Belgium's Leopold II, and Alfonso XIII of Spain. The evidence is paltry as to which royal(s) gained her favor that night, but I'm guessing, no matter what, La Belle Otero was compensated generously for her efforts on that occasion.

Once proclaiming, "I have been a slave to my passions, but never to a man," La Belle Otero retired to a sprawling French mansion in 1922. "Women have one mission in life: to be beautiful," said Otero after squandering her vast fortune on a lavish lifestyle that included way too much time in casinos. Toward the end of her life, she said, "When one gets old, one must learn how to break mirrors. I am very gently expecting to die." While we may raise an eyebrow at her decidedly anti-feminist view on the "mission" of women, the part about breaking mirrors is pretty damn clever.

CASANOVA

PROFILE
DAY JOBS: Author; adventurer; slut
CLAIM TO FAME: The "World's Greatest Lover"
THEATER OF OPERATIONS: Italy/Western Europe

What exactly does it mean when people conjure up the epithet "Casanova" to describe you, perched there on a bar stool in your fancy brocaded vest over a shirt with puffy sleeves and a row of lace on the cuffs? And why can't you tell us when you're going to perpetrate that preposterous ensemble? But more to the point, who *was* this eponymous gigolo whose sexual antics in Europe during the eighteenth century still resonate with us today? Well, let's first be charitable and say he was active. At one time or another, this *homme du monde* was a friend to everyone in Europe who mattered at the time, from popes and royalty to Benjamin Franklin, Voltaire, and other pillars of the Enlightenment.

Born in Venice, the young Casanova was abandoned by his travelling carnie parents to a grandmother who, convinced witches were giving the youngster nosebleeds, shipped him off to a boarding school in Padua. Casanova turned out to be a brilliant student and eventually enjoyed a number of careers: priest, poet, philosopher, translator, lawyer, military brass, gourmand, occultist, mathematician, government informer, theater manager, pimp, violinist, and notary public, among other even more dubious endeavors. But where, you ask, does it say he was a prostitute?

Casanova the prostitute is a tricky question. He certainly frequented ladies of the evening, picking up a wide and colorful array of venereal diseases along the way, but did this legendary seducer really do it for the money? Kind of. Cash transactions of the kind negotiated on dark street-corners weren't really Casanova's style—he recounts in his autobiography *The Story of My Life* countless instances in which he employs love as leverage, seducing women who beg him to stay. They would offer him "linen and sheets" and then eventually "diamonds and all the money [they] had," but they also provided entree into wealthy and influential families and significant political power.

The legend of Giacomo Casanova, refined and knowledgeable as he may have been, is largely horseshit. Widely held to be one of, if not *the* world's greatest lover, this well-dressed ogre in a fussy vest made elaborate plans to seduce his own daughter. It was the old son-and-a-grandson-in-one-go trick, a crime against nature that wipes the sheen off this multitalented member of the sexual aristocracy, and makes you want to kick him in his withered, diseased testes. Casanova, however, seems to be pretty proud of himself, pointing out that he performed that particular act of mortal depravity "only two or three more times" before putting a stop to the affair.

On the flip side of the groin, Casanova once explained that he used his condom as a "prophylactic against melancholy," and with Casanova being such a happy fellow, one can assume his condom was put to substantial use. It was. Although, that he apparently toted around just one condom, reusing it with multiple partners, is of particular hygienic concern.

In the end, like so many iconic pedestal-loafers, Casanova was little more than a brilliant man with a trash dick. His final bed tally, while impressive (122 women and an untold number of men, whom he failed to factor into the arithmetic), Casanova just sort of looks like a more articulate though less-discriminating version of Bill Clinton.

Chapter II

PROMINENT PIMPS AND MANDARIN MADAMS

With the advent of the Internet and other leading-edge prostitution software, life for the sex worker has become decreasingly dependent on pimps and madams. Unless your pimp is a seventy-wpm typist or you work at a brothel/wi-fi café where the madam is more of a barista than a switchblade-wielding tyrant, most working boys and girls can make all their amorous arrangements in the comforts of home. That's probably a net positive. Some of the following characters will fit with your preconceived ideas of what a whoremonger is and does (beats up people and is manipulative and sometimes wears a fancy hat); but then there are the gentle, the clumsy, the brilliant, and the benign flesh-peddlers who smash stereotypes and give us hope that if there's ever like a global Internet crash and we're back to rotary phones, somebody will know what the hell to do about offline sex. From the new-jack pimp to the old-school procuress, here are the head honchos behind the whores.

JESSIE WILLIAMS AND EDNA MILTON

PROFILE

DAY JOB: Owners/proprietors of "The Best Little Whorehouse in Texas"

CLAIM TO FAME: See above

THEATER OF OPERATIONS: And see above again, y'all

Born Faye Stewart in 1881, "Miss Jessie" was owner and proprietor of the storied "Best Little Whorehouse in Texas," made famous by the Broadway musical of the same name (an inferior movie version was also made in 1982, starring a moustache and two enormous breasts). When she took over the brothel in 1905, it was a fledgling operation, but Jessie, who had escaped a wretched life of poverty in nearby Waco, set out to turn her little establishment in La Grange into the West Texas capital of fornication.

The bordello did exceedingly well during World War I, but like every business, it took a hit during the Great Depression. Jessie, entrepreneurial spirit that she was, changed the name of her floundering enterprise to "The Chicken Ranch," and she was back in business with a vengeance. "What in the F is a whorehouse doing calling itself 'The Chicken Ranch,'" you ask? Yes, the name does carry with it the suggestion of barnyard bestiality, but it made perfect sense at the time. In 1932, the fee for services was about $1.50 per "poke," a lot of money when Wall Street bankers have taken all of your savings and your farm. You have nothing left except these stupid chickens—maybe a heft of manure, but that's pushing things. But, wait. Have you heard? Miss Jessie is trading pokes for poultry! That's right, Miss Jessie tweaked her business model a bit, and the brothel was back.

For years, Miss Jessie and the gang at the Chicken Ranch also had a tacit arrangement with the local police, which was essentially this: The girls and I will be on the outskirts of town doing business if you will look the other way. That worked out for everybody, including the entire Texas A&M football team (allegedly), for a very long time. When Miss Jessie died in 1961, she bequeathed the brothel to her favorite prostitute, Edna Milton. Edna ran the place as a tribute to Miss Jessie, helping out with civic projects like Little League baseball teams and the community hospital. Local legend and long-time sheriff of La Grange, Jim Flournoy, used to state with pride, "That Chicken Ranch has been here all my life and all my daddy's life and never caused anybody any trouble."

"If a woman hasn't got a tiny streak of a harlot in her, she's a dry stick as a rule."
—D. H. Lawrence, British author of the controversial
Sons and Lovers and *Lady Chatterley's Lover*

In 1973 trouble eventually found Edna, Sheriff Flournoy, and the girls of the Chicken Ranch, when a local reporter out of Houston, Marvin Zindler, went and ruined things for everyone. Marvin was an odious and officious presence on the Houston news. He was also an ugly man, a plastic surgeon's dream, whose nipped-and-ripped-within-an-inch-of-its-life visage made this lunatic resemble nothing so much as a constipated orc. Marvin and his local news team arranged a sting, and the Chicken Ranch was forced to shut its doors. The ghost of Miss Jessie Williams, a host of happy johns, and a legion of innocent chickens pecked a hole in the sky that day. Even then-governor of Texas, Dolph Briscoe, resisted closing the ranch, but Zindler made such a stink on air about it, that Governor Briscoe's hands were tied—and not in the good way. Edna stayed behind and tried to go legit, but with little success. She eventually gave up and moved to East Texas.

Zindler, positively orgasmic over his newfound fame, did a follow-up report eighteen months later, in which a hopping mad Sheriff Flournoy grabbed Zindler and then ripped off the newsman's wig. With cameras still rolling the sheriff galloped down the street in circles waving the hairpiece over his head in imitation of a Native American warrior flaunting a freshly cut scalp. It was poetic justice for Zindler, and mighty fine comedy all the way around.

For early '70s nostalgia and/or more information on the Chicken Ranch, put on ZZ Top's "La Grange" and rock out.

SNOOP DOGG

PROFILE

DAY JOBS: Youth League basketball coach; Crip

CLAIM TO FAME: Multiplatinum rap artist; porno entrepreneur

THEATER OF OPERATIONS: The LBC and beyond

The S-N-Double-O-P D-O-Double-G's tales of pimpin' and hos and the gangsta lifestyle all figure prominently in his lyrics, but is he for real? Was Snoop *really* a pimp? Here it is straight from the hustla's mouth on FUSE TV in an interview with music journalist Touré:

> Yeah, I'm talking like really going in and getting girls to bring you back money for their services. . . . And I was running with real pimps and getting the understanding of pimpin'. 'Cause I don't do things for fake, I do it for real.

Snoop began to cotton to his new profession. He tells *Rolling Stone* magazine that shortly after his entrée into the pimp hustle, he was delighted to discover, "That shit was my natural calling and once I got involved with it, it became fun. It was like shootin' layups for me. I was makin' 'em every time." Snoop Doggy Dogg—just making ho buckets.

In 1971 Calvin Broadus Jr. was born in Long Beach, California, and he grew up to be a man of many talents. Over the years he has proven himself to be remarkably skilled as a petty thief, a drug dealer, an actor, a marijuana legalization activist, a rap star, and host of *Doggy Fizzle Televizzle*, a sketch comedy show that ran from 2002 to 2003, on which Snoop played characters such as Cap'n Pimp. The central message of his show revolved around the notion that pimping is a viable career option. Moreover, children who had the gumption to develop proficiency in this line of work could presumably grow up to live in a world of bright colors, money, and hos. However, after the show fizzizled, the pretend Cap'n Pimp felt compelled to take on pimping for real from 2003 to 2004 while working on a series of porn videos and simultaneously coaching his son's Pop Warner football team.

While much of Snoop's musical oeuvre is an homage to the gangster life—shooting people, dealing drugs, driving around, clockin' hos, and being rich (*see* "Who Am I [What's My Name?]," "Snoop's Upside Your Head," and "Serial Killer,")—his later work shows a kind of maturity as Snoop the family man made a concerted effort to shed the guns-thugs-and-drugs stereotype and whole-heartedly embrace his true calling, that of a pimp and pornographer.

If you've ever been involved in a philosophical debate, you've undoubtedly found the conversation winding back to the ageless question: Who would make a better prostitute? Britney Spears or Christina Aguilera? In that case, you need the Doggfather. With his storied eloquence, Snoop resolves the question, asserting that "Britney would make a better prostitute than Christina," because "She's thicker." So, big propers to the Doggfather for settling yet another existential quandary.

With *Snoop Dogg's Hustlaz: Diary of a Pimp* erotic video series and other "Snoop Dogg's Doggystyle Productions," Snoop made tremendous inroads into the porn industry, with *Diary of a Pimp* eventually becoming the bestselling erotic video of 2003. In *Diary of a Pimp*, Snoop, dressed like a parody of a pimp, goes around enlisting women, many of whom are hip-hop journalists, to join his crew of hos. All forty seem persuaded by the Doggfather and then, well, you know how these things unfold. And so it goes, and so it went.

Today, Snoop still supports youth football and family, and he seems contented to sit around counting money and blowing blunts, making the occasional appearance as a guest host on WWE Raw or endorsing "Chronic Candy," a line of sweet treats that taste like marijuana.

Snoop eventually had to give up the pimp lifestyle. As Ice Cube asserts, "pimpin' ain't easy," and Snoop concurs. Sometimes the whole pimping endeavor can be just too much trouble—the government red tape, the Feds, health insurance, Roth IRAs, etc.—who can maintain a music/youth football/pimp/actor schedule and stay sane? We can't blame Snoop for getting out of the game. Reminiscing about his time as a pimp, Snoop was often faced with what Kierkegaard might have called a "pimpological suspension of the ethical," with regard to slapping hos. Correction: "Bitches."

> I made sure my bitch would never talk shit to me. She always got all the money upfront, she never looked in another pimp's eyes, she kept her head down. But I wasn't a gorilla pimp where I was beatin' the girls up. I was more finesse with it, just givin' you a comfort zone and providing you with opportunity 'cause I know so many motherfuckers who like buyin' it, so if you come fuck with me, it's not as much of a risk as bein' with a gorilla pimp. He gon' be hard on you and rush you, as opposed to a nigga like me who's gonna relax and let you go get it. And if you don't go get it you just gon' be replaced.

Way to keep it classy, Calvin.

LULU WHITE

PROFILE

DAY JOBS: Owner and operator of the famous Mahogany Hall brothel

CLAIM TO FAME: "Queen of the demimonde"

THEATER OF OPERATIONS: Storyville, New Orleans

Ladies and gentleman, I've worked in advertising and "branding" long enough to know compelling ad copy when I see it. I've also suffered countless "focus groups," typically a collection of confused, half-drunk people trying to say nice things about a shitty product. The resulting brainfart typically yields a pamphlet or brochure that makes *Silas Marner* look like a page-turner.

"Storyville" was the official name for the red-light district of New Orleans from 1897 to 1917. The area is named for Big Easy alderman Sidney Story, who, taking a cue from Dutch and German prostitution ports in Europe, set up a special district where prostitution could be regulated and given a measure of oversight. Storyville was a thorough operation, where folk could get an idea of Storyville's services—including maps, recommendations, and available ladies—by perusing one of the handy "blue books" given to visitors and tourists and printed by the local government. These blue books gave critical information about individual houses of ill repute and their attendant employees. Think of it as a kind of hard copy adultfriendfinder.com with a fancy logo. Emblazoned on these blue books was an oath: *Honi soit qui mal y pense,* or "Evil be to him who evil thinks," or, in today's parlance, "Y'all can be freaky people, just don't be *nasty* people."

Every once in a while, however, I come face-to-face with an advertising campaign that inspires me and renews my faith in creativity *and*
commerce. It would behoove advertising students and business owners
alike to take a lesson from Ms. Lulu White: procuress, madam, queen
of bling, and for the early years of the twentieth century, the owner of
Mahogany Hall bordello in Storyville, New Orleans. Here's an excerpt
from the Mahogany Hall ad campaign:

> The New Mahogany Hall . . . was erected specially for Miss Lulu
> White at a cost of $40,000. . . . The entire house is steam heated and is
> the handsomest house of its kind. It is the only one where you can get
> three shots for your money:
>
> The shot upstairs,
> The shot downstairs,
> And the shot in the room.

Eschewing convention, Lulu doesn't even add an exclamation point
after the word "room." Daring! Although, who the hell wants to spend
valuable time traipsing up and down a bunch of stairs on the way to a
romp in the hay? Of course, the denizens of Storyville at the turn of the
twentieth century had no HDTV, Angry Birds, art crawls, or faith that
on the street they wouldn't be shanked with an ice pick before lunch,
so they had far fewer distractions and probably only a mild sense of
urgency about gaining a little carnal knowledge.

Continuing on with her brochure, the alarmingly straightforward
ad agency gives us a pretty good picture of Miss Lulu and her lair:

> This famous West Indian octoroon first saw the light of day thirty-one
> years ago. Arriving in this country at a rather tender age, and having
> been fortunately gifted with a good education it did not take long for
> her to find out what the other sex were in search of. In describing Miss
> Lulu, as she is most familiarly called, it would not be amiss to say that
> besides possessing an elegant form she has beautiful black hair and

blue eyes, which have justly gained for her the title of the "Queen of the Demimonde."

Her establishment, which is situated in the central part of the city, is unquestionably the most elaborately furnished house in the city of New Orleans, and without a doubt one of the most elegant places in this or any other country. She has made a feature of boarding none but the fairest of girls, those gifted with nature's best charms, and would, under no circumstances, have any but that class in her house.

Unfortunately, Lulu had a voracious appetite for diamonds, which she wore in such abundance that her promotional pamphlet described them as "like the lights of the St. Louis Exposition." Such extravagance eventually took a toll on her bankroll. Moreover, Lulu was a reckless investor; she lost over $150,000 on shady investment schemes. Lulu was destitute when she fled New Orleans in 1917 after the permanent closing of Mahogany Hall.

While Lulu and the Mahogany Hall brothel will be celebrated forever in Louis Armstrong's "Mahogany Hall Stomp" and the various representations of Storyville in film, art, and literature, the end of Lulu's life and career—very much like the "art" of advertising—is a depressing mystery, and one for someone else to probe.

HEIDI FLEISS

PROFILE

DAY JOBS: Laundry operator; reality TV presence

CLAIM TO FAME: Madam to the stars

THEATER OF OPERATIONS: Los Angeles

To some, she is a venerable feminist who took back the night. To others, she's nothing but a common trollop who stayed afloat mostly thanks to

Charlie Sheen's insatiable penis. But to most of America, and maybe the world, Heidi Fleiss endures as *the* face of upscale prostitution in the latter half of the twentieth century, despite a face that some say resembles an albino jack-o-lantern with fjord teeth.

Born in California in 1965, Fleiss learned her craft from a covey of top-notch L.A. madams before striking out on her own in 1990. She made her first million only four months into her career as a madam. Heidi's long list of famous clients is rumored to include: Charlie Sheen. That's right, out of all the heads of state, royals, and celebrities that counted themselves part of her clientele, only Charlie Sheen got pinched, and this is why we love him. There is something endearing about such carelessness.

Alas, it was carelessness along with jealousy on the part of less successful pimp-hooker-madam types in Southern California that put Heidi away. In 1993, she fell victim to a sting operation and was finally prosecuted for money laundering, attempted pandering, and tax evasion. Fleiss served twenty-one months in jail, where she spent much of her time playing chess and throwing chairs at fellow inmates as well as prison guards who were not easy to keep at bay. The pandering charges were eventually dropped, and Heidi came back strong.

A true whorrior, these days Heidi Fleiss is fighting addiction on numerous reality shows, including appearances on such gems as *Celebrity Big Brother, E! True Hollywood Story: Charlie Sheen*, and the Dr. Drew apocalypse, *Sober House*. Today, Fleiss lives in Nevada, where she keeps a pandemonium of twenty exotic macaws for her current show, *Heidi Fleiss: From Prostitutes to Parrots* on Animal Planet after an ill-advised attempt to open an all-male-staffed "Stud Farm," which was exactly what it sounded like. Heidi has also set up a coin-operated dry cleaners called "Dirty Laundry" on the outskirts of Sin City. Who knows what's in store for Heidi Fleiss—a natural-born grifter, we've not heard the last of her. Wait. Just found her again. According to TMZ.com, Heidi was recently evicted from her "Dirty Dog Laundry" business space for turning the place into a "dungheap." Luckily, she's also in the works with "Pimpmaster General" Dennis Hof (don't worry; he has his own entry) to open a sci-fi-themed whorehouse next to Area 51 to be christened, the "Alien Cathouse." Space whores for nerds. Genius.

MADAME GOURDAN

PROFILE

DAY JOB: *Entremetteuse extraordinaire*

CLAIM TO FAME: Running Paris's most notorious brothel

THEATER OF OPERATIONS: Eighteenth-century Paris

If you think the sunburn, tattoo, and genital carbuncles you brought home from Spring Break Cancun 1998 constitute the zenith of good times, you're an idiot. No matter where you vacation, it will never get as rowdy as eighteenth-century France. German philosopher Georg Hegel sums up the epoch in his weighty tome, *The Philosophy of History*:

> [A] mad state with which, at the same time, was bound the highest depravity
> of morals and spirit—an empire of injustice with the growing consciousness of
> that state.

You know the party got way out of hand when somebody puts things all philosophical like that. If you were up for the really juicy action, however, you came to the Château de Madame Gourdan, the most brazen *maison de tolerance* in all of France.

> *"So do not think of helpful whores as aberrational blots;*
> *I could not love you half so well without my practice shots."*
> —James Simmons, Irish author and poet

While Gourdan initially tailored the offerings of her *château* to serve the niche markets of lesbians and those who embrace sex toys, she soon expanded, turning the place into an all-out bordello, a combination of Willie Wonka's S&M Factory and Saw's house. Follow along as we walk through the Château de Gourdan room-by-room with none other than Pidanzat de Mairobert, an unimportant, prerevolutionary blowhard, as he recounts what he saw on a tour given by a local official after authorities shut down the sordid château temporarily in 1779. *Allons-y?*

The Piscine: "There was *'Essence a l'usage des monstres'*; it's a very strong astringent, with which Madame Gourdan treats the most tattered beauties and restores what can only be lost once."

Ballroom: "It's where everyone plays masquerade, where the peasant is metamorphosed into bourgeoisie and the noble lady sometimes into a chambermaid. . . . Wives—hiding their rank and their titles . . . could receive the vigorous assaults of crude rustics selected to assuage their burning lust."

Infirmary: "[T]he main concern here is not venereal diseases but rather aging voluptuaries whose jaded senses need to [be] revived . . . he showed me a little ball made out of stone, called a *pomme d'amour* [a ben-wa ball, probably] . . . so effective that if a woman inserts it into her pleasure center, it will start titillating her and giving her so much enjoyment that she will have to remove it before it kills her. . . . I saw next a quantity of little black rings, that were much too big to be finger rings . . ."

Chambre de la Question: "It's a closet where through secret peepholes the mistress and her confidants can see and hear whatever is said and done there."

Salon de Vulcain: "I found nothing unusual there except an armchair, whose singular design caught my eye. 'Sit down,' the president told me. . . . Just as soon as I threw myself there, the movement of my body tripped a counterweight. The back flipped backwards and so did I. I found myself spread-eagled, legs bound apart and arms as well, in a sort of cross . . . called the 'trap of Fronsac' because it was dreamed up by this Seigneur, to overcome a virgin who . . . had resisted all his seduction attempts, all his gold and his threats."

Now, we don't know much about Madame Gourdan's background, but the "little countess" addressed the refinements of her depraved décor in a manner almost as obsessive as Martha Stewart. The Madame had a sense of style and a real knack for "French hospitality," a throbbing oxymoron today, but back then, it was an accurate description of the Château de Gourdan business model. That assumes your idea of the red-carpet treatment includes masked perverts, peep holes, cock rings, orgasmically deadly apple balls, virgin juice, and being trapped in a rape chair. *Vive la Résistance*!?

ISAIAH AND CAROL REED

PROFILE

DAY JOB: Christian ministers

CLAIM TO FAME: Rising from the dead

THEATER OF OPERATIONS: Richmond, Texas

Sometimes, in order to get your ass off the street, you've got to get your mind on Jesus. It's been that way for millennia, the most famous case of conversion being St. Augustine, whose *Confessions*, written around A.D. 397, is a primer for how to cut a swath of fleshy capers and then shape up later: No harm, no foul. This seems like a cheap trick, but when we're into the mind of God and out of our depth, it's best to keep cosmological quandaries away from issues of prostitution. But sometimes, there's just no helping it.

Isaiah and Carol Reed weren't always evangelists at the Christian Vision Ministries. No, Isaiah and Carol were once, according to their website, "entwined in an international web of drugs and prostitution," with Isaiah as a pimp to seventeen hos, including Carol, his favorite. Life was good. "I was very good at being a drug dealer and a pimp," admits Mr. Reed in an interview with himself on the Reeds' website, also boasting that a newspaper once called him "the most vicious pimp in the state of Hawaii." As a prostitute, Carol was equally effective, though profligate. She could earn anywhere from $900 to $1,500 a night, but that usually went to drugs and other accoutrements necessary to maintain the sinful lifestyle. "When I bought my Rolls Royce I was so drunk drinking Courvasier [*sic*]," continues Isaiah. "I brought [the bottle] in with two prostitutes in a brown paper bag. Paid for it cash. Drove down the street drinking Courvasier [*sic*], looked at the Mercedes Benz place and bought a Benz with the change," he adds. Dangling modifiers aside, I'm concerned about what extraction of prostitute fits two to a paper bag. And do they mint larger bills especially for pimps? It's like Isaiah in Wonderland up in here, but that's of minor importance.

What is important is Isaiah's "come to Jesus" moment (Carol's conversion, indeed her life, is glossed over in the couple's bio, giving one the impression that prostitution and pimping may sometimes extend beyond the ho stroll to the house of the Lord). According to *www .isaiahreed.com*:

> **Isaiah Reed** was pronounced DOA at Denver Hospital from 2 bullet wounds and 16 stab wounds resulting from a drug deal gone bad. They did an autopsy on him and afterwards remembered they had not notified the next of kin. Once on the phone with Isaiah's mom, she refused to accept her son's death because of a promise God had made years back that Isaiah was going to be a preacher.

Now, I washed out of pre-med with organic chemistry, but it seems like if being killed didn't kill you, an autopsy would. Luckily, Isaiah came out of this unfortunate *contretemps* in one piece. For three more years, Isaiah "continued to live in sin after God raised him from the dead." Even for St. Augustine, that's pushing it. But Isaiah didn't get where he is without a strong woman to support him. No, sir. That's where Carol's story comes in! Somewhere on the website, maybe. . . . Okay, still nothing. She looks nice in the pictures, though.

The Reeds maintain a simple ethos: "To reach out and be a service to the drug addict, Prostitute, the lost and afflicted by way of 12 hour 5 days a week service with the word of God through outreach. No contribution small or large will go unnoticed. If you our [sic] interested please make your monthly, one time or yearly donation out to Christian Vision Ministries." Well, at least they get to the point. And while Christian Vision Ministries is located in Richmond, Texas, if you're interested in giving them your money, you'll have to track them down. They continue spreading the gospel with a rigorous travel schedule, including a number of upcoming trips planned to Hawaii. Jesus wept.

JAMES LIPTON

PROFILE

DAY JOBS: Writer, critic, poet, producer, professor, demi-pimp

CLAIM TO FAME: Exquisitely pedantic host of *Inside the Actor's Studio*

THEATER OF OPERATIONS: Paris; New York

If you are not by now familiar with Mr. James Lipton's ponderous, addictive show, *Inside the Actor's Studio* on the Bravo network, you might as well deposit your boorish head in the oven. James Lipton would want it that way, though he would probably explain it to you in Latin, maybe French. The man has become an institution, using *Inside the Actor's Studio* to educate legions of film aficionados, celebrity gawkers, and stoned couch-blisters about the finer points of acting and film and sometimes, even *cinéma*.

Born in 1926 in Michigan, Lipton first found radio voice-over work on *The Lone Ranger*, originally broadcast on WXYZ in Detroit. He soon went on to Hollywood where he toiled as a scriptwriter for numerous soap operas, including *Guiding Light* and *Another World*. But how, one might ask, did a naïve kid from Detroit come to appreciate the melodrama of life as depicted on daytime television? Easy. He goes to Paris, learns French (not the French other people speak, but a more pretentious, Frenchier patois), he becomes enchanted by life in the City of Lights, and he finds the few extra sous he needs to live that life by working as a midlevel pimp. Lipton explains in his memoir, *Inside Inside*:

> This was when I was very, very young, living in Paris, penniless, unable to get any kind of working permit. . . . I had a friend who worked in what is called the Milieu, which is that world and she suggested to me one night, 'Look, you'll be my meck' . . . We would translate it perhaps . . . as pimp. We were earning our living together, this young woman and I, we made a rather good living, I must say.

The old blowhard reveals that he would also arrange sex shows and other insipid displays. He writes,

> I had to accompany my clientele to the Rue Pigalle, and then I'd take them up to the room and I had to remain there because they were very nervous, they were young Americans for the most part . . . and they didn't speak French. I offered them a full bill of fare: two women or a man and woman. A man and woman was much more costly than two women: the law of supply and demand—not to mention the law of diminishing returns; the women could perform countless times each day, the men only two or three.

Pompously put insights such as these make it nigh on to impossible to take Monsieur Lipton seriously no matter what he is talking about. Indeed, his comments here raise certain obvious questions: James, were you really just a *translator* for prostitutes? You can never tell with students of the Stanislavski School. The method to their madness is surely just Method, which makes their madness even more maddening, especially off-screen.

Today, James Lipton is looking down the barrel at his ninetieth birthday, but all indications are that this histrionic Methuselah may continue pursuing the Holy Grail of Cinema long after solar flares have consumed the rest of us. He's no Snoop Dogg, but James Lipton and his supercilious baritone, along with his feast of insights and inanities, no doubt sent home from Paris countless young Americans with a thriving colony of Cupid's cysts after looking for love in all the wrong plazas.

WYATT EARP

PROFILE

DAY JOBS: Sheriff, boxing referee

CLAIM TO FAME: Throwing it down at the OK Corral; sweet moustache

THEATER OF OPERATIONS: Peoria, Illinois; Tombstone, Arizona

You may think you learned everything you need to know about Wyatt Earp from *Tombstone* with Kurt Russell. That's fair. *Tombstone* is the capstone of Wild West badassery. But know this: You were cheated.

That's right, instead of the lurid and historically accurate brothel scenes we deserved as serious cineastes, Hollywood cooked up the usual "romance" shtick, depriving us not only of *veritas* but also of the sex and nudity we crave. In real life Wyatt Earp owned and operated a number of brothels with his equally pimpalicious brothers, an egregious omission from the celluloid story.

How can we be so sure about this forgotten bullet point on Wyatt's resume? For one, in February of 1872, Wyatt and his brother Morgan were arrested for "Keeping and Being Found in a House of Ill-Fame" at a bagnio in Peoria, Illinois, which Wyatt was clever enough to list as his home address. Then, three months later, the brothers were pinched again over at the McClellan brothel. This from the *Daily Transcript* of May 11, 1872:

> That hotbed of inequity [*sic*], the McClellan Institute on Main Street near Water was pulled on Thursday night, and quite a number of inmates transient and otherwise were found therein. Wyat [*sic*] Earp

and his brother Morgan Earp were each fined $44.55 and as they had
not the money and would not work, they languished in the cold and
silent calaboose.

Are you as scandalized as I am? Even though the official *Oxford
English Dictionary* says it's only "a jail cell," the mention of a "calaboose" had me blushing. And as for his lack of liquidity, we're only
saying Wyatt was a pimp, not necessarily a *good* one. A pimp without *any* kind of bankroll is just embarrassing, so it's just as well Wyatt
turned to something for which he was better suited: killing people at
close range.

Born in Monmouth, Illinois, in 1848, Wyatt was the fourth of
eight brothers and sisters (including a half brother and sister). A rest-
less soul, Wyatt tried unsuccessfully to sneak into the Union army at
the age of thirteen. Before the famous gunfight at the OK Corral with
the "The Cowboys," a gang of thugs led by Ike Clanton, Earp worked
as a lawman, gambler, farmer, saloonkeeper, boxing referee, and of
course, a pimp.

The gunfight at the OK Corral was essentially a bunch of tired,
hung-over guys confused about their role in civic matters who got a
little trigger-happy. Oh, and Virgil Earp, *not* Wyatt, was the police mar-
shal that day. Regardless, Wyatt, along with some of his brothers and
Doc Holliday, saw fit to draw steel from six feet away, laying waste to Ike
and his cowboys. Though reports differ about who fired first, we can
assume Wyatt got the drop on his man. According to famous frontier
lawman Bat Masterson, who once worked with the Earps:

> Wyatt's speed and skill with a six-gun made almost any play against
> him with weapons "no contest." . . . I never saw the man in action
> who could shade him in the prime essential of real gun-fighting—the
> draw-and-shoot against something that could shoot back.

You know the rest. Every few years Hollywood trots out some
tough actor in chaps and a trench coat, and every few years down goes
the Clanton gang. Somebody rides off into the sunset, and in the end

we probably don't even get a decent full frontal shot. Wyatt Earp died in 1929 after a successful career pimping his wildly exaggerated legend all over America.

SABRINA ASET

PROFILE

DAY JOBS: Devoted mother; scientist

CLAIM TO FAME: High Priestess of the "Church of the Most High Goddess"

THEATER OF OPERATIONS: West Los Angeles

Are you familiar with the Greek term *hieros gamos*? In English, it translates to "sacred marriage," but this isn't like when Beyoncé married Jay-Z—this is holy, sort of. The notion behind *hieros gamos* is that it is a special kind of sacrament, a union of god and goddess. And since such unions are so hard to come by, in the mid 1980s, a druid-looking fellow named "Wilbur" crowned his new-age yuppie wife, Sabrina Aset "High Priestess of the Church of the Most High Goddess," and now she is busy taking back the night. And the day. And, it turns out, most mornings. The process involves performing a series of cleansing sexual rituals, adhering strictly to the tenets of a creed she and husband Wilbur invented for a new order called the "The Cult of Isis." The idea seems to be that she, as a "sacred prostitute," is able to cleanse men of their wickedness.

Sabrina is a highly accomplished, multitalented, complicated woman. She was born in 1943, and like so many "sacred prostitutes," she has earned a postgraduate degree. In addition to being a high priestess, Ms. Aset is also a lion tamer, and in one of the numerous articles on the church's website, she claims to have "sucked cocks through the open window of my car and through a hole in a wall," which, granted, doesn't sound all that impressive, unless it was through the open window of a moving car with a lion in the front seat. The point is, she's a sexjack deity with no patience for palliated storytelling. Plus, sometimes you just can't beat the real thing, so here's Sabrina on her website, *www .goddess.org*, to provide her own quick resume:

> I graduated high school with a straight A average, graduated the University of Miami, cum laude in chemistry . . . attended the University of Oregon Medical School and received my masters in Environmental Sciences/Chemistry from Portland State University. I am a mother first and foremost. . . . In my calling as a priestess, I have sex with men . . . every day, several times a day (and even more often would be better). To date I've had vaginal sex with over 2,779 different men, oral sex with over 4,000 different men, and being bisexual, I have eaten a couple of hundred pussies along the way.

Perhaps you're thinking she's not a prostitute, she's just a confident woman having a high ol' time for herself. Well, this is where Wilbur comes in. In the Church of the Most High Goddess, a sacred whore comes with a price. According to High Priest Wilbur, "Church members must contribute money or services to participate in rituals that involve sexual intercourse." Hey, tithing is a long tradition among the faithful, and besides, while the Church of the Most High Goddess lacks a fancy pipe organ, a nude picture of Sabrina does hang discreetly over the altar. You can play along with your own organ, if you can't afford the happy-ending-complete-absolution package.

PROFILE

DAY JOB: Gubernatorial candidate; successful hedge fund manager

KRISTIN DAVIS

CLAIM TO FAME: "The Manhattan Madam," kicked former NY governor Eliot Spitzer's freaky ass to the curb

THEATER OF OPERATIONS: Manhattan

Kristin Davis, "The Manhattan Madam," ran a first-class cathouse. She treated her women well, and when complaints started piling up regarding New York Governor Eliot Spitzer's "condom problem" (specifically, his tendency to be "a real weasel" about wearing one), Kristin lost patience with Spitzer and blacklisted him from her operation. She also exposed clients if they became violent or aggressive toward her employees. Kristen treated the ladies like family, acknowledging prostitution as an inevitably short career arc and helping them cultivate skills that might serve them well in the future. And, with a client-book of over 10,000 names, including: business moguls, sports stars, Hollywood celebrities of every ilk, and plenty of satisfied politicians. In fact, in January 2012, Davis testified that she provided women for currently in-deep-shit French politician Dominique Strauss-Kahn. According to Davis, in 2006, when Strauss-Kahn was head of the IMF and in the middle of a presidential candidacy, the Whoreback of Notre Dame blew up her cell personally, agreeing to front $1,200 cash for a hotel tryst in New York.

So you see, Kristin Davis was more than a run-of-the-mill madam—she was an empresario.

After a few perfunctory stints in Los Angeles as an escort, Kristin saw an opportunity to improve the business, and she moved back to the Big Apple. To be fair, her goal was well within reach, as most escort services were presided over by a glorified pimp and boasted a few telephones, a nice batch of herpes, and low-grade blow. Kristin had always been smart. She finished high school at fifteen, went to college graduating with a business degree and later a master's in psychology. Furthermore, before she opened shop, Kristin honed her business skills as the vice president of a New York hedge fund. With her business acumen, her people skills, and two enormous boobs, Ms. Davis's business would, at its peak in the mid 2000s, bring in over $5 million a year. She offers a glimpse of her business model in her bestselling memoir, *The Manhattan Madam: Sex, Drugs, Scandal and Greed Inside America's Most Successful Prostitution Ring*.

> *"A professional politician is a professionally dishonorable man.*
> *In order to get anywhere near high office he has to make*
> *so many compromises and submit to so many humiliations that*
> *he becomes indistinguishable from a streetwalker."*
> —H. L. Mencken, American satirist, essayist, and critic

Like any good cult of personality, she first needed a badass madam moniker:

> I chose my madam name, Billie, after the teenage outlaw Billy the Kid. I was a young woman living outside the law, but working in a man's world, profiting from the illicit desires of all types of men, from blue-collar workers to celebrity millionaires. I needed a name that was both sexy and ballsy; a name that said, "Don't mess with me, buddy"; a name for a vigilante and an enforcer of the peace. And so to the more than 10,000 clients I accumulated in five years as the leader of the most successful call girl game in Manhattan, I was Billie.

So she was Billie the Trick, a sharpshooting reverse cowgirl with a bright future. Ms. Davis was right. Nobody ever messed with the great outlaws, like Billy the Kid or Ned Kelly or, indeed, *Whore Stories* favorites like Butch and Sundance. Until somebody did. The inevitable vice crackdown obliged the Manhattan Madam to move to the less-forgiving confines of Riker's Island for a four-month getaway. Today, though, Kristin is an advocate for women's issues and for reform. In a wildly ironic move, she staged a failed, yet spectacularly salacious gubernatorial campaign in 2010 running on an "Anti-Prohibition" ticket and urging the legalization of pot and prostitution. She also has plans to open "Hope House," a nonprofit facility offering support and shelter for victims of sex trafficking.

Through it all, Kristin also found time to date future Hall-of-Famer Alex Rodriguez, an inexcusable lapse on her part, A-Rod's mammoth dingers and hot-frosted tips notwithstanding. But we'll let that one slide, Madam Manhattan—you're a piece of all right.

DENNIS HOF

PROFILE

DAY JOB: Star of the HBO docudramedy, *Cathouse*

CLAIM TO FAME: America's Pimpmaster General

THEATER OF OPERATIONS: Nevada

Dennis Hof is a shrewd businessman with an uncanny prescience about how to make money off of all things prurient. Known far and wide as "America's Pimpmaster General," this horny, bald, fat man with cherub cheeks and hairy man-boobs down to here, appeared in the HBO reality series *Cathouse* saying things like "Guys know what they think sex is worth. . . . But they don't know what it's worth to dress up in women's underwear." Insights like that are the reason Dennis Hof gets to hang out in the Nevada desert with a harem of beautiful women performing metrics on panties, while you and I continue to slog away at our day jobs.

Hof made his fortune in San Diego real estate before buying the Moonlight Bunny Ranch in 1992 and turning it into a veritable Disneyland of sex. Indeed, Hof's motto at the Bunny Ranch is "Not Just Sex—An Adventure," which sounds suspiciously like that trip to

Veracruz where you learned the Spanish word for gonorrhea, *gonorrea*, which doesn't make it much easier to take. But Hof insists his sporting house is a good clean establishment—no festering diseases here. He claims it's more like a time-share, just a little fleshier, a little more ambitious. In an interview with FRED Entertainment (formerly "Movie Poop Shoot") Hof says:

> My vision, my dream is to close up half the Starbucks in America and make mini-Bunnyranch Expresses out of them. Stop by for a little tension release. Starbucks has everybody amped up on caffeine. I want to bring 'em down a notch. A guy can come out of his office, go to the Bunnyranch Express and fifteen minutes he's back in his office and it's not so bad of a day for him.

So far he hasn't said anything about screw-thru windows, but I'm sure he'll figure it out soon enough.

Hof is mum on his early life, offering only that he grew up around Tempe, owed a chain of gas stations, and had two sons whom he's disowned for "disrespecting the family," a grievance some may find ironic. Hof, on the other hand, may count these among his achievements:

1. Enjoys referring to porn king Ron Jeremy as "my bitch."
2. On again/off again boyfriend of Heidi Fleiss.
3. Resembles the character of "The Judge" in *Blood Meridian*.
4. His "good friend" Larry Flynt refers to him as "Pimpmaster General."
5. Is proud to be, in his estimation, "The Colonel Sanders of Pimps."

Today, Dennis Hof, *Cathouse*, and the Moonlite Bunny Ranch are all going strong. One of the novelties at the Bunny Ranch is the porno "fantasy camp" where folks with a load of disposable income have the opportunity to do unspeakable things with real-life porn stars. If that's not their cup of shit, however, they can join Hof and the girls on "Armed

Forces Appreciation Day," when soldiers ride for free, or they can attend "Freak of the Week" parties, where the "bar is raised," whatever that means. Over 500 Hof-approved hos are available twenty-four hours a day, seven days a week; however only 40 to 50 are actually onsite at any given moment.

The battle against legal prostitution continues in Nevada, with Senate Majority Leader Harry Reid (D. Nev.) threatening to limit and tighten laws on whoring, but Dennis Hof isn't going down without a fight. "Harry Reid will have to pry the cathouse keys from my cold, dead hands," he cocks crowily. Currently getting preparations in order for the "Alien Cathouse" he's opening with Heidi Fleiss, Hof is keeping the Comic-Con contingent on edge as to whether or not he will be successful in finding intergalactic whores with standards low enough to take on the Trekkie hordes.

FILLMORE SLIM

PROFILE

DAY JOB: Blues musician

CLAIM TO FAME: "The Pope of Pimping"

THEATER OF OPERATIONS: San Francisco

Clarence "Fillmore" Slim just wanted to play the blues. And he did that, but he also became a legendary pimp on the streets of San Francisco, where he seems to have had no choice. "Pimps are born, not made," he asserts. You hear that people are born to play the blues, too, so maybe you can be born to do more than one thing. If you were fortunate enough to catch him in the documentary *American Pimp*, however, it is hard to imagine Clarence as anything but a "fancy man."

Born in New Orleans in 1934, young Clarence came from humble beginnings, picking cotton and plowing fields with a mule, eking out

some facsimile of a life by day, but entranced in the evening with the blues
lore and legend his grandmother provided. By 1955 Clarence had taken
his leave of Louisiana and moved to Los Angeles, where he made a small
dent in the music scene, but one night on tour in Midland, Texas, everything changed. In an interview with *SF Weekly*, Slim explains, "We played
a smoky blues dive in Midland. I noticed this little girl who kept coming
in, then going out. Finally, she came up to me and said, "I like you. I want
you to have this money.'" Slim, quite naturally, was confounded. "I asked
her how she got all that money. She finally told me she was a hooker. I
asked her what a hooker did, and she broke it on down for me." Not one
to miss an opportunity, Slim took off for San Francisco where the future
for a blues singin' booty slanger was decidedly rosier.

In San Francisco, Slim opened for BB King, Dinah Washington, and
other blues icons. He even released a successful single of his own called
"You Got the Nerve of a Brass Monkey." Slim waxed a flurry of somewhat less well-received 45s in the ensuing years, while somehow finding the time to cultivate a reputation as the premiere pimp of San Fran's
Fillmore district. Eventually the intricate financials associated with a
dual career playing the blues and pimping got to him, and "Fillmore
Slim" had to hang up the guitar, embrace supply-side economics, and
hit the streets in earnest.

Slim claims that at the high point of his career he had twenty-two
"bitches" working for him. It's one thing to manage, like, four imbe-
ciles at a Kinko's, but twenty-two bitches running around lawless on the
streets of San Francisco? That's a job to inspire a blues ballad if there
ever was one. But then again, as Fillmore so elegantly puts it, "pussy
gon' sell when cotton and corn don't."

Today, Mr. Slim has allegedly reformed himself. He's playing the
blues again and coming up on eighty years old. Gone are the days of
schlepping around the streets of San Francisco, looking for "bitches" to
turn out, and trying to keep his hos off "dog food." Today, Fillmore has
left the life of the loins behind, but he has his nostalgic moments:

> I still do miss the game sometimes, but I'm also glad I'm still here
> to talk about it. These days the game is dangerous. I'm glad I'm still

OG—paid my dues and lived through the days. But now I'm doing something that society accepts me for.

Like writing some of our most cherished floozy anthems, including: "Street Walker," "Hooker's Game," and the timeless ode to pimp frustration, "The Girl Can't Cook."

POLLY ADLER

PROFILE

DAY JOB: Bestselling author

CLAIM TO FAME: Classy cathouses drew everyone from Joe DiMaggio to Dorothy Parker

THEATER OF OPERATIONS: New York

Talk about pulling yourself up by the bra-straps, Polly Adler's life in many ways represents everything the American dream has to offer: sex, wealth, power, and just enough drugs to be fun but not go completely outer limits. Of course, as the movies and to a lesser degree, history, have taught us, you have to go through a whole bunch of horse shit first, before you can realize the American dream. Polly had to make compromises in her quest for the dream, and those compromises led to more than a dozen collars for running houses of ill repute and other lesser indiscretions all over New York City.

Pearl "Polly" Adler was born in Russia at the turn of the twentieth century and immigrated to the United States just before the outbreak of World War I. Having alienated her traditional family by getting pregnant without the benefit of marriage and then having an abortion, Ms. Adler found herself lost in a sea of immigrants living in the squalid tenements of 1920s New York City. Luckily, Polly understood a thing or two about the universally spoken language of harlotry. She tried eking out a living at a shirt factory in Brooklyn, but soon turned to renting (then renting-out to concupiscent clients) individual apartments throughout New York City, where discretion and anonymity ruled the day and ass ruled the night. Eventually Adler had enough clients to open up a full-fledged bordello.

Ms. Adler ran a different kind of place, a classy joint where the rich and famous could frolic on a first-class passion playground. According to Polly, in her autobiography *A House Is Not a Home*, when men would take one of her girls for a date on the town, "I insisted that on such occasions they dress quietly and use a minimum of makeup. The days of the flagrantly dressed, flagrantly 'refined' tarts who tossed down their snorts of rotgut with the little finger well out were long past."

These days, the Internet is making it easier for prostitutes to ply their trade and keep one step ahead of the police. But that's not to say the fuzz doesn't try to limit prostitution in certain areas by using certain legal loopholes. In Washington, D.C. (and *especially* during inauguration ceremonies and other diplomatic fêtes), lawmakers have instituted "Prostitution Free Zones," (PFZs) where prostitutes can't hang out unless they're offering sex for free or if they ply their thighs outside of the ten-day PFZ enforcement periods, a bit of seedy political wrangling that make the PFZs quasi-constitutional. Cyndee Clay, the executive director of Helping Individual Prostitutes Survive (HIPS), a nonprofit group in Washington, D.C., argues that "A Prostitution Free Zone allows the loitering standard to be so low that anyone who doesn't look like they belong in a particular neighborhood [is] rounded up." And the battle of the sexers continues.

Adler's bordellos often had to change locations abruptly in order to elude police, but the big-name New York personalities always seemed to know exactly where to find her. Members of the Algonquin Round Table, including Robert Benchley and Dorothy Parker, frequented Adler's classy cathouse, and so did mob boss Dutch Schultz, Joltin' Joe

DiMaggio, and even the famously depraved and corrupt mayor of New York City, Jimmy Walker.

Prohibition was the law of the land, but Adler served up bootleg liquor and good times until a bunch of buzz kills including the Feds, the vice squad, and the temperance movement ruined everything. Ceaseless raids and constant fear that she might be "taken out" by some gangster eventually proved too much for Polly, who gave up on the life of an iconic New York City madam for a relatively chaste life in California, where she eventually went to college and wrote the bestselling *A House Is Not a Home*. Polly Adler was one hell of a woman; intelligent, insightful, pragmatic, financially successful, and brutally realistic to the very end. In her autobiography, she gives an eloquent argument in defense of her "tainted" past:

> If I was to make my living as a madam, I could not be concerned either with the rightness or wrongness of prostitution, considered either from a moral or criminological standpoint. I had to look at it simply as a part of life, which exists today as it existed yesterday. . . . The operation of any business is contingent on the law of supply and demand, and if there were no customers, there certainly would be no whorehouses. Prostitution exists because [people] are willing to pay for sexual gratification, and whatever [people] are willing to pay for, someone will provide.

Ms. Adler died in 1962 in Hollywood, California.

ROSEBUDD BITTERDOSE

PROFILE

DAY JOBS: Memoirist; pool hustler

CLAIM TO FAME: Scene-stealing turn in Hughes Brothers' documentary *American Pimp*

THEATER OF OPERATIONS: Los Angeles

Don't let his paradoxical and bewildering *nom de pimp* fool you—Rosebudd Bitterdose ("with two 'Ds' for a double-dose of this pimpin'") is a bewildering paradox. This wily whoremonger can appear to be an old sage of the streets who gets all misty-eyed talking about the tragic death of the first bitch he pimped. Rosebudd claims a bunch of bank-robbing LAPD cops killed her so she wouldn't talk. In an instant, however, he can morph seamlessly into a stone-cold moron reinforcing all the worst stereotypes. For instance, just try picking up what Rosebudd's putting down on the illusive concept of "game" in this interview with *Suck.com*:

> You don't see real game. . . . That's the part of it that's still a secret, and you cannot imagine how motherfuckers get a hold of girls, besides tricking them with drugs. And let me tell you, a pimp thinks like this: "I don't want no motherfucking drug addict counting my money before I do." A pimp is selfish. . . . A real pimp isn't thinking, "I got to stand over here to keep an eye on her." There are pimps who think like that. But those be little pimps. Those be pimps that are not willing to risk losing a broad over their principles. I'm willing to risk it for my principles.

What in the Sam shit does that even *mean*?

You may be thinking to yourself, "Why, I don't want no motherfucking drug addict counting my money before I do either!" but don't flatter yourself that you are a legitimate pimp. If you are a quasi-rational person, and even moderately aware of the hazards associated with drug use, such as jail time and death, you are suffering from delusions of grandeur, and you most assuredly do not have what it takes to be a pimp. Even if you are so morally steadfast you would be willing to risk losing a broad over your principles, I have to ask, "Do you even have a broad to risk, man?"

Well, pimps have to start somewhere, and young Mr. Bitterdose (born John Dickson) started by hustling pool in Hollywood. Hustling pool turned into hustling women, and by the 1970s, Rosebudd was *the* pimp of Sunset Strip. He was, in fact, the star and the most compelling and preposterous pimp of the bunch in the Hughes Brothers' documentary, *American Pimp*, as Mr. Bitterdose proclaims to care about his "hos" and "bitches," even though he feels that sometimes he's forced to beat the stank out of them.

In his memoir, *Rosebudd: The American Pimp*, the author writes about how he "has to" slap a bitch who has stepped out of line. The young ho wants an off day, so he smacks her "four or five times" while thinking to himself, "An off day, hummmmmm, what a concept." But then, he comes to his senses, remarking "Bitch, if you wanted a designated off day, you should have been a secretary or something!" Rosebudd attempts to justify himself saying, "Now to a hustler, being a motherfucker is what you strive for. So when someone say, 'Rosebudd's a motherfucker,' that's the highest compliment you can get because they've run out of adjectives."

It looks like we're all run out of adjectives up in here, Rosebudd.

JASON ITZLER

PROFILE

DAY JOBS: *Page Six* magazine favorite; prison bitch

CLAIM TO FAME: Self-proclaimed "King of All Pimps"

THEATER OF OPERATIONS: New York

If you've ever heard of Jason Itzler, it's probably because he was the founder of a notorious prostitution ring called NY Confidential. The last time most people heard anything about this lecherous miscreant was in September of 2011 when the authorities charged him with promoting prostitution and selling drugs through an escort service called Rockstar Models & Partygirls. Pleading not guilty, Itzler stood before the court, and, in one of the more satisfying turns of events in recent memory, his pants fell down. The bailiffs snatched him up, and he scampered awkwardly back to jail.

French writer André Gide was spot-on when he said that, "Nothing is so silly as the expression of a man who is being complimented." Well, Itzler was a man who, for a time, spent all of his waking hours being toadied to and basking in compliments inspired by stark terror, so imagine the guy Gide is talking about, scoff at him, and then picture his pants around his ankles. That vision will make everything right with the world; this is why we need Jason Itzler. We need the fall. We need justice, even if it's only the poetic kind.

Itzler was born Jason Sylk in 1967, and he was raised in a cosmopolitan atmosphere. His family was hooked up with everyone from notorious Mob accountant Meyer Lansky to the then prime minister of Israel, Golda Meir, who stayed with Jason's family on trips to the United States. However, Jason early on developed much more of an affinity for the Lansky lifestyle.

While enrolled at George Washington University, Jason had little time for class; he was busy, busy, busy making his first fortune as "the

22-year-old phone-sex king of South Beach." Tax issues and bankruptcy soon laid waste to the phone-sex operation, and he suffered some serious blowback from getting caught on his return from Amsterdam with 4,000 tabs of ecstasy, a purchase Itzler admits correctly was a "totally retarded idea." The judge gave him seventeen months in the hoosegow to reflect on his crimes and to ponder how to become a better citizen. Inspiration did not arrive, however, until he was on parole in Hoboken, a long-standing setting for the hatching of bad ideas. He would start an escort service—the best. It would be called NY Confidential, a lazy branding campaign if there ever was one, but Itzler had a dream, not unlike MLK, except for Itzler's dream was so rapturously stupid:

> At NY Confidential, I told my girls that the pressure is on them because we have to provide the clients with the greatest single experience ever, a Kodak moment to treasure for the rest of their lives. Spreading happiness, positive energy, and love, that's what being the best means to me. Call me a dreamer, but that's the NY Confidential credo.

For a while, the dream came true. The ladies in Itzler's NY Confidential stable spread more positive energy around swanky hotel rooms and the NY Confidential headquarters in Tribeca than one cares to imagine. And in a daring display of chutzpa he took out full-page ads in a number of upscale NYC publications, flying his floozy-flag in full view and almost daring the police and the politicians to shut him down. The thing was, many of them were his customers. Ashley Dupré, former governor Elliot Spitzer's go-to gal, was once an NY Confidential Escort, as was Natalia, the $2,000/hr sex sorceress (see entry on Natalia McLennan).

In 2005 the cops could not ignore the obvious any longer, and they took down Itzler and NY Confidential. After serving his eighteen months, Itzler bounced around, running lower-key escort services and dealing a little coke, but those enterprises also came crashing down, along with his pants, after the cops found him wandering around W. Fourteenth wearing a jaunty fedora and carrying a trombone he didn't know how to play, which is not a crime, but prostitution and drug-dealing still are. Hobbling ignominiously out of the courtroom in handcuffs with his pants around his ankles, Itzler had one last flash of inspiration: He wailed in psychosis, "I saved Billy Ray Cyrus's life, that's what this is about!"

Oh, come *on*, man. That's not even *trying*.

Chapter III

HUSTLING FOR
A HIGHER CAUSE

Some people just can't ever be satisfied. You must be familiar with this species of ambitious creature: the medical assistant training to be a doctor, the waitress waiting to be discovered as a model/actress/singer, or the prostitute pounding the pavement, hoping the Fortuna wheel of the street will eventually give him or her that lucky spin toward something loftier. So on that note, let's meet the overachievers, the busybodies, and the multitalented call girls, rent-boys, and common streetwalkers who came to distinguish themselves not only in the field of floozies, but by other, more newsworthy achievements than just lying down to take it and fake it.

THEODORA

PROFILE

DAY JOB: Politician

CLAIM TO FAME: A trick with a goose; ruling the Western world

THEATER OF OPERATIONS: Byzantium

Meet Theodora, the whore who once held dominion over the Western world. She was born a Greek Cypriot with a bear trainer for a father and a "scandalized" mother. Her fate, it seemed, was to be stuck in a dead-end gig as a mime/nudie dancer, but in A.D. 527 Theodora managed to work it all the way to the throne of Byzantium.

The ancient scholar Procopius in his *Historia Arcana*, which lay hidden for centuries in the Vatican archives, recounts one of Theodora's signature moves:

> She would sink down to the stage floor and recline on her back. Slaves to whom the duty was entrusted would then scatter grains of barley from above into the calyx of this passion flower, whence geese, trained for the purpose, would next pick the grains one by one with their bills and eat.

Luckily for Theodora, Justinian, the open-minded emperor of Byzantium, also commonly referred to as "The Emperor who never sleeps," was smitten with this courtesan's beauty and her willingness to get a little freaky. Theodora and Justinian married, and it is Theodora, by most accounts, who is credited with being the brains of the operation to restore Rome to its former glory. Justinian insisted that his bride share the throne and that she serve as a spearhead in all decision-making processes. They were well on their way to glory when the bubonic plague thwarted their grand vision by decimating the population.

An ardent champion of women's rights, Theodora spent much of her life working to reform Byzantium, starting with a prohibition on forced prostitution. In Rome and abroad she successfully lobbied to expand women's legal rights in domestic proceedings, property issues, and guardianship, while showing no quarter to criminals convicted of rape (think lions) and other crimes against women.

HERBERT HUNCKE

PROFILE

DAY JOBS: Junkie; poet

CLAIM TO FAME: "The Mayor of Forty-Second Street"

THEATER OF OPERATIONS: Forty-Second Street

If you look closely, you'll notice prostitution is a theme that emerges in the lives of many figures from the "Beat Generation," the group of post–World War II writers and artists that includes Allen Ginsberg, Jack Kerouac, William S. Burroughs, and Neal Cassady, among others. However, perhaps the "beatest" of the Beats, was the man who coined the term, the man who operated in the shadows, the man with the perfect name for a back-alley prosty: Herbert Huncke (pronounced "hunky").

Herbert was born in 1915 in Massachusetts, but his family soon relocated to Chicago. There, Huncke thumbed his nose at the authorities and dropped out of school to hustle wide-eyed Windy City tourists, then hopped trains and lived the hobo life, which was tough, because where the hell are we supposed to deliver your paper, Mr. Caboose? The reality was that Herbert Huncke had no need for, or interest in, reading a newspaper; he was one of those unique life forms who exist purely in the ethereal space between life, time, and the local news.

In 1939 Huncke hitched a ride to the Big Apple and took up residence on Forty-Second Street, where for the next decade he would be a fixture known as "Huncke the Junkie," and/or "The Mayor of Forty-Second Street." It was here, in Times Square, that Huncke the prostitute blossomed. Huncke was an open-minded, gender-blind working boy who offered his services to men and women desperate enough to enlist a homeless addict sporting a wilted *boutonnière*, and attracting the kind of attention usually reserved for fistfights and devastating apartment fires.

In the autobiographical *Junky*, William S. Burroughs remembers seeing Huncke (called "Herman" in the book) for the first time:

> Waves of hostility and suspicion flowed out from his large brown eyes like some sort of television broadcast. The effect was almost like a physical impact. The man was small and very thin, his neck loose in the collar of his shirt. His complexion faded from brown to a mottled yellow, and pancake make-up had been heavily applied in an attempt to conceal a skin eruption. His mouth was drawn down at the corners in a grimace of petulant annoyance.

Of course Burroughs was trying to sell Huncke some morphine and a submachine gun at the time, a pitch that may have contributed to Herbert's "waves of hostility and suspicion." And while the temptation is to talk about how insane it is to name a child "Herbert", it's time to get back to the call-boy boogie.

Before Huncke could serve as an inspiration to his Beat contemporaries, live off their charity and regale them with stories of slanging every iteration of the word "junk" in Times Square, he had to live the life. In a 1949 journal entry, Allen Ginsberg wrote of Huncke:

> I appreciated [his] activities as touches peculiar to Huncke alone, and therefore valuable, lovely and honorable. They were part of his whole being and "life force." I also enjoyed mythologizing his character. It is a literary trick which Kerouac, the novelist—who has written much about Herbert Huncke—and I exploited in the past.

As a literary muse, Huncke was unparalleled. To be sure, he was a junkie and thief, but the man was also a Times Square Prometheus who imparted his own brand of fiery wisdom to the poets and then suffered the wrath of the gods while flaunting his opiate-saturated booty along Broadway. As a prostitute, maybe he just needed money for dope, or maybe he was indeed, as Jack Kerouac described him, "martyred. Tortured by sidewalks, starved for sex and companionship." In his autobiography *Guilty of Everything* we are given Huncke the writer, which if you are interested, offers a certain tedium and explains why he had to have lots of other day jobs.

> *"Hustlers of the world, there is one Mark you cannot beat: the Mark Inside."*
> —William S. Burroughs

Shakespeare poses the question, "What's in a name?" With a name like Herbert Huncke, you'd better be ready to go knuckles out on the playground, and often, or make your entrance from around the back. For better or worse, Herbert made his choice.

JEAN GENET

PROFILE

DAY JOBS: Writer; political activist; scamp

CLAIM TO FAME: Colossus of French modernism

THEATER OF OPERATIONS: France

Doesn't the name "Jean Genet" make you yearn for a trans-Atlantic tryst with an artsy Frenchman? Maybe he's also mysteriously reticent, wearing a beret and a black-and-white striped shirt. Wait, no. Those are mimes. Different fantasy.

Although not a mime, Jean Genet is known as the powerhouse dramatist of French modernism. He was also controversial for his political activism, for his alliance with the Black Panthers, and for the graphic portrayal of homosexual sex in his plays and novels. Born in 1910 and abandoned at seven months by his mother, a destitute prostitute fighting a losing battle on the rancid rues of Paris, Genet was charged with his first crime (theft) when he was only ten. He spent most of his early years in state-run institutions and reformatory "schools," where he got by on his prodigious intelligence and a certain facility for theft, drug-dealing, and, of course, prostitution.

You may call it the grundle, taint, gooch, choad, nifkin, or durf, but the area bridging the divide from your anus to your genitalia is actually called the *perineum*. Scientists and freaks are wont to measure this fleshspan, called anogenital distance (AGD), with longer AGDs linked to increased fertility in men (the average AGD is around two inches, or 52 mm). For the ladies, studies indicate that massaging the perineum with warm olive oil toward the end of the third trimester can reduce tearing and the need for an episiotomy. And yes, I'm referring to the pregnancy trimester, not the trimester where your proposal to major in "choad measuring" was declined by the biology department, the narrow-minded fools.

Living for a time in Gibraltar during the 1930s, Genet sometimes sold his body for sardines and a loaf of bread (literally) to English seamen. He would often dress as a woman to aid in his petty thievery, and presumably, to make the sailors of the stuffy English armada feel less guilty about dorking a master of modernism on a dirty wharf. Genet recounts many of these buoy-toy experiences in his seminal novel, *Our Lady of the Flowers*, which he wrote while in prison for "vagrancy" and "lewd acts." In this worthy tome, Genet graphically details all the ins-

and-outs of a man-whore subculture, along with one of the best odes to a choad you'll read this week:

> There was in his supple bearing the weighty magnificence of a barbarian. . . . The most impressive thing about it is the vigor, hence the beauty, of that part which goes from the *anus* to the tip of the penis.

Our Lady of the Flowers had worldwide influence, inspiring participants in the New York Stonewall uprising and the Tokyo Street riots, both turning points in the fight for gay liberation. The legendary philosopher Jean-Paul Sartre praised Genet's novel as "an epic of masturbation . . . a matchless, unholy trinity of scatology, pornography and the legitimate study of evil." One would think an author could pen only so many weighty epics on masturbation, but Genet would continue for years to explore themes of sex, politics, prostitution, and society, most notably in *The Balcony*, a masterpiece of modern theater in which a brothel serves as the focal point for a violent revolution in the streets. The prostitutes featured in *The Balcony* are well-developed characters, full of humanity and righteousness, unlike the morally bankrupt characters that represent the status quo. Genet remains often imitated but never duplicated, and his influence transcends time and culture, which only occasionally results in misbegotten mime fantasies. A towering figure in both the art world and the tart world, Jean Genet gave a voice to the dispossessed, and he offers a frustrating reminder of how, if one is dead-set on creating meaningful art, one should probably catch a case and go to prison for a while.

ANNIE SPRINKLE

PROFILE

DAY JOBS: Sex icon

CLAIM TO FAME: Prostitute/porn star turned artist/ sexologist

THEATER OF OPERATIONS: San Francisco

Camille Paglia calls Annie Sprinkle a "feminist revolutionary"; Sprinkle calls herself a "metamorphosexual"; and I hereby proclaim her "Queen of the Golden Shower Ritual Kits." But Annie Sprinkle would have merited none of these titles if she hadn't first distinguished herself as a prostitute.

Born Ellen Steinberg in 1954 in Philadelphia, Annie Sprinkle never shied away from her past. In fact, her trailblazing porno film, *Deep Inside Annie Sprinkle*, which made her the "second-best selling video star of 1981," is largely autobiographical. The film features a character named Ellen Steinberg, a shy little Jewish girl from Philly with dreams as big as her breasts. The movie follows the bashful Ellen as she grows up to be the inimitable Annie Sprinkle, exploring her sexuality with a host of talented costars, including Ron "The Hedgehog" Jeremy in one of his first roles!

In a 2000 interview with *Salon*, Sprinkle recalls "feeling ugly and wanting to be touched" as a child, and she believes these feelings were the driving force behind her entrée into porn and prostitution by her late teens. Whether it was nature or nurture, according to Annie, "Porn was exactly what I needed, and up 'til my mid-20s, I really liked being a prostitute." That's something you don't hear every day, and they are strong words from the former Girl Scout, but Annie is nothing if not unconventional. "I'd do something that was so-called taboo and say 'that doesn't feel bad.' It's like growing up with a religion you end up rejecting," she adds, although the analogy strikes me as a bit strained. This would be more like growing up with a religion you end up fisting.

Annie's provocative one-woman show, *Annie Sprinkle's Herstory of Porn*, is a performance and film diary that explores Sprinkle's thirty-year odyssey of orgasms, orgies, and orifices, from her sexual awakening around the time of the sexual revolution of the sixties, to her "discovery" as a porn starlet while "fluffing" Harry Reems, and then on to her present vocation as a "modern media whore" and lecturer. Highlights from *Herstory* include the aforementioned fisting, along with golden showers (I'm serious about those Golden Shower Ritual Kits), sex with amputees and dwarves, bondage, and "rainbow showers," which is code for barfing on people—almost anything you can think of, really.

Believe it or not, according to Sprinkle, after a while, "straight-porn directors didn't want to work with me anymore; they said I was too kinky." And where do we take it to when we get "too kinky"? That's right, we take it to the "performance art" scene and join up with other horny neo-Dadaists and Fluxus artists to make avant-garde nudie flicks, author a journal on "piss-art," and then move on to more lucrative instructional videos like *Annie Sprinkle's Amazing World of Orgasm*. You may think, "That's just cashing in on the notoriety that comes with being filmed nude and drinking pee," and you may think right.

But in 2002, Annie Sprinkle not only talked the talk, she walked the walk *and* chalked the chalk, receiving her PhD in Human Sexuality from the Institute for Advanced Study of Human Sexuality, in San Francisco. Prostitute. Porn Star. Provocateur. Professor. Never let it be said that Annie Sprinkle didn't cover all the bases. But let's just hope she covered the mattress with a tarp or something.

CALAMITY JANE

PROFILE

DAY JOB: Cowgirl, but don't call her "girl"

CLAIM TO FAME: Pioneer badass; good with the six-shooters

THEATER OF OPERATIONS: The Wild West

Of all the picturesque figures out of Wild West lore, Calamity Jane stands out as the one who probably gave the most head. Born Martha Jane Canary Burke in 1852 in Missouri, Calamity Jane is said to have earned her epithet not by some misguided sexual escapade involving Wild Bill Hickok's unruly moustache, but through the perception that to offend her would be to invite calamity, venereal and otherwise. Some reports claim she was given the name because of her tendency to roar "What a calamity!" when bested at poker. Nobody can say for sure. However, what we do know is that Martha Jane was a well-known, often drunk, cross-dressing tranny prostitute who was well acquainted with the vicissitudes of life for a woman on America's frontier.

After intense scrutiny from their vantage points in various wood-paneled American libraries, professors ultimately determined that Calamity Jane was not the Indian-killing, bank-robbing gunslinger the movies and *Deadwood* have led us to believe. Even so, the woman was a character and most certainly, as you've likely guessed by now, a card-carrying hooker.

Described by frontiersmen Jesse Brown and A. M. Willard in their 1924 *Black Hill Trails* as "nothing more than a common prostitute, drunken, disorderly and wholly devoid of any conception of morality," Calamity Jane nevertheless possessed a humanitarian bent. In 1878 during an outbreak of smallpox in Deadwood, this scourge of polite society came through huge for the townsfolk. Jane girded up her overtaxed loins, rolled up her sleeves, downed some cocktails and proceeded to nurse the afflicted patients ceaselessly, even as other, more upstanding and God-fearing citizens stayed away claiming the plague was probably biblical and no doubt beyond their control. Also, they didn't want to die.

Moreover, Calamity Jane lent her unique services to the United States Army at the "Three-Mile Hog Ranch," Fort Laramie's fabled house of ill repute. According to one lieutenant, the place was populated by "as hardened and depraved [a] set of witches as could be found on the face of the globe," adding, "In all my experience I have never seen a lower, more beastly set of people of both sexes."

Our Calamity Jane eventually managed to get off of her back, eschew whoring, and land on her feet in the history books, but at fifty-one she died broke and hammered in the Calloway Hotel of Terry, South Dakota. On her deathbed, she asked to be buried next to Wild Bill Hickok, who, according to many sources, found her company excruciating. But, Calamity Jane got her wish.

SALLY STANFORD

PROFILE

DAY JOB: Former mayor of Sausalito, California

CLAIM TO FAME: "Dean of San Francisco Prostitutes"

THEATER OF OPERATIONS: San Francisco

You don't survive eleven heart attacks, three decades as the grand madam of San Francisco, and a career as an elected politician without being one hardy hooker. Sally Stanford was born in Oregon in 1903. Christened Mabel Janice Busby, the precocious vixen quite understandably moved on as quickly as possible to her *nom de horizontale*, and would prove herself to be one of the most resourceful, resilient, and savvy harlots around.

At the age of sixteen young Mabel eloped with a machinating dip-shit who claimed he was the grandson of Colorado's former governor. Granted, his alleged credentials were not all that impressive, even if true, but Mabel thought she saw an opportunity, and she took it. She soon found herself caught up in a failed robbery scheme orchestrated by her dunce husband, and the judge sentenced her to two years in the Oregon State prison. Mabel, however, carried out her sentence hanging out with the warden's wife in their house. Apparently, when Sally was taken to Salem, the warden said he had no place to care for a child and turned the young girl over to his wife, so Sally lived in the couple's house for two years. I agree. That makes absolutely no sense, but one gets the impression things were even weirder back then, when the law was vague enough to allow for creative (but not in the Guantanamo kind of way) forms of punishment or "rehabilitation."

Bouncing back after her brief "incarceration," Mabel changed her name to Sally, made a handsome nickel in the speakeasy business, and invested in hotels, first in San Francisco's shadier Tenderloin but eventually setting up shop on Nob Hill. She then quickly became the Bay City's main madam. By all accounts Sally's girls were refined, gorgeous, loyal, and discreet. If anyone got blitzkrieged on booze and raised a stink, Sally promptly had their ass thrown to the curb, and that would include even the likes of such luminaries as Humphrey Bogart, a notorious sot, whom she hated (by many accounts a terrible drunk and a prissy diva) and had booted for disorderly conduct.

Sally was also an early pioneer in the sphere of globalization. Nowadays that term is something of a hackneyed buzzword, but in 1945, when Sally and her girls entertained the delegates from the United Nations Organizing Conference, there was nothing "hackneyed" about her operation. In fact, according to the Pulitzer Prize–winning *San Francisco Chronicle* columnist Herb Caen, "The United Nations was founded at Sally Stanford's whorehouse." Strong.

After suffering countless collars for the usual "lewdness" charge, Sally became weary of visits from the SFPD vice squad, and she bowed out of the game gracefully. The retired madam opened a high-profile restaurant, and eventually ran for the city council of Sausalito. She was defeated in her first five attempts, but as Sally always said, "Sinners never give up!" She won the mayoral race in 1976 on—what else?—a pro-business ticket.

In 1978, when the inevitable movie was made of her juicy autobiography, *The Lady of the House*, Sally famously dissed Dyan Cannon's portrayal of her, saying, "She just didn't have it in her to play me," although Sally, always a player and a politician conceded, "I have to admit, it's a hard act to follow." Upon news of her death from her twelfth heart attack, all the flags in Sausalito flew at half-staff, an erectile dysfunction rarely, if ever, witnessed in Sally's old place at 1144 Pine Street.

DEBRA MURPHREE

PROFILE

DAY JOBS: Stone-cold streetwalker

CLAIM TO FAME: Brought Assemblies of God minister Jimmy Swaggart to his knees.

THEATER OF OPERATIONS: New Orleans

When the wildly popular televangelist Jimmy Swaggart was caught with a prostitute in 1988 at a dingy Travel Inn, he got on TV and wept, "I have sinned against you, my Lord, and I would ask that your precious blood would wash and cleanse every stain until it is in the seas of God's forgetfulness, never to be remembered against me." You know the drill. And while we remember Swaggart, one wonders: What happened to the prostitute? We have no idea. During the scandal in the late 1980s, the hooker Debra Murphree remarked to reporters that she might go back to live with her children in Indiana, maybe do some interior decorating. Then she posed nude for *Penthouse*. This was followed by the obligatory cyclone of tax problems faced by a $20-a-session hooker becoming a world-famous centerfold, and then, like Amelia Earhart, she disappeared. Well, not exactly like Amelia Earhart. Maybe she's just working on wallpaper arrangements and custom nesting tables. But for a few fleeting moments at the close of the twentieth century, Debra Murphree was at the center of the media universe.

When Jimmy Swaggart's former rival and fellow Assemblies of God minister Marvin Gorman (against whom Swaggart had earlier made a concerted effort to expose as a philandering sinner) came equipped with a telephoto lens and a private detective to the Travel Inn, he photographed Jimmy *in flagrante* with Debra, a working girl just trying to make a life for herself and her nine-year-old daughter in the unforgiving alleyways of New Orleans. A familiar face in the New Orleans trick tank, maybe a small problem with the drugs, and not the best example for her daughter, Debra Murphree nevertheless was integral in bringing down Swaggart (temporarily), and these days, well, sometimes all we can manage is to embrace our angels on their descent.

Erototalia, is the act of sexy talk. Research shows that over 70 percent of couples engage in some kind of erototalia to keep things interesting during intercourse. Well, that's all very interesting, but what the hell do you call what passes for sweet nothings in Rev. Swaggart's world? I'll tell you what those are; they are "pieces of mouth diarrhea" or "coprolalia," (the obsessive use of scatological language) and very rarely a turn on.

Murphree was born Debra Hedge and raised in Patoka, Indiana (pop. 735), where classmates, in a 1988 *Dallas Morning News* article, recalled that she "went to school," "wasn't involved in any extracurricular activities," and once even "left town with a biker named Dick," among other dazzling recollections. Well, things were about to change for the high school dropout and small-town girl.

At its apostolic apogee in the mid-1980s, the Swaggart Ministry was a $140 million-a-year business, taking in $500,000 every *day*. And each week, his television program, *The Jimmy Swaggart Telecast*, attracted 8 million viewers across the globe. However, for Swaggart, with smoking-gun photographs and revelations such as the ones dished out by Ms. Murphree in the pages of *Penthouse*, the pastor's popularity began to wane. Speaking of her dalliances with Swaggart, Murphree noted:

> He'd ask me if I'd ever let anyone screw my daughter when she was that young, and I said, "No, She's only nine years old." He asked me if she started developing [breasts] or if she had any hair down there. . . . I didn't know what to say. I thought, "This man's got to be sick."

Sick is one way to put it. A loathsome pig too tainted even for the abattoir is another. After the scandal broke and Swaggart was whimpering like a simpleton, the Assemblies of God moved quickly to defrock—Swaggart's exploits were too much even for the church of too-much. Of course, after Debra Murphree made the media rounds, she faded back into obscurity. Swaggart, on the other hand, managed to return to the limelight, coming out shamelessly for encore after frustrating encore.

In his new iteration as a Pentecostal minister, Swaggart has come forward to claim that the prophet Mohammed was a "pervert" and a "sex deviant." Ever the hypocrite, this perverted con artist and would-be Christian asserts that gay marriage is an "abomination" and that if a gay person ever "looks at me like that" he plans to "kill him and tell God he died." So things are actually pretty much as they were, I guess.

As for Debra, you can't even track her down on Facebook or Linkedin, for Christ's sake. Swaggart, now seventy-seven years old, continues to broadcast his *Jimmy Swaggart Telecast* to 104 countries around the world. God, why art thou so far from helping us, and from the words of our roaring? You're not even listening, are you?

RAVEN O

PROFILE

DAY JOB: Performance artist; hustler

CLAIM TO FAME: Being famous

THEATER OF OPERATIONS: New York

Be it ballet, traditional hula, or whoring, Raven O is a man of many talents. A one-time member of the pliable *Cirque du Soleil*, Raven O hit the streets of New York at age eighteen, a fresh-faced, Hawaiian Adonis, ready to conquer the world. About an hour or so later, Raven-O found himself addicted to crack and whoring himself, while go-go dancing at the now-defunct Limelight Club. In an interview with OutinJersey.net, Mr. O explains, "I began my career as a singer-actor-dancer and fell into whoring to pay for my drug habit," but luckily for us, he adds, "where there is the elite, there are whores. Both worlds are one in the same. [sic] As I say in my show, everyone's a whore one way or another."

Proving his point, Raven O eventually hooked up with the likes of Keith Haring and Grace Jones, and joined that ethereal realm of the "artist" whose precise talents appear to lie primarily in their ability to consume vast quantities of cocaine, though who can forget Grace Jones's stunning performance as "May Day" in the third-best James Bond 007 movie, *A View to A Kill*?

> *"It is a poor family that hath neither a whore nor a thief in it."*
> —Proverb

Raven O's prodigious talent, along with his remarkable networking skills, drew him out of New York's druggy underbelly and put him on the path to regional stardom. Blessed with a beautiful voice and a willingness to showcase it while wearing devil horns and a cock ring, Raven O eventually wound up at the Box, a Lower East Side nightclub where confused frat boys go to be gay, but was once an interesting venue for performance art and celebrity sightings. There, he captivated audiences with provocative stage acts and an impressive boner. Talking to the *NY Press*, he elaborates:

> When I was at The Box, we wanted to do a number to say "fuck you" to the press . . . to the Nirvana song "Rape Me." When the curtain opened, my back was to the audience and I was completely naked. I decided to be completely erect, so when I turned around I was singing with a hard on. I've always been about going for it. Nothing's off limits with me.

In 2010, Raven O's one-man, off-Broadway production, *Raven O: One Night with You*, opened to critical acclaim, and then closed to critical acclaim. As of this writing, the artist is spending way too much time on Facebook: "I realize I don't have a 'job,'" writes Mr. O in a recent Facebook post, but he's writing from Cannes, Ibiza, and London, and it's hard to sympathize with that kind of frictional unemployment. Raven O nevertheless remains an electrifying performer and an accomplished vocalist, although I might add that it's not really that daring to expose yourself if you are possessed of an outsized penis. Where is the fear?

NEAL CASSADY

PROFILE

DAY JOBS: Merry Prankster; thief; oral historian

CLAIM TO FAME: Inspiration to the Beats

THEATER OF OPERATIONS: Pretty much anywhere "On the Road"; Mexico

If you could bottle up all the outrageous plaudits, moony remembrances, and bong-loaded questions surrounding the life and times and death and drugs of Neal Cassady, you would have a bottle filled with a pestilent clash of truth and myth, and it would most likely taste like gnatty communion wine and camphor. Let's drink it!

That's the kind of initiative a guy like Neal really would have appreciated—and the reason why nobody ever had a clue as to what in the smash he might be going on about. But it doesn't matter. Neal Cassady was fast, beautiful, and real, and you were lucky enough just to have him gust through your groovy transom. Cassady was the inspiration for countless depictions of hipster-speak, gigolo swagger, blasted genius, and what Kerouac called the "energy of a new kind of American saint." In fact, for the uninitiated, the character of Dean Moriarty in Jack Kerouac's Beat classic, *On the Road* (still the standard-bearer of puff-puff-give hipster quips and New Age dharmic ooga-booga) was based entirely on Neal Cassady.

Born in 1926 in Salt Lake City, after Cassady's mother died when he was only ten he was left with an alcoholic father, who eventually zig-zagged the family across America to Denver, where Neal began a life of car thefts and prostitution in earnest. According to some, Cassady just couldn't get enough sex, and the money was a nice perk for satisfying his satyriasis. Others attribute Neal's flesh-life to his living purely "in the moment," attracted to the basic urges of human functioning, led by what Kerouac dubbed his "enormous dangle." Allen Ginsberg, completely and desperately smitten (Ginsberg and Cassady would remain occasional lovers for twenty years) wrote in his poem "Many Loves" that Cassady, "brought me to my knees/and taught me the love of his cock and the secrets of his mind."

Neal was one of those visionaries who not only had a huge dong, but a huge intellect, as well. Even when money was not in short supply, Cassady would prostitute himself for "knowledge" and tutoring, writing once to Ginsberg that he slept with the poet only "as a compansation [*sic*] to you for all you were giving me," which caused Ginsberg to call Cassady a "dirty, double-crossing, faithless bitch." Lesson: You can take the man out of the dirty truck stop, but you can't take the dirty truck stop out of the man.

Dad was right when he chastised, "Moderation in all things." Too much of a good thing—including solo sex play—can turn *deadly*. Consider the story of Rev. Gary Aldridge, pastor of Montgomery, Alabama's Thorington Road Baptist Church and one of the Rev. Jerry Falwell's bosom buddies. The holy man met a particularly diabolical end when, in 2007, police discovered his body "clothed in a diving wet suit, a face mask . . . a second rubberized suit with suspenders, rubberized male underwear. . . . There are numerous straps and cords restraining the decedent. . . . The hands are bound behind the back. The feet are tied to the hands. . . . There is a dildo in the anus covered with a condom.

Call me crazy, but wearing *two* wetsuits smacks of overkill.

Jack Kerouac would state that, for Neal, "sex was the one and only holy and important thing in life." Indeed, Neal's sexual appetite was so gargantuan that he was often forced (perhaps "forced" isn't exactly the right word) to masturbate six or more times a day, in addition to his normal sex load. Neal Cassady was many things to many people. In "Howl," Ginsberg writes of Cassady that he is the

> secret hero of these poems, cocksman and Adonis of Denver—joy to the memory of his innumerable lays of girls in empty lots & diner back-yards, moviehouses' rickety rows, on mountaintops in caves or with gaunt waitresses in familiar roadside lonely petticoat upliftings & espe-cially secret gas-station solipsisms of johns, & hometown alleys too.

Today, Neal is still celebrated, venerated, and occasionally reviled as a crank and a druggie loser, but "The Holy Goof" serves as a veritable avatar for an entire generation of dispossessed Americans. Neal Cassady seemed to have done it all, and at the age of forty-two, he lay down on some train tracks outside of San Miguel de Allende and died, finally and completely beat.

BELLE DE JOUR

PROFILE

DAY JOBS: Forensic pathologist; child health researcher

CLAIM TO FAME: Blogstitute

THEATER OF OPERATIONS: London

For years the question remained: Who is this mysterious "Belle de Jour," and does she take Diner's Club? For the better part of the 2000s, the blogosphere was abuzz with chatter about *Belle de Jour: Diary of an Unlikely Call Girl.* The book is a wildly popular account of a hardworking British university graduate who ditches the daily grind for a life of gaping and rimming and occasionally beating the shit out of people for the low, low price of $400 (and sometimes maybe a little more) per hour. More bestselling books were to follow, including *The Intimate Adventures of a London Call Girl,* and *The Further Adventures of a London Call Girl,* and each was adapted into a hit TV series. But who was this duplicitous demimondaine?

In 2009, Dr. Brooke Magnanti, a forensic pathologist, child health researcher, and Yank no less, outed herself as the Belle de Jour. After years of speculation and threats from an ex-boyfriend, Dr. Magnanti succumbed to pressure and revealed that for fourteen months during her postgraduate studies at the University of Sheffield, she'd arched it for an escort service in order to pay for her studies, and she admitted to being the author of the bawdy blog. After an interview with the *Sunday Times* in which Magnanti revealed her true identity, she posted on the Belle de Jour blog:

> It feels so much better on this side. Not to have to tell lies, hide things
> from the people I care about. To be able to defend what my experience
> of sex work is like to all the skeptics and doubters. Anonymity had a

purpose then—it will always have a reason to exist, for writers whose work is too damaging or too controversial to put their names on.

We all owe Dr. Magnanti, the Belle de Jour, an enormous debt of gratitude. Since revealing her identity, she remains active in research medicine, while continuing to address important issues relevant to the sex-trade industry. Through her blog and subsequent writings, she has been instrumental in dispelling puritanical myths about sex and pornography, and she has lobbied for sex education and the unbiased study of sexuality through science.

LUPE VÉLEZ

PROFILE

DAY JOB: Actress

CLAIM TO FAME: Married Tarzan, died with her head in a toilet

THEATER OF OPERATIONS: Mexico, Hollywood

Lupe Vélez is a difficult woman to get a grip on. Christened María Guadalupe Villalobos Vélez in San Luis Potosí, Mexico, sometime around 1908, her father was a strict military man who died when Lupe was in her early teens, while her mother appears to have been an opera singer, a prostitute, or both. Vélez was a difficult, rambunctious child, and for a time her parents sent her off to a convent school in Texas, which they expected would force her to reform. Lupe, however, would have none of it. According to Kenneth Anger's sensational *Hollywood Babylon*, Lupe was a sex leviathan: "Whenever I see a man," says Vélez, "there is something in here which must make me winkle my eyes at him. . . . When I cannot flirt with some mens, I get a fever." You wonder what exactly Lupe meant by "winkle my eyes," but you get the impression her temperature ran a pretty consistent 98.6°F.

After Lupe's father died, young Lupe's mother suggested her daughter carry on the family tradition. In his autobiography *Moving Pictures*, the Academy Award–winning screenwriter and novelist Budd Schulberg writes,

> Lupe's mother had been a walker of the streets. . . . Lupe herself had made her theatrical debut in the raunchy burlesque houses of the city. Stagedoor Juanitos panted for her favors and Mama Velez would sell her for the evening to the highest bidder. Her price soared to thousands of pesos.

Moreover, Anger, in *Hollywood Babylon*, calls Vélez, "the gyrating cunt-flashing Hollywood party girl." Yeowch! Vélez was also known as "The Mexican Spitfire" and remembered as a pioneer who brought Latinos to the silver screen, advanced the feminist cause, and boned just about everyone in Hollywood. Gary Cooper? Check. In *Lupe Vélez and Her Lovers*, author Floyd Conner quotes Vélez as saying "[Cooper] has the biggest organ in Hollywood but not the ass to push it in well."). Errol Flynn? Check. Johnny Weissmuller, aka Tarzan the Ape Man? Check. And the list goes on.

Vélez's first screen appearances were bit parts in Hal Roach comedies, but soon she found her niche onscreen as the recurring Mexican Spitfire; her character, like she herself, was vulgar, voluptuous, and occasionally violent. Of course, her act provided endless entertainment for those of the quasi-racist, moviegoing public who (like now) found the shortcomings and malapropisms of a vixen speaking English as a second language rather humorous. But offscreen, Lupe Vélez's life was one of torment. In 1944, Spitfire found herself pregnant with the child of a B-list actor who rejected the idea of marriage. Devastated, Lupe made up her mind to kill herself. She arranged flowers and scented candles, and she went to get her hair and nails done—an elegant exit for an eccentric young woman. She took a lethal dose of barbiturates and wished her life away.

Well, wish in one hand and shit in the other and see which fills up first, say the experts. Here's the description from *Hollywood Babylon* that describes what happens when you eat too many enchiladas then try to kill yourself:

> The bed was empty. The aroma of scented candles, the fragrance of tuberoses almost, but not quite masked a stench recalling that left by Skid-Row derelicts. Juanita traced the vomit trail from the bed, following the spotty track over to the orchid-tiled bathroom. There she found her mistress, Senorita Velez, head jammed down in the toilet bowl, drowned.

To paraphrase the Scottish poet, Robert Burns, "The best-laid schemes of mice and men [also starlets]/ Often go awry, / And leave us nought but grief and pain, / For promis'd joy!" That's true shit.

DENHAM FOUTS

PROFILE

DAY JOB: Socialite

CLAIM TO FAME: Muse to the likes of Gore Vidal and Truman Capote, among others

THEATER OF OPERATIONS: Worldwide, indeed

Truman Capote once fawned, "If [Denham] Fouts had slept with Hitler, as Hitler wished, he could have saved the world from the Second World War." Now that's high praise, even if it does come from the author of *In Cold Blood* during his quasi-coma-toasted-on-codeine phase. Unfortunately, there's no documented proof that the Führer made a play for Denham's drawers, but nobody pursued good gossip like Capote.

Denham Fouts was born. From there, the details get murky. One story asserts that at age sixteen he was liberated from behind the counter of his father's Jacksonville, Florida, bakery and shuffled off to Berlin by a

German baron, perfume magnate, and cruller aficionado. After a Christ-like ellipsis in the early years of Mr. Fouts's biography, he emerges more or less fully grown in the 1920s. At this point we find him shagging a Greek shipping tycoon, robbing him, landing in jail, and then being res-cued from the pokey by Evan Morgan, aka Lord Tredegar, a Welsh poet who took a shine to Fouts. And, even though Lord Tredegar provided more than enough cold hard cash for the young gigolo (not to mention legendary parties that included, among other bewildering creatures: a baboon, Aleister Crowley, a bear, H. G. Wells, and a parrot trained to fly out of the nobleman's britches), Fouts soon ditched the penny-ante entertainments of British royalty for another, decidedly more influen-tial, Greek luminary, the future king, Prince Paul. With World War II looming and Prince Paul presumably vexed about the Greek Orthodox Church's stance on homosexuality, Fouts headed back across the pond for an American tour. He came armed with Picasso's *Girl Reading* under his arm and "severance pay" from one Peter Watson, a satisfied cus-tomer and margarine mogul.

The word *tapette* in French typically refers to a fly-swatter. However, in colloquial usage, *tapette* is often used to refer to a person who is flamboy-ant, in particular, a homosexual male who publicizes his sexual orientation ostentatiously, perhaps even taking the metaphor to its inevitable conclu-sion: swatting meddlesome squares who insist on buzzing around asking for fashion tips, a squirt of Jean Paul Gaultier's Le Male, and/or wine recommendations (or garden-variety assholes that perpetuate gay stereo-types about fashion, cologne, and/or wine recommendations).

Stateside, Fouts came face-to-face—and to other, less conven-tional geometries—with the A-list of American literati: Gore Vidal, W. Somerset Maugham, Truman Capote, and Paul Bowles, among other luminaries. In his role as artistic muse, Fouts again played the part to per-fection, regaling his audiences with ribald tales from his past and look-ing at them with "eyes set on different levels, as in a Picasso painting" or like "Dorian Gray emerging from the tomb" in the words of part-time lover and British novelist Christopher Isherwood, who went on to add that Fouts was "the most expensive male prostitute in the world," and "the last of the professional *tapettes*." Fouts even found time to study medicine at UCLA for a brief period, but he eventually tired of America and travelled to Paris, where he could be found shooting flaming arrows out of his apartment window. He was a skilled archer, and it is always advantageous for a man of the evening to have a side gig if he's going to walk the Champs-Élysées.

Isherwood, Capote, Vidal, Bowles, and others lionized Fouts as a lover and an Adonis, but his early thirties were marked by drug abuse and more sinister nighttime adventures. Illustrator and painter Bernard Perlin remembers Fouts lying in an opiate-induced stupor, "in bed like a corpse, sheet to his chin, a cigarette between his lips turning to ash. His lover would remove the cigarette just before it burned his lips. At night Fouts took out his cigar box of drugs, injected himself and . . . came to sparkling life for the evening." In 1948, after years of hard living, Fouts expired in Rome of congenital heart failure, a condition that was surely exacerbated by ingesting enough opium along the way to dope up most of Western Europe. A sour endnote for a savory stud: Denham Fouts lives brilliantly in the great literature of his time, while his real life was a fog of sex, drugs, and a little archery.

SCOTTY BOWERS

PROFILE

DAY JOBS: Gas station attendant; prostitution ring leader

CLAIM TO FAME: Lover of Cary Grant and Spencer Tracy, among others

THEATER OF OPERATIONS: Hollywood

If you pictured the celebrated actors of Hollywood's Golden Age, as a bunch of randy whoremongers, you'd be right. The question is: Who had the talent, the moves, and the mojo to take on Hollywood's most famous actor/fornicators? The answer: World War II Marine GI, bartender, gas station attendant, and whore to the stars Scotty Bowers.

Scotty Bowers was born and raised on his family's farm in Illinois. He moved to Chicago, where he made a modest living turning tricks, until duty called and the young Bowers shipped off to Iwo Jima as a paratrooper. By this time he was a hardened, streetwise, battle-tested kid, but there was still nothing to suggest that Scotty would someday run a prostitution ring that catered to the Tinseltown elite out of a Richfield gas station at the corner of Hollywood Boulevard and Van Ness, but there rarely is. In the end, kids just grow up to be themselves.

After the war, Scotty went to California, Hollywood specifically, where he found work at the service station and ran a brisk side business setting up newly returned GIs with older men. Word of this new enterprise quickly spread throughout the city, where Bowers forged a "friendship" with heartthrob Tyrone Power and a host of other stars, eventually morphing into the most celebrated pimp/prostitute in a town pulsing with pimp/prostitutes. Scotty's clients and sexual partners allegedly incorporated much of the A list, including: Edith Piaf, Spencer Tracy, Vivien Leigh, Cary Grant, Edward VIII, Tennessee Williams, Charles Laughton, Katharine Hepburn, Rita Hayworth, Errol Flynn, Noël Coward, Mae West, James Dean, Rock Hudson, and J. Edgar Hoover, and that's just the appeteaser.

In his tell-all book, *Full Service: My Adventures in Hollywood and the Secret Sex Lives of the Stars*, Bowers' gives a firsthand, warts-and-all account of screen idol screwballs and their sordid sex lives. On Katharine Hepburn, he noted that "she had skin like a dead crocodile," and as for James Dean, he was "a fucking little prick." Ouch. Such is the danger of pissing off your prostitute.

Speaking of crocodiles, sex, and Katharine Hepburn, it's probably a good idea to turn to birth control for a moment. We've all had scares with torn Trojans, diced diaphragms, and misplayed pull-and-prays, but in ancient Egypt, the science of birth control was still stuck in the Dark Ages, and those hadn't even happened yet. If you were a female prostitute (or anybody trying not to get pregnant) in Ancient Egypt, the preferred method of contraception was to insert crocodile excrement into your vagina. Nope. That's it. You just went and found an alligator, encouraged it to poop in your hand, and then sought out a private place to make the necessary application. I'm all for safe sex, but I think if it were up to me, I'd just take my chances with the lunar cycle.

Before gay liberation, before this new wave of STDs started withering our genitals and before the paparazzi lurked around every corner ready to Tweet the grade of gasoline you chose, if you wanted sex and you wanted discretion, you found yourself low on fuel near the Richfield station. Now pushing ninety, Scotty still lives in Los Angeles with his wife, who must be frustrated knowing that no matter what, the best-case scenario is that she's got the second-best stories at the party.

QUENTIN CRISP

PROFILE

DAY JOBS: Writer; raconteur

CLAIM TO FAME: "The Naked Civil Servant"

THEATER OF OPERATIONS: Old Compton Street, London

Before we get rolling, I'd like to introduce you to one of the best little monologues on masturbation ever.

> As soon as I was old enough to wash myself, I had begun the habit of staying in the bath until my body passed from lobster-pink to scum-gray. While lying in one of these semi-submerged trances, in a boarding house in Queen's Gate to which my parents moved temporarily, I discovered the only fact of life that I have ever fully understood. Masturbation is not only an expression of self-regard: it is also the natural emotional outlet of those who, before anything has reared its ugly head, have already accepted as inevitable the wide gulf between their real futures and the expectations of their fantasies. . . . Vice is its own reward.

The source of the passage is the controversial, bestselling memoir, *The Naked Civil Servant,* by English eccentric and former rent-boy, Quentin Crisp. But let's be clear about this; Quentin Crisp was more than an intellectual pioneer in the philosophy of self-flagellation. The man was as comfortable with the trick-towel as he was with the spankerchief.

Born Denis Pratt in 1908 to "middle-class, middle-brow, middling" parents in Sutton, Surrey, our young hero was sent to school, or what he described as "a cross between a monastery and a prison" in Derbyshire where he was understandably bullied for cross-dressing. Pratt soon left school and settled in London, where he got rid of his Victorian birthright and adopted the truly fabulous sobriquet, "Quentin Crisp."

An easily recognizable figure in London's queer scene, Crisp would often find himself beat up, ridiculed, reviled, and ravaged—and that was on the slow nights. However, some people can't be faded—not at their core—and that was Quentin. *The Naked Civil Servant* was published in 1968, and in addition to ruminations about how he might do in his enemies, he also includes stories about chicken hawking, nude modeling, book designing, and good old-fashioned English manners.

One particularly charming yarn involves Crisp's adventures during the London Blitz of 1941. On one notable night during the German attack, he sprang into action for God, for country, and for men in uniform everywhere. He hurriedly applied the last of his makeup, left his flat, bought five pounds of henna, and then sashayed about the bombed-out streets of London in the dark, picking up American G.I.s. While never investigated for war profiteering, the fact that the self-proclaimed "Stately Homo of England" went out trolling for doggers and ducats during a Luftwaffe strafing is enough for us to let it slide. As you might imagine, however, the good citizens of Great Britain were scandalized by his behavior, but then everything from flatulence to wet cement seems to scandalize the average Brit.

By the time Crisp made his move to New York in 1981, most of his tranny antics seemed pretty ho-hum, but his quill, scroll, and most of all his voice really made the old rent-boy resonate here in the Colonies. A champion for gay rights, a unique presence in a knee-jerk, fall-into-rank world, and a sure bet for a sound-bite until his death in 1999 at the age of ninety, Quentin Crisp was a gentleman, a scholar, and a sexpot for the ages.

REGINA SAVITSKAYA

PROFILE

DAY JOBS: Master's candidate at Moscow State; Bolshoi ballerina

CLAIM TO FAME: Devotchka

THEATER OF OPERATIONS: Moscow

With surprising candor for a Soviet, Yuri Brokhin explored the dark underbelly of sex and crime in Moscow in his 1975 exposé, *Hustling on Gorky Street*. During the Cold War paranoia many Americans thought all Russians were busily making uranium isotopes in their bathtubs as part of a plan to blow us back to the Stone Age. We imagined that any Soviet not so engaged would be carted off by the KGB and relieved of his eyelids.

According to Brokhin, however, the Soviets were more like us than we thought; murders, the mafia, drugs, prostitution, and corruption were all rampant for the Commies, too. If we had known, we could have been singing a Cold War "Cumbayá," but we didn't. It would take another decade and a half before the Iron Curtain rose dramatically, and a parade of Frederick's of Hollywood models would march toward Moscow like lemmings in lingerie.

> *"He that has neither fools, whores nor beggars among his kindred, is the son of a thunder-gust."*
> —Benjamin Franklin, American statesman, Founding Father

Hustling on Gorky Street provides a rogues gallery of floozies, but Regina Savitskaya stands out from all the rest. She was a Bolshoi-trained ballerina who earned a master's degree from Moscow State University and a fat roll of rubles from her real calling, *interdevochka*, or "international girl," a fancy term for a prostitute who can demand the high hard currency. Regina got around, but she always came back to her old haunt at the ballet. She tells Brokhin:

> In the evenings, I worked the Bolshoi Theatre. My favourite ballet was *Swan Lake*: four intermissions to spend time working the crowd in the lobby. . . . I've been screwed by such famous pricks as John Steinbeck, Yevgeny Yevtushenko . . .[and] clergy from the Vatican.

One must obviously ponder which (if not all) definitions of the noun "prick" Ms. Savitskaya intends to convey here, but Regina goes on to explain how the rigid Soviet-bloc training she received on the way to earning her master's degree gave her an advantage over the ogling johns and Steinbecks lurking under the ominous shadows of Moscow's onion domes:

> Later in the day, I'd stand on Kutuzov Prospekt, where the foreign residents live, and pretend to hail cabs, keeping an eye open for Mercedes Benzes or Cadillacs, wearing my best Simone-de-Beauvoir expression. (My study of existential philosophy came in handy for hooking foreign suckers that starved for an intellectual cunt.)

That the Soviets possessed an arsenal of nuclear weapons aimed at our armpit, *and* they had a hot-to-trot *devotchka* with her existential ass aimed at some of our most important novelists failed to result in a global apocalypse, and for that we're lucky. It would have been a twentieth-century Trojan War, with Regina of Moscow replacing Helen of Troy in the role of beautiful woman whose charms threaten to tear the world asunder. And instead of a Trojan horse, it's a big Soviet bear stuffed with hookers, nuclear bombs, and Yakov Smirnov. The Americans are aware of the caveat, "Beware of Greeks bearing gifts," although the slightly lesser known adage, "Beware of Soviets gifting bears" hasn't made the rounds. Just like that, the Bolshoi bombshell could have become a destroyer of worlds.

These days, Regina Savitskaya manages an international road transportation and shipping company out of the Czech Republic. I'm not sure if that's the same Regina Savitskaya we've been discussing here, so if it is, nice work. Hell, even if it's not, nice work—not everybody can perpetrate upper management.

NATALIE "NATALIA" MCLENNAN

PROFILE

DAY JOB: Tap dance champion

CLAIM TO FAME: Once known as NYC's "#1 Escort"

THEATER OF OPERATIONS: New York

When you're on the cover of *New York* magazine and printed over your picture is the headline "N.Y.'s #1 Escort," well now, that's just making momma proud. Although, according to her tell-some memoir, *The Price: My Rise and Fall as Natalia, New York's #1 Escort*, winning the 1996 Canadian Junior National Tap Dancing Championships may have been a greater source of pride for Natalie's mother. After her daughter's terpsichorean triumph, Natalie's mother beamed, "Honey, I am so proud of you," to which Natalie later responded, "I wish I could have bottled up that moment and put it under my pillow."

Natalia, at her swankiest charged $2,000 per hour. Wait a sec, you say. $2,000 per *hour*?! Well, according to TheEroticReview.com, Natalia achieved a level of prostitutional perfection bordering on apotheosis. The website encourages clients to "rate," on a scale of 1–10, his or her experiences with various sex workers about town. To receive a rating of "10" is rare, something akin to a "10" on the uneven bars at the Olympics. During one incandescent streak in 2004, however, consummately satisfied clients awarded Natalia seventeen straight 10s, a "once-in-a-lifetime" distinction. It defies logic that one girl could be so preternaturally gifted in her tap shoes and out of her knickers, but that's Natalia.

Before she fell under the spell of "The King of All Pimps," Jason Itzler, and his torrid team at NY Confidential, she found work bartending, acting off-Broadway, and "crawling across the floor like a horny hyena" while posing for photographs taken by legendary *bon vivant*, Peter Beard. It was Beard who introduced Natalie to Itzler, and the next thing she knew, she had transformed into "Natalia" and even better, Jason's "bottom-bitch," which, in escort jargon, counterintuitively refers to the "top draw."

It was all fun and games and money and Manolos until somebody— Itzler mostly—fell victim to harem hubris and the whole house of cads came tumbling down. Among the throngs of hedge-fund managers, NFL quarterbacks, rock stars, and politicos turnstiling in and out of Natalia's lair, there were also large, conspicuous Con Edison vans outside NY Confidential headquarters in Tribeca, the place she and Itzler called home. The heat was on. Cops began to show up daily to root around, gawk, and pass judgment before eventually taking their leave. Any reasonably alert working girl would have taken this action as a sign to put the brakes on. But by this time, egad, Natalia was so coke-addled, paranoid, and devoid of hope, she "slumped down on the floor of Macy's and burst into tears." Sure enough, NY Confidential headquarters was raided, with cops taking computers, credit card receipts—even the goddamned fog machine! Naturally, Natalia and many other members of the old Tribeca gang were arrested for prostitution, money laundering, and a host of other no-nos. Natalia pleaded guilty to attempted money laundering in 2010 and now lives in Montreal, where she was offered a much more lurid and disturbing role than any she had played before either on stage or in the bedroom: the lead in a play by Ayn Rand.

ASHLEY DUPRÉ

PROFILE

DAY JOB: Rapper/singer

CLAIM TO FAME: "Brought down" former New York governor Eliot Spitzer

THEATER OF OPERATIONS: NYC

What must it be like when you're an aspiring pop singer from Jersey; Dad is mad 'cause you so wrecked the Porsche and you've got to get out of town; you've been abandoned by your boyfriend and you're all alone on 5th Avenue with nothing but your wits and a line of credit? It's like being Ashley Dupré, except that you probably don't have a job servicing a man resembling the love child of Frankenstein's monster and Yoda who just happens to be Eliot Spitzer, governor of the great state of New York. Clearly, Ms. Dupré worked hard for the money, too. Her court testimony reveals Governor Spitzer was almost as much of a pain in the ass in the bedroom as he was in his job at CNN: refusing to wear condoms and refusing to shut up, respectively.

Just when Dupré was building up a nice little grub-stake, making some strong sales and emerging on New York's "scene," along comes Spitzer, or Client #9, and the ensuing scandal/media frenzy. Was all that notoriety a good thing or a bad thing for Ashley's career? If you're familiar with Ms. Dupré's musical oeuvre, you know why even the hype surrounding the little *ménage* with Governor Spitzer didn't move her Pussycat Dolls–influenced jams up the download charts more than a trifle. Her beats are hackneyed and Ms. Dupré's lyrics, if not an overt nod to Ezra Pound's fascist-era doggerel, seem inspired by a similar brand of delusion.

So, what has all the fuss come to? There's Spitzer droning on CNN, and there's Ashley making the rounds of the reality TV show circuit, most recently on VH1's *Famous Food*. Also, trading the upscale ho stroll for a quill and scroll, Ashley now serves as the dating and sex columnist for the *New York Post.* Her advice column, "Ask Ashley," offers solutions to probing existential questions:

> Q: My boyfriend insists on showering immediately after sex. What's a girl gotta do to get some cuddle action?

> Ashley: I get the whole needing-to-shower-off-all-the-gooeyness factor (especially if you use lube), but physical touch plays a huge part in any relationship—most importantly after intercourse. . . . What about hopping in before him? If he's so particular about being clean, I bet he'd want you to be, too. Then, let him rinse off after you. This way, you can jump back into bed naked and prepare to lure him back into your clean arms.

Nuh-uh. The boyfriend insists on showering after sex because he's got to get back to the office, and he doesn't want to reek of Dream Angels, that *eau de by-the-hour* Victoria Secret fragrance so popular among call girls, and a veritable smoking gun of poor decision making and adultery. This is just the kind of advice column grandstanding that brought Dear Abby down. That's not entirely true. Alzheimer's, then death, brought Dear Abby down, but the sentiment remains.

MIKE JONES

PROFILE

DAY JOB: Masseur

CLAIM TO FAME: Blowing the whistle (among other things) on evangelical bowel movement, Ted Haggard

THEATER OF OPERATIONS: Denver

On Ted Haggard's website the disgraced minister invokes the words of Genesis 50:20 where Joseph speaks to his brothers after they sell him into slavery saying, "You intended to harm me, but God intended it for good to accomplish what is now being done, the saving of many lives." The passage, claims Haggard, has "become a source of life to us," "us" being Haggard and his long-suffering wife. Welcome to the world of people who are plum out of their goddamned minds!

Lucky for us, through all the meth, masturbation, and mendacity, one person emerges from the Ted Haggard sex scandal as a voice of quasisanity: Mike Jones, masseur, muckraker, and drug-dealing prostitute.

In 2006, Mike went on a Denver radio show and "outed" reverend Haggard, a vocal opponent of homosexuality who vigorously supported Colorado Amendment 43, which bans same-sex marriage in the state. Hey, Mike! You can't go around outing people for being meth-snorting, closeted homosexuals with a thing for Stars and Stripes–patterned he-thongs! I understand your impulse, but Ted Haggard wasn't just anybody: He had a standing meeting with George W. Bush on Monday mornings to talk about the evangelical movement and what to do about evil gay devils.

Haggard's church, the 14,000-member New Life Church in Colorado Springs, was thriving, and Ted held sway over legions as president of the 30 million–strong National Association of Evangelicals. Well, if you're determined to spread hate, bigotry, and intolerance under the guise of, well, anything, I think we can all agree you've got a little media scrutiny coming to you.

"Men will pay large sums to whores for telling them they are not bores."
—W. H. Auden, American poet

Jones outed Haggard at a time of great political importance. "I took the vibrator and greased it up while he put some lube inside his rectum," reveals Jones in his tell-all, *I Had to Say Something: The Art of Ted Haggard's Fall*. How is that grotesque image of Haggard even remotely related to political importance, you ask? Well, while Haggard was dispatching Astroglide into his party portal, Colorado was primed to vote on Amendment 43, with Haggard serving as one of the most influential and fervent supporters of the same-sex marriage ban.

Jones saw through the lube and he felt it was his civic duty to expose Haggard, whose annoying habit of leaving globs of meth under his own nose while roaring, "Jack me off, now!" had become intolerable. Jones elaborates on why he chose to reveal the unctuous underbelly of one of America's most influential men:

> People forget why I exposed him. . . . Not because he was ranting about gays, but because he was a hypocrite . . . and still enjoy[s] the benefits of marriage. What a lucky man. Should gays be so lucky to marry the one they love and be totally devoted.

When the scandal broke, columnist and sex-advice sage Dan Savage hailed Mike Jones as a "Gay American Hero" and Mike was instantly revered throughout the community. No, not just the "gay" community, but also the community of people who are not stark raving mad, right-wing "fundamentalist charismatics." The ultimate irony, and perhaps the best argument there is that God really doesn't exist, is that Haggard has established another wildly successful church and made tons of money appearing on *Celebrity Wife Swap*, while our hero Mike Jones has been reduced to putting on eBay the massage table he used to pleasure Haggard.

Also, Amendment 43 passed with 53 percent of the vote. Now there's something truly scandalous.

NINON DE L'ENCLOS

PROFILE

DAY JOB: Philosopher; writer

CLAIM TO FAME: Epicurean hardbody; *Mademoiselle Libertine*

THEATER OF OPERATIONS: Paris

Like so many of the French, Ann "Ninon" de L'Enclos's main occupation was to be artsy. Well, unless you were Marcel Marceau or Cardinal Richelieu or were lucky enough to have been born wealthy, you needed a second line of work so you could eat *fromage* and buy unfiltered cigarettes. For some the option was taking to the bimbo banks of the Seine in Paris, vying for spots near the Pont Neuf with the other hookers until you found Prince Charming, or if you were not lucky, until the riled-up Reformation gestapo threw you in a gutter. Anne de L'Enclos was one of the fortunate few who had relatively smooth sailing in her ascent to the heady heights of harlotry.

Anne de L'Enclos, born in Paris in 1620, came into a family divided. Her father was a broke nobleman, a neo-Epicurean, lute-playing, early hippie who encouraged "Ninon," as he called her, to pursue an even more dubious career than his own. This fatherly advice didn't jibe well with Ninon's mother, a devout Catholic and a yawn who was trying mightily to bring up her daughter according to the austere and arbitrary moral codes of the Counter-Reformation. Fortunately for history, Ninon listened to her father. She mastered the lute and embraced wholeheartedly the four tenets of Epicureanism:

1. That pleasure which produces no pain is to be embraced.
2. That pain which produces no pleasure is to be avoided.
3. That pleasure is to be avoided which prevents a greater pleasure, or produces a greater pain.

4. That pain is to be endured which averts a greater pain, or secures a greater pleasure.

Translation: Let's slip into something naughty.

As luck would have it Ninon's beloved father had to hightail it after getting his ass handed to him in a duel. Ninon was left to fend for herself in a convent, from which she escaped after a year for fear she was losing out on the party. But let us be clear about this, Ninon was not just a ditzy party chick; she was Mensa material and could outwit and out-culture you to the point of embarrassment, or orgasm. She was also fluent in half a dozen languages, a skilled musician, and particularly taken with the progressive philosophy of that old moth in the moral molasses, Montaigne.

During her reign in Paris, she was known as "Mademoiselle Libertine," open and willing to do anything that bumped up hard against the sexual mores of the day, while writing some of the most compelling philosophical tracts of the era. She befriended the dramatists Molière and Racine, and her bedroom talents were reserved for "men of rank and station or of high talents." But it wasn't a trick pelvis or some honeysuckle-scented homemade lubricant that kept the men coming back to Ninon. It was her complete familiarity with the best techniques for bursting every sinful cyst of desire, for anticipating every nascent want—conscious or unconscious—that festers in a red-blooded man.

In a letter to one of her *paramours*, a dense Marquis, Ninon is forced to elaborate because it just isn't sinking in with this titled buttplug. She writes:

> It is women who have taken upon themselves to dissipate these mortal languors by the vivacious gayety they inject into their society, by the charms they know so well how to lavish where they will prove effectual. A reckless joy, an agreeable delirium, a delicious intoxication, are alone capable of awakening your attention, and making you understand that you are really happy; for, Marquis, there is a vast difference between merely enjoying happiness and relishing the sensation of enjoying it. The possession of necessary things does not make

a man comfortable; it is the superfluous which makes him rich, and which makes him feel that he is rich.

The "superfluous" could be anything from like a hand job to a jet ski, in case you're wondering.

QUEEN SEMIRAMIS

PROFILE

DAY JOBS: Socialite; queen

CLAIM TO FAME: Hanging Gardens of Babylon honoree; pioneer in the use of eunuchs

THEATER OF OPERATIONS: Assyria

Most of what we know about Queen Semiramis is from a Hellenic writer named Ctesias. Ctesias is famous for writing a bunch of semi-plausible "histories," one of which is called the *Assyriaká*, which recounts the tale of Queen Semiramis, an ample hussy who married King Ninus, the founder of Ninevah.

Ctesias tells us that Semiramis was born in a city called Ascalon, next to a big lake full of fish. One of these fish had the head of a woman, so she was very much the big deal around town. Her name was Derceto, and she was a ghetto mermaid who wound up pissing off Aphrodite. The Goddess uses her mysterious powers to help Derceto jump the bones of a Syrian peasant, thereby causing the young woman to turn up pregnant, shamed, and pissed. Derceto kills the baby daddy, and she leaves the newborn Semiramis out on some rocks to die. Derceto then jumps into the sea. But a bevy of public-spirited doves "nurtured the child in an incredible and miraculous manner," and thus kept Semiramis alive.

All right, meat-crease, our more discriminating readers might say, *you've obviously put this Shama-semi-rami-dingdong piece in the wrong section.*

What kind of historical document has part-fish sluts and babies fed by doves and then all-of-a-sudden Aphrodite shows up? Please. This account doesn't reflect the airtight logic of the Bible in which Men are Men, Women are Women, and in Mark 5:10, pigs turn into demons. Okay, two out of three ain't bad.

Let's try another story. This one is recounted by an anonymous eleventh-century writer in Harriet Brien's *Queen Emma and the Vikings: Power, Love, and Greed in Eleventh-Century England*. In this iteration, we learn of a paradoxical Semiramis, a call girl who is so picky that she only goes for gods and planets (if you're Roman), but who will endure the indignity of her main john, Zeus (Jupiter), insisting that he morph into a bull for their hourly sessions. No matter. Semiramis took sex columnist and activist Dan Savage's advice to be "Good, Giving, and Game" (GGG) to new heights, or depths—it's hard to decide which. Here's our Norman scribe:

> What prostitute in the whole world could have been more debased?
> His dewlaps make her purple robes seem worthless, in the green grass
> Semiramis learns to low, under a young moon [she] delights[in] the
> bull's mounting.

First of all, it's great that Zeus has dewlaps. Secondly, don't you get the impression the writer is maybe just a bit jealous? I mean, it's Zeus, for crying out loud. And the bull thing? Well, it's like my dad always yells, "Ah, just eat it! It all goes down the same hole anyway." I never knew what that meant, and like Semiramis, the beasty-prosty from Babylon, Mt. Olympus, Cleveland—wherever—her meaning and cryptic origins are ripe for endless speculation.

For instance, The *Assyriaká* may have Semiramis confused with a queen called Shamuramat who lived around 800 B.C. How this mix-up might have occurred, we have no idea. Okay, I have no idea. Does it matter? The point is that in the always-entertaining clash that occurs when East meets West, things get lost in translation. For some, Semiramis remains a sacred prostitute goddess, for others, a bull-banging creep; and still for others, she's the inspiration for the Hanging Gardens of Babylon. Dante, in Canto V of *Inferno* describes her as an

Empress of many tongues [sweet]. With the vice and luxury she was
so broken, that she made lust and law alike in her decree, to take away
the blame she had incurred. She is Semiramis, of whom we read that
she succeeded Ninus, and was his spouse. She held the land which
the Soldan rules. The other is she who slew herself in love, and broke
faith to the ashes of Sichaeus.

Sichaeus? Soldan? Ninus? Who are these people? Dante is not the
only one confused by this tale. Egyptians worshipped Semiramis as Isis,
Babylonians called her Ishtar, the Israelites called her Ashtoreth, she
hooked as Isi in India, and the list goes on. Perhaps we should just pick
one myth and stick with it.

HAWK KINCAID

PROFILE

DAY JOB: Slam poet

CLAIM TO FAME: Founder of *Hook* magazine, a publication
for male sex workers

THEATER OF OPERATIONS: New York City

It's true that for some of us, slam poetry remains an enigma, if not
the arts and entertainment equivalent of mouth herpes. Why are these
poets so peripatetic on the stage? And have you ever seen so many
white people with dreadlocks? If you're going to rap, let us hear some
music. And stop making hand gestures that mimic shooting a gun
while spouting what you hope will pass for slant rhymes about your
devastating breakup sophomore year at Amherst—the disconnect is
too great. No one is moved.

   On the other hand job, if you get a poet up on the mic who has actually endured some real-world experiences, the poetry slam can take on
a decidedly different timbre. Hawk Kincaid is this kind of poet. Born in

Illinois, Hawk was a chubby, red-headed kid, who, in an interview with
author and activist David Henry Sterry, cops to "terrible memories of
getting hard-ons in church." So I guess it's not just the priests.

Now, what "made" Hawk a prostitute isn't a particularly unusual
or compelling story. What is compelling is Hawk's contribution to the
improvement of sex worker culture, through *Hook*, an e-zine for and
about the male sex trade (*www.hookonline.org*), and his slam poetry performances, which are not riddled with the usual doggerel about thug
life at Choate. Hawk has played the game and he knows it well. In fact,
Hawk is one of those rent-boys who managed to get a grip on that ever-
dangling carrot of the business world—the *niche* market. His milieu was
known as B&E, and involves being paid to break in to a paying cus-
tomer's home, tie him up, then sex the nonsense out of him. Hawk
recounts his ass antics with clinical detachment:

> Bondage was definitely my thing. And spanking, paddling and abuse.
> I preferred bondage, though, because I could tie them up and leave
> for a bit, come back and be mean, hit them and then leave. Low
> maintenance.

Do not judge this man too harshly, however. Hawk maintains that
all that beating the crap out of folks was just taking care of business.
"My real identity is more cuddly and fuzzy. I am softer than I let on,
especially when working," he says. That's refreshing. Indeed, we can
see Hawk's tender side in his verse. One needs only to peruse Kincaid's
ode to ass equations, "Anal Geometry," which essentially articulates the
prostipoet's wish to give nice people larger penises than scoundrels.

"The whore and gambler, by the state Licensed, build the nation's fate."
—William Blake, English poet, mystic

Using this logic, the nicest person in the world could sport a
75-foot-long penis. This sounds a bit unwieldy to me, but who are we
to mine the mind of mathematics? Whether he's breaking into your

house to fuck you, or just stopping by to drop poetry and knowledge and maybe other things on that ass, Hawk Kincaid is a talented artist and a pioneer in bringing male sex work issues and information to the people who need it.

Chapter IV

SURPRISE STREETWALKERS

What could be more satisfying than discovering that many of your idols, at some point in their ultra-glamorous careers, were compelled to do a little whoring? This storied crew does not disappoint. From rock stars to revolutionaries to Roseanne Barr (WTF?), history is riddled with accounts of our most venerated figures going horizontal to keep the heat on. The road to hell is paved with untapped talent, but no one in this group ever gave up. They all bared their flesh to ensure a place in the pantheon, and then they bared their souls about what they did to get there. Be surprised. Be very surprised . . .

AL PACINO

PROFILE

DAY JOB: Thespian

CLAIM TO FAME: Perennial Oscar contender (1 win); screaming some of the most famous lines in cinema

THEATER OF OPERATIONS: Sicily

Dog Day Afternoon, The Devil's Advocate, Scent of a Woman, The Insider, Sea of Love . . . Cruising? Perhaps it shouldn't come as much of a surprise that at one time, the uber-actor Al Pacino made his daily bread by slanging himself as a sexual *spazzino* on the island of Sicily. That's right, before the accolades and before his acting "style" devolved into either whispering or screaming his lines, Pacino the prostitute was a lead role.

In the 1980 flop *Cruising*, Al Pacino plays a sexually confused NYPD undercover officer out to catch a serial killer terrorizing the Meatpacking District, specifically the call-boy community. Pacino may have drawn heavily from his gigolo days in Sicily to prepare for the role (in which he goes under covers to go undercover), though if he did, who knew the halcyon days of Palermo were full of so much fisting, amyl-huffing, and whatever that tempo-thrashing "dance" is Pacino insists on doing during the disco scene?

Born in 1940 in New York City, young Alfredo grew up on the rough streets of east Harlem, mostly acting like an asshole, flunking his classes, dropping out of high school, his application to the famed Actors Studio rejected. But did Pacino give up? Hell no. "I'll show *you* out of order!" he surely yawped, as he packed up, moved to Sicily, and suggested that anyone willing to pay might enjoy saying hello to his little friend.

Pacino revealed in a 2009 interview in the *San Francisco Chronicle* that "at 20, I lived in Sicily by selling the only asset I had—my body. An older woman traded food and housing in return for sex. I woke mornings not really loving myself." We all know the feeling: You're a twenty-year-old flesh peddler, you're living in Sicily *shtupping* a bronzed, well-seasoned Mediterranean woman who pays you for it, and you feel like the whole world is conspiring against you. It's like *Serpico*, without the beard and the hole in the head. But bedding down with elderly Sicilian women who pay you and keep you in cigarettes, alluring as it may be, does not get you your Broadway break, much less the iconic Hollywood roles for which Pacino would come to be known.

So what is to be done? Pacino took whatever money he'd saved, moved back to America, and ground it out in the off-Broadway trenches until his breakthrough role in 1968 in Israel Horovitz's *The Indian Wants the Bronx*. In the end, Al Pacino ended up becoming Al Pacino, and the rest is just nostalgic whorestory. Hoo-ah!

NANCY REAGAN

PROFILE

DAY JOB: First Lady of the United States

CLAIM TO FAME: Just Say No; "The Blowjob Queen of Hollywood"

THEATER OF OPERATIONS: Hollywood, Washington, D.C.

If the Clinton/Lewinsky scandal taught us anything as a nation, it's the importance of maintaining a healthy oral sex life within one's marriage. Failure to heed this message can lead to a stain on our nation, not to mention on your best blue dress. Well, there's one president who never scandalized the country by hauling some intern into the oval office for a face full of pubes, and that's Ronald Reagan.

Sure, there was Iran/Contra, where Ronnie hooked up with some dubious drugs and arms deals. Okay, and maybe he wrecked the environment, sodomized the economy, threw the mentally ill out on the streets, and pushed us to the brink of nuclear war. At least he knew that ketchup was a "vegetable." That is, of course, until his own near-vegetative state began to kick in somewhere in the nascent moments of his second term.

But it's Nancy Reagan (née Davis) we have to thank for keeping our kids on drugs and the president with some degree of compos mentis. Why was he happy? Because Nancy Reagan was at one time known as the blowjob queen of Hollywood.

In Kitty Kelley's biography of the former First Lady, *Nancy Reagan: The Unauthorized Biography*, Kelly writes that the young Nancy Davis "was renowned in Hollywood for performing oral sex." That's right, patriots. Our First Lady of the United States was allegedly quite the First Lady of Fellatio back in the day. Eager to make it in the Machiavellian world of starletry/harlotry, young Nancy "performed that act [blowjobbing] not only in the evening but in offices. That was one of the reasons that she got a contract and that was one of the reasons that she was very popular on the MGM lot."

Being pillars of 1980s conservatism who did their best to promote paranoid misconceptions about sex, religion, and moral values, it's curious that both Nancy and Ronnie had such sordid skeletons in their closet. "Now, hey," you're assuredly asking, again, "this is unauthorized information we're talking about here. You don't have *film* of Nancy Reagan sucking off Peter Lawford and his buddies on a road trip to visit Nancy's parents; you're going by Lawford's wife's steamy, vengeful biography, which asserted Nancy was 'known for giving the best head in Hollywood.'" You're damned right I am.

No, it's not on YouTube, and you can't find it on Twitter. Once upon a time, we had to rely on something called "the rumor mill" for our gossip, and if there's one thing experience taught us, it's that rumors and gossip are probably true. Moreover, the more outrageous they are, the more likely they are to be true. So give it a rest, children of the new millennium, with your iThings and your e-shit.

If we didn't know better, we'd call the paragons of conservatism and family values, Ronald and Nancy Regan, a couple of hypocritical charlatans, with deceit (and other protein-rich unmentionables) dripping from their chiseled, Hollywood chins.

BOB DYLAN

PROFILE

DAY JOB: Musician

CLAIM TO FAME: Voice of a generation; American rock icon

THEATER OF OPERATIONS: Greenwich Village, New York

Believe it or not, Bob Dylan once claimed to have prostituted himself when he first arrived in the Big Apple. This story seems extraordinarily unlikely, as it's hard to imagine anybody paying to have sex with a famous Bob Dylan, much less a dead-broke Bob Dylan. Fame has its charms, but an out-of-control fro and a grill like a jaundiced gnu could not have been the tremendous draw that Dylan would have us believe. "Sometimes we would make one hundred a night, really, from four in the afternoon until three or four in the morning," Dylan said in a 1966 *New York Times* interview. "Cats would pick us up and chicks would pick us up. And we would do anything you wanted, as long as it was paid. . . . I almost got killed. . . . I didn't come down to the Village until two months later. Nobody knew that I had been hustling uptown."

One gets the impression that this is utter horseshit. Bob Dylan has offered so much disparate, unverifiable, and bogus information to interviewers that it's a wonder anyone even tries anymore. That's the problem with being the voice of a generation: People listen to you. Of course, it is entirely possible that Dylan really did wear the pink pants while boning up on his clientele and his songwriting skills. The lore or the whore, which is it? If Dylan has his way, which he normally does, we'll never know.

A tuning fork's nightmare, celebrity chameleon, and grizzled old troubadour who is no doubt still reeling from getting stoned and seduced by the infuriatingly mellifluous voice of Joan Baez, Bob Dylan deserves mention only as a minor whore in the canon of the flesh trade, but for his lyrics and poetry (*not* his fiction; if you're looking for a fast-working emetic, give his "prose poem" *Tarantula* a read), he is a perennial candidate for the Nobel Prize in Literature, but let's hope the Swedish Academy skips over passages like this sentence, from the aforementioned *Tarantula*: "Now's not the time to get silly, so wear your big boots and jump on the garbage clowns." In the 2003 *Spin* magazine piece, "The Top Five Unintelligible Sentences from Books Written by Rock Stars," Dylan won the blue ribbon for that obscenely indecipherable brain fart. But hey, Bob Dylan is only human, despite his Martian appearance.

CARY GRANT

PROFILE

DAY JOB: Actor

CLAIM TO FAME: Tinsel Town "everyman"; Academy Award winner

THEATER OF OPERATIONS: Hollywood; New York; North by Northwest

Cary Grant wasn't known for playing diverse roles in the course of his long and storied film career. In fact, he never once played a villain, and his only Oscar was one of those honorary "Lifetime Achievement" statues given out to people who are semiconscious and sure to crumble a hip in the next few years if they haven't already. However, the life of Cary Grant (born Archibald Leach in Bristol, England in 1904) was far from one-dimensional.

An ardent supporter of the Allied war effort in World War II (donating his salaries from both *Arsenic and Old Lace* and *The Philadelphia Story* to fight fascism), a vocal proponent of gun control, a dexterous former acrobat, an outspoken fan of LSD, and later in life a staunch Republican, Grant was one of those larger-than-life figures who spent many of his early years in New York as a struggling actor and doing a little whoring on the side.

Cary Grant may never have won an Oscar, but plenty of other actors took home the Oscar for their turns as prostitutes. Take a look at these Oscar winners and their respective performances:

- Janet Gaynor in *Street Angel* (1928)
- Helen Hayes in *The Sin of Madelon Claudet* (1931)
- Anne Baxter in *The Razor's Edge* (1946)
- Donna Reed in *From Here to Eternity* (1953)
- Susan Hayward in *I Want to Live!* (1958)
- Melina Mercouri in *Never on Sunday* (1960)
- Shirley Jones in *Elmer Gantry* (1960)
- Jo Van Fleet in *East of Eden* (1955)
- Elizabeth Taylor in *Butterfield 8* (1960)
- Jane Fonda in *Klute* (1971)
- Mira Sorvino in *Mighty Aphrodite* (1995)
- Kim Basinger in *L.A. Confidential* (1997)
- Charlize Theron in *Monster* (2003)

"Archie was rapidly gaining a name as the number one gigolo in town," notes Grant biographer Marc Eliot, adding that "His good looks had made him quite popular among the wealthy women around town, and it was an open secret among them that the 'social services' of this handsome young actor could be acquired for an entire evening at quite a reasonable cost." I never saw Cary Grant coming off as a cheap date, but that's acting for you.

Worried that his burgeoning escort career was interfering with his dead-in-the-water acting career, young Archie took a series of "legitimate" jobs, one of which included standing in the middle of the street wearing a sign that advertised a Chinese restaurant located across from Macy's in Herald Square. The destitute Archie would soon morph into the leading-man Cary, but for a long time, the master thespian maintained that during this period when he was supposed to be prostituting himself in New York, he'd actually been in London.

Hollywood's likeable "everyman" certainly had a few bones in the closet, as they say. But at the end of the day, Grant is revealed to be truly a man of many talents and an inspiration not only to whores everywhere, but also to those who see a well-rounded life and a chin-dimple as the key to enduring happiness. The legend himself once said, "I've often been accused by critics of being myself on-screen. But being oneself is more difficult than you'd suppose." It all makes sense now.

MALCOLM X

PROFILE

DAY JOB: Hustler; activist

CLAIM TO FAME: Pioneer in civil rights; controversial Muslim radical

THEATER OF OPERATIONS: Boston; New York

It is often history's job to ruin all the fun, and so here it is: Malcolm X was once a whore. This doesn't mean he wasn't other things. It is not the intention here to judge the character of Malcolm X, or to opine about his political, personal, or political legacy. That's for academic prostitutes on the History Channel, airing their opinions to basic cable in the hope that a TV appearance will somehow count with the tenure committee as a publication.

No, here we're just interested in Malcolm X's legacy as a paid lothario. If we've learned anything by now, it's that prostitutes are relentless multitaskers and capable of so much more than just hocking ass. During his days in Michigan, Malcolm Little was a jack-of-all illegal trades: dope dealer, pimp, thief, and well-known hustler. But, according to the record, Malcolm Little even managed to supplement his income with pecuniary payments for services rendered as a party boy.

Little evidently managed to stay current on his rent by charging a more venal kind of fee to a moneyed tyrant on the other side of town. Then, upon his move to New York, the misguided youth occasionally stopped by the local YMCA, where he administered blowjobs to the local gym gentry, making the lyrics to the Village People's classic anthem inspire us even more than usual.

In 1978 when disco sensations and gay icons, the Village People had a number-one hit worldwide with "Y.M.C.A.," they garnered praise from mainstream America and the Y.M.C.A organization itself (who later adopted the tune as their official song). The Christian organization seemed oblivious to the seedier undertones of the song, not realizing that Y.M.C.A.s were popular cruising and trolling locales for the gay community. The next year the Village People pressed their luck and recorded a clarion call to arms, legs, and military man-love with "In the Navy." The Navy planned to use the number in a recruitment video, but for some reason, all that leather made the admirals suspicious.

And in a decidedly tame (yet lurid in their vividness) series of encounters in Boston, author Manning Marabel, in his controversial *Malcolm X: A Life of Reinvention*, allows that Little's services were often solicited to sprinkle talcum powder over one particular john until the man reached orgasm. Surely this is the easiest money ever made by a rent-boy.

Malcolm X made a few more false starts in his life, but by the time he was murdered in 1965 at the age of thirty-nine, the man had reached iconic status. Even today, his religious teachings and his civil rights activism continue to inspire. But, whatever your thoughts on Malcolm X the man, Malcolm Little the panderer is an indispensible inclusion in the canon of flesh-peddlers.

MARILYN MONROE

PROFILE

DAY JOBS: Miss California Artichoke Queen; actress

CLAIM TO FAME: Being Marilyn f'ing Monroe

THEATER OF OPERATIONS: Hollywood; sundry Kennedy compounds

Oh, Marilyn. What an odd specimen you were. Born Norma Jeane Mortenson (her mother had her baptized as Norma Jeane Baker—apparently there was some sort of paternal confusion), Marilyn entered the world in the charity ward of the L.A. County Hospital on June 1, 1926, and left it in a barbiturate blowout, just thirty-six years later. But Marilyn is still *the* defining icon of Hollywood, if not postwar America at large.

Marilyn may have gone in for a devil's threesome with John and Robert Kennedy, but like much of Marilyn's life (and death) the whole tragic affair is shrouded in myth and mystery. She was politically conscious, allegedly talking atomic apocalypse with JFK just weeks before the Cuban missile crisis. She appeared to have actually read *Ulysses*, something most of us only pretend to have done. But her legacy is that of the dumb blonde, a clumsy, clueless goddess astride a steam vent in *The Seven Year Itch*, her panties just out of eyesight and legions of fans straining to see as they silently or not so silently howl, "Blow steam, blow!" Marilyn was blessed with rare comic timing, and she had an undeniable screen presence. Contrary to popular belief, she also had smarts to go around, and would later prove herself more than worthy in dramatic roles such as *Bus Stop* and *The Misfits*.

Norma Jeane's early years were grim. Perhaps you know the stories: a lunatic mother and an absent father; raised in foster homes and ultimately declared a ward of the state; in a loveless marriage by fifteen and divorced by nineteen; plagued by incessant health problems real and imagined. With Hollywood showing little interest, she posed for nude photographs, made stag films, and allegedly worked as a high-priced call girl. The one bright light in all of this came when she was named the 1947 Miss California Artichoke Queen.

> *"Every government is a parliament of whores.*
> *The trouble is, in a democracy, the whores are us."*
> —P. J. O' Rourke, American satirist, humorist

While Marilyn never confirmed her stint as a call girl, she readily admitted to engaging in another phyla of prostitution: the Hollywood Hustle. Here is Marilyn quoted by journalist Jaik Rosenstein in Sarah Churchwell's *The Many Lives of Marilyn Monroe*:

> You know that when a producer calls an actress into his office to discuss a script that isn't all he has in mind. And a part in a picture, or any kind of a little stock contract is the most important thing in the world to the girl, more than eating. She can go hungry, and she might have to sleep in her car, but she doesn't mind that a bit—if she can only get the part. I know, because I've done both, lots of times. And I've slept with producers. I'd be a liar if I said I didn't.

One would like to think that the California Artichoke Queen would not have to succumb to such pressures just to get a leg up in Hollywood. Marilyn Monroe had the looks, the talent, the skills, and God knows she had the sex appeal, but apparently such gifts would only get you so far in 1950s Hollywood.

Maybe Marilyn cut corners. Maybe she was a self-absorbed star, frothing at the mouth from enough Nembutal to drop a rhino. Maybe she whored around to pay the bills. Who are we to judge? Consider the final, cryptic line from Osgood Fielding III, the eccentric millionaire in one of Marilyn's most successful films, *Some Like It Hot*: "Well, nobody's perfect!"

And how in the fuck does a candle in the wind cling to anybody? It's metaphors like this that make me think Elton John is just lazy.

BARBARA PAYTON

PROFILE

DAY JOBS: Starlet

CLAIM TO FAME: Classic cautionary tale of rags to riches to rags

THEATER OF OPERATIONS: Sunset Blvd., Hollywood

At one point Barbara Payton looked like she had a bright future in Hollywood. She made the obligatory "spec" shots (meaning she paid for them) that got her press in some of the higher-end 1940s and '50s jack-off rags like *Spy* and *Brief*. Payton spent the obligatory amount of time bent over couches in casting agents' and producers' offices, and she finally wound up a leading lady, starring with James Cagney in *Kiss Tomorrow Goodbye* and Lloyd Bridges in the noir classic, *Trapped*, among other films.

Ms. Payton lived fast and died young (1927–1967), but during the 1940s and '50s she was a paparazzo's wet dream. She got her swerve on with Howard Hughes and tore up the Sunset Strip like a riled-up hellspawn of Christina, Lindsay, Britney, and the rest of those half-assed party girls combined. She owned luxury cars and mansions, and she made $10,000 a week on the movie set. Then it all came back to bite little old Barbara Lee Redfield from Cloquet, Minnesota, in her steepled Nordic hindquarters.

It's a familiar story—one that every aspiring young actor and actress should bear in mind before becoming swallowed up by the Hollywood machine, addicted to drugs and alcohol, and dispensing rim-jobs for ripple wine outside the 7-Eleven. Here's Barbara in her 1963 tell-all autobiography, *I Am Not Ashamed*, summing up her meteoric rise and equally meteoric crash, from the glitz and glamour to fat and drunk:

> I went out with every big male star in town. They wanted my body and I needed their names for success. There was my picture on the front pages of every paper in the country. . . . I live in a rat infested apartment with not a bean to my name and I drink too much Rosé wine. I don't like what the scale tells me. The little money I do accumulate to pay the rent comes from old residuals, poetry and favors to men. . . . Does it all sound depressing to you? Queasy? Well, I'm not ashamed.

For an ex-starlet who used to date Bob Hope (there is speculation that Barbara was his "kept" woman), this kind of admission was unorthodox and career-ending—a testament to how desperately she needed the $1,000 book advance. In those days there were no reality shows to exploit one's addiction and cultivate a new, equally annoying yet sober personality.

In just a few short years, Barbara Payton went from superstardom to squalor, with arrests for, among other peccadilloes, passing bad checks, public drunkenness, shoplifting, drunk and disorderly conduct, and prostitution. Living in abject poverty, fraught with dipsomania and morbidly obese, Barbara moved in with her alcoholic parents, clearly not a good idea. Payton died at the dawn of the sexual revolution (she would have enjoyed it) at the age of thirty-nine of heart and liver failure. And, like so many of our finest talents gone to meet their reward too early, Barbara Payton's life came to a close while sitting on the shitter. I mean *damn*, y'all.

CLARK GABLE

PROFILE

DAY JOB: Actor

CLAIM TO FAME: "The King of Hollywood"

THEATER OF OPERATIONS: Hollywood

"Frankly, my dear, I don't give a damn; I'm going to scrub my penis until it bleeds, go gay-for-pay, and bang my way to the top of Hollywood despite my chronic bad breath, hepatitis, and false teeth," is something Clark Gable never said, but certainly may have thought, if we are to believe some of the reports. These Hollywood transformations can be amazing. The cosmic volte-face that propels some people from lowly civilians like us who are just trying to get through the day without cutting our boss with scissors to iconic screen stars like Clark Gable is something I'll always be bitter about—especially since I gargle regularly, I don't think I have hepatitis, and my grill contains 100 percent real teeth.

According to numerous reports, Gable allegedly compensated for his shortcomings by having sex for money and other favors in various bathrooms, bedrooms, and boudoirs of Beverly Hills. In fact, Clark was a fixture in the men's room at the Beverly Wilshire Hotel (not an actual bathroom fixture, like a urinal), as well as the seedier area around Pershing Square, where an up-and-coming actor could get into some "rough trade" and disaster capitalism hawking his hindgut with the career cruisers.

Are you telling us that Clark Gable . . . "The King of Hollywood" . . . Rhett Butler . . . was a man-whore? Don't look so devastated. Would you feel any better with some tasteless details? Me too. "In those days," writes Gable biographer David Bret in his *Clark Gable: Tormented Star*, Gable was "not averse to charging for his services." In fact, his colleague and sometime paramour, the silent-screen star Billy Haine, is quoted as telling Gable's frequent costar Joan Crawford, "Cranberry [Crawford's nickname], I fucked [Gable] in the men's room at the Beverly Wilshire Hotel. He was that desperate. He was a nice guy, but not a fruitcake." Let's savor this awkward silence for a moment.

Now, let's move on to the following revelation from one of Gable's friends, quoted in William J. Mann's *Wisecracker*: "Billy fucked *him* in the men's room. Billy was the *fucker*, never the *fuckee*." First of all, what's a fuckee? A yoga mat, or some new-age ethos? And secondly, Wow! This doesn't do much for Gable's macho reputation, but it does make him a more interesting character. Ultimately, if you're a guy hung up on your leading men being big hunks of rough, oozing masculinity, and you refuse to acknowledge that most of the male stars you identify with and look to for inspiration are heavy into dudes, well, perhaps the homophobe doth protest too much.

At the end of the day, what we have is Gable's work. Sure, he may have whored it out a little, but when you've got the talent, sometimes you've got to make your own luck. With a best actor Oscar in 1935 for *It Happened One Night*, and two more nominations for his performances in *Gone with the Wind* and *Mutiny on the Bounty*, Gable's legend as an actor is secure. As for his sexuality, clearly there are some discrepancies. Doris Day once swooned "[Gable] was as masculine as any man I've ever known, and as much a little boy as a grown man could be—it was this combination that had such a devastating effect on women." Day's remarks stand in stark contrast to Bret's assertion that before his star rose, "Gable's more serious relationships had been with three homosexuals." How could a figure as public as Gable manage to trick so many manly men into growing stereotypically gay moustaches? It's almost like Gable was *two* people at the same time. Get used to it. It's called "acting."

KURT COBAIN

PROFILE

DAY JOB: Musician

CLAIM TO FAME: Grunge pioneer; unwitting Gen X spokesperson

THEATER OF OPERATIONS: Seattle

At twenty-seven, Kurt Cobain, tentative spokesman for a generation and front man for Nirvana, once one of the biggest bands on the planet, killed himself, leaving legions of fans and admirers lost, bereaved, and confused. To date, Nirvana has sold more than 50 million albums worldwide, and they continue to function as the flagship for the tortured and confused members of Generation X, who pine for the revolution that never happened and, it must be noted, are looking a little swollen and bald these days. In spite of it all, none of Cobain's Gen X minions may have been more tortured, confused, and maniac than Cobain himself. Okay, Courtney Love—a solid point.

The "poet of grunge" was born in 1967 in Aberdeen, Washington, to a musical family. After his parent's divorce when he was nine, Cobain moved between two different homes; made forays into born-again Christianity, homosexuality, and the junior high wrestling team; then dropped out of high school with only two weeks to go before graduation. This last vintage punk rock move caused Cobain's mother to kick him out of the house, and he began in earnest his grunge odyssey, living under a bridge down by the river, probably smelling like teenage shit.

In one interview Cobain imagined an employment scenario straight out of an updated and grungy Seattle Dickens: "I always wanted to move to the big city. I wanted to move to Seattle, find a chicken hawk [an older gay man] . . . sell my ass, and be a punk rocker." Of course, as anyone familiar with Cobain's interview persona will recall, the young man was not reliable, especially when the subject turned to sex or sexuality. Some even claim that Cobain was the inspiration for River Phoenix's character Mike, the gay hustler in Gus Van Sant's movie, *My Own Private Idaho*. In fact Van Sant later chronicled events at the end of Cobain's life in the aptly titled, *Last Days*. It does seem plausible that Cobain could serve as a model for the tortured gigolo. In Christopher Sandford's biography, *Kurt Cobain*, we're told how Kurt was said to have enjoyed numerous "dalliances in the back alleys of Seattle," and this coupled with his willingness to sell his ass, presumably for money and drugs, makes him a likely candidate. But to say Kurt Cobain was at any time a full-fledged prostitute is a stretch, if not total crap. Sure, murmurs persist and the possibility is certainly there, but with every year that passes, Cobain's legend devolves into more legend, leaving us with questions, speculation, and gossip—and, alas, Courtney Love, who appears here to stay.

If drugs and prostitution are inexorably linked, and Courtney Love is linked inexorably to drugs, then by the transitive property of equality, Courtney Love must also be linked to prostitution. Why are we not surprised that Courtney managed to incorporate the two in a novel, albeit desperate, way. In an interview with British chat show host Alan Carr, a sober Love reflects:

> I had this rock and roll trick that I would do. I'd be in . . . like Cleveland or Cologne, Germany. . . . I would call up a hooker agency and I would ask for the ugliest hooker, because the ugliest hooker would know [how to find drugs]. They would think I was a lesbian . . . and I'd be like, "No, no put [the sex toy] down, I just want to know where the drugs are."

With Ms. Love, it's not always choices for healthy living, but you have to give it to her—it's always ingenious and usually rock star as hell.

MAUREEN MCCORMICK

"Marcia! Marcia! Marcia! . . . What the *hell* happened?" asked fans who read Maureen McCormick's 2008 memoir, *Here's the Story: Surviving Marcia Brady and Finding My True Voice*. Maureen, as you know, unless you spent 1969–1974 hermetically sealed in a cultural vacuum, was the oldest sister, "Marcia," on the TV series *The Brady Bunch*. Marcia is beautiful and one of the more popular girls at Westdale High, and she has an innocent little crush on Davy Jones, lead singer of a sonic abortion called the Monkees, which some characterize as the N'Sync of the late '60s. But according to Maureen, "Peter Tork was always my favorite Monkee. That was the difference between Marcia and me. She was predictable, a straight arrow. My taste was quirky, offbeat, and different." Peter Tork lovers, consider your sorry selves redeemed.

On *The Brady Bunch* Marcia also has a fragile ego, is a little conceited, and she's not particularly resourceful. This, subsequently, is in stark contrast to her real-world counterpart, the actress Maureen McCormick, who was at the time doing enough cocaine to line a baseball diamond.

You know the drill, starlets: win the Miss San Fernando Beauty Pageant; come to LA; make some inroads; get on a popular TV show and attract boyfriends, including everyone from your pimpled and randy cast mates to Steve Martin and Michael Jackson. You become a fixture at the Playboy Mansion. You're rich. . . . You're even richer. . . . And then you meet cocaine, which is all you'd ever hoped it would be, except for expensive and addictive as hell. In her memoir, Ms. McCormick describes a common Hollywood trajectory:

I sought refuge in seemingly glamorous cocaine dens above Hollywood. I thought I would find answers there, while in reality I was simply running farther from myself. From there, I spiraled downward on a path of self-destruction that cost me my career and very nearly my life. . . . Over the years I battled drug addiction and bulimia. I was treated in a psych ward, went in and out of rehab, and looked to God for answers.

While McCormick didn't need to prostitute herself to become a household name, she did to afford her drug habit. "I would have sex to get the drugs," she reiterated on NBC's *Today Show*, confirming her sordid hooker past, a time when McCormick did so many drugs she was often called "Hoover," a reference to her propensity to suck up pills, coke, mushrooms, and other chemical detritus. "It was my lowest point. It was awful," she says, not unsurprisingly.

McCormick goes on to recount more tales of trading sex for drugs, of stealing handfuls of amyl nitrates or "poppers" at one of Sammy Davis Jr.'s late-night bashes, and finally of freaking out Steven Spielberg during an audition for *Raiders of the Lost Ark*. She was so tweaked after a bouncing eight-ball binge that the director offered her an orange and showed her the door. Seriously though, Marcia, you don't take Smokey's drugs!

Maureen, foolish but no fool, eventually recognized she had a problem, and she has been clean and sober since the late '90s. She has also been tediously "born again," an insidious and oftentimes dangerous drug in its own right. Thanks to reality flotsam like *Gone Country*, where wayward celebrities try to become country and western singers and season five of *Celebrity Fit Club*, where wayward celebrities try to become less fat, you can still catch glimpses of the old Marcia all grown up, a little more mature, a little wiser, and significantly chubbier. But Ms. McCormick is a fighter and ★★★SPOILER ALERT★★★ she wasn't as portly at the end of the show as she was at the beginning. In fact, she won! C'mon everyone: "Maureen! Maureen! Maureen!"

No, you're right, "Maureen" sounds funny. She'll always be our little Marcia (sniff) . . . (snort).

ROSEANNE BARR

PROFILE

DAY JOBS: Comedienne; actress

CLAIM TO FAME: "Domestic Goddess"; universal nuisance

THEATER OF OPERATIONS: Colorado

Did anybody catch an episode of *Roseanne's Nuts*? In 2011 the Lifetime Channel's reality series featured Roseanne, her son, some other people, and "celebrities" ranging from Phyllis Diller to one of Ike Turner's former "Ikettes" living, working, and being stupid on a macadamia nut farm in Hawaii. No? You missed it? Not surprising. They only had the nuts to air a few episodes.

Well, things were different back in 1989, when Roseanne was appearing on more magazine covers than anybody in America. She broke ground first with her stand-up comedy act, opening for Julio Iglesias (yes, you read that correctly), then she was on a hit TV show, *Roseanne* (1988–1997), where she cultivated her identity as "Domestic Goddess," a streetwise, wise-cracking tough gal with a distinctly un-Hollywood edge. Her character was believable, because it was true. Roseanne wasn't brought up with a silver spoon in her mouth; she was brought up with a tasteless joke in her mouth.

Raised in your typical working-class Mormon/Jewish family, Roseanne did stints as a child preacher for the Mormon Church from the age of six until she turned sixteen, at which point she was hit by a car and went "nuts." In both of her bestselling autobiographies, she describes how after the accident, she refused to sleep, went into convulsions and was briefly placed in a Utah state mental hospital, where Roseanne and her twenty-one distinct personalities lingered for nearly a year.

Upon her release, Roseanne was changed. She thumbed it to Colorado where, at twenty-six, she met her first husband, a hippie called Ed, and settled down to live in a cramped, 600-square-foot house, working as a cocktail waitress, a maid, a window dresser, and, yes, a prostitute.

In the February 1994 issue of *Vanity Fair*, Roseanne delivered a fairly philosophical perspective on her efforts to help support her family by "turning tricks in the back seats of cars in the parking lot between comedy gigs." She adds:

> I think prostitution should be legal because the way any society treats its prostitutes reflects directly on how it treats the highest, most powerful women. . . . It has always been here, and women should be able to control it and regulate it. . . . Prostitution is business.

Roseanne goes on to explain that, for her, prostitution was about being "powerful and in control," but somewhere along the way that control went away. As success, wealth, and fame came to the comedy star, instead of sticking to her blue-collar guns, she came to symbolize just the kind of Hollywood feculence she claimed to loathe. She became the ultimate diva, and the set of *Roseanne* became well known as the most unpleasant place to work in television. She got plastic surgery, spouted new-age Kabbalah-babble, and became so outrageously self-absorbed as to think great numbers of people would stay glued to their television sets fascinated while she picked macadamia nuts in Hawaii.

We can applaud Roseanne for her success, and we can strive to make our own lives remarkable, whether earning $20 a hand job in the back seat of a car, or over $20 million a year on the set of a TV show. But watching Roseanne today, one comes to doubt her former husband and partner in mediocrity, Tom Arnold, who described the pair as "America's worst nightmare—white trash with money." No, America's worst nightmare is not white trash with money; America's worst nightmare is watching Roseanne in a tank top, straining to pick a macadamia nut and screaming at us—the American television Janes and Johns—for a gimme.

DEE DEE RAMONE

PROFILE

DAY JOB: Musician; abysmal rapper

CLAIM TO FAME: Bassist for punk trailblazers the Ramones

THEATER OF OPERATIONS: Fifty-Third and Third, Manhattan, New York

The second single of the Ramones' debut album *Ramones* is a breakneck punk assault called "53rd and 3rd."

Yes, it's another song about what happens on a Manhattan street corner, but this little ditty is about a *real* place, one that once radiated debauchery and ejaculated good times. There's a Barnes & Noble at that corner now. (Are you there? Are you taking this book into the stalls to masturbate in the hope there are some lurid pictures? You'd be better served going over to the magazines and putting a *Hustler* inside a *Financial Times*, but since you've already fondled this one, you probably ought to go pay for it now. Not my rules, B&N's.)

What made the corner of Fifty-Third and Third such a fine spot for a shady soiree was that in the mid-1970s, that intersection was the sexual nexus of slanging that ass, and young Dee Dee Ramone (born Douglas Colvin) wasn't afraid to go down there and ram it in the name of punk rock, a drug habit, and habitual insolvency. According to an interview for the photography book and collection of essays *Addict out of the Dark and into the Light*, Dee Dee notes:

> I would work as a mail clerk in the daytime and that didn't give me much money because it was a low paying job, to support an apartment in Manhattan and a drug habit, a heroin habit. And at night I would go to the street corner called 53rd Street and Third in Manhattan and hustle and pick up men and go to their homes for twenty dollars and have sex with them so I could buy a couple of bags of dope. And this

went on for a few years and I became a miserable full blossom drug addict. All the friends I circularized with were hustlers and addicts.

On the occasions when Dee Dee wasn't paralyzed by drug and alcohol addiction, he managed to write such punk staples as "Chinese Rock," "Rockaway Beach," and "Teenage Lobotomy," to name a few. His particular genius was the ability to merge his angst and his humor with three chords, and in the process create a scream-along catchiness.

> *"Behold, thou shalt sleep with thy fathers;*
> *and this people will rise up, and go a whoring after the gods of the*
> *strangers of the land, whither they go to be among them, and*
> *will forsake me, and break my covenant which I have made with them."*
> —The LORD to Moses, in conversation

Dee Dee continued to write songs for the Ramones after he broke with them in 1989 to embark on one of the dumbest ventures the music world has ever seen: Dee Dee King, rapper. Gems like "Mashed Potato Time" and "Funky Time" failed to crack the mainstream. In the Ramones documentary *End of the Century: The Story of the Ramones*, Dee Dee speculated about the reason for his caustic reviews, opining, "Maybe it was because I'm not a Negro." When your brain is that addled, death can't be far behind. And it wasn't.

In 2002, Dee Dee died one of those horrible Hollywood rock star deaths—a spike in his veins, still gripped by the heroin addiction that haunted him throughout his life.

RUPERT EVERETT

PROFILE

DAY JOB: Thespian (like an actor, but British)

CLAIM TO FAME: Token unthreatening Hollywood homosexual; that scene where he starts singing in *My Best Friend's Wedding*

THEATER OF OPERATIONS: London

You all know Rupert Everett. For a while he was the gay guy. What is that supposed to mean, "the gay guy"? Well, there was a time in Hollywood not long ago when there was only one openly gay guy allowed as a major screen presence at any given moment. Of course, closeted gay actors could play gay men or straight men—even samurais and fighter pilots. Then in *My Best Friend's Wedding,* another one of those Julia Roberts films where she's sad then at the end she's happy, Rupert went and stole the show with his portrayal of George, a loveable queen with a penchant for singing. The real Rupert Everett is much more interesting.

In a 1997 interview with *Us* magazine, Everett says, "I didn't set out to hustle, but this guy offered me such a massive amount of money, well, it was like a year-and-a-half's pocket money," going on to explain how he "sort of fell into" prostitution after a man solicited his services outside the London Underground. It mustn't have been a particularly grueling decision, though, considering Everett's noble extraction.

Everett grew up in a house of privilege with barons and whatnot peppering the family tree. His father was a military man, and he sent young Rupert to study piano with Benedictine monks. Later London's Central School of Speech and Drama expelled Rupert for insubordination, but he scratched and clawed and whored himself until he finally caught a break. He was cast as an eccentric homosexual schoolboy at a stuffy English private school, a role that allowed him to draw heavily from his own experience. It was a West End performance of *Another Country*, and the crowds as well as the critics went wild. His performance became legendary, which was a good thing for Rupert, as his rent-boy gig did not provide the financial safety net one needs. Rupert confessed to *The Telegraph*:

> Actors make bad lovers. Their most important kiss is for the camera. Not in a superficial way, in a really deep way. They can only give everything if they know someone is going to shout cut! Oh, I am a pathetic lover, I never had the right cards in my hand. Being Catholic, coming from a military background, then having that dawning, nagging feeling that I was not going to be on the right side of the fence.

Everett was not only a bad whore, he could also behave like a big, annoying diva. After the success of *My Best Friend's Wedding*, Everett's star began to rise stateside. He was the Adonis from across the pond, and both men and women fawned over him as if he were a gay James Bond. He'd been famous as a pain in the ass in England for years, but even Americans will tire of pompous prigs eventually, and they did. In fact, he got so diva that he out-divaed his sometime friend, the diva of divas, Madonna. She unfriended him, and Facebook hadn't even been invented yet. After the obligatory autobiography, in which Everett admitted affairs with everyone from Susan Sarandon to Sir Ian McKellen, the Hollywood machine has tempered its enthusiasm for the ravishing former rent-boy, the paragon of "gay best friends," but that seems to be okay with Everett. "You should be able to putter off and have a breakdown or a heroin addiction, whatever it is, your particular problem of choice. That's what makes you an interesting actor, anyway. We're more interesting if we are dysfunctional," he tells the *New York Times*, reinforcing the notion that actors are difficult, uninteresting, and prone to puttering.

MAYA ANGELOU

PROFILE

DAY JOBS: Author; activist; intellectual

CLAIM TO FAME: Former U.S. Poet Laureate

THEATER OF OPERATIONS: St. Louis; California

Maya Angelou once said, "Laugh and dare to try to love somebody, starting with yourself." Let's turn that around a bit and dare to try and laugh at somebody we love, namely Maya Angelou herself.

You probably thought Maya Angelou was just that older lady with a grandmotherly grin and an uncanny ability to compose stanzas of haunting poetry that include profound insights into the human condition. Also, you may have taken issue with her manner of speech since she often comes off as a haughty gnome, but, in spite of her grandiloquence, the woman is unquestionably a great American poet. She is more than that. Much, much more.

How can there be anything like a "scheme of things" or "laws of the cosmos" if a madam and a common prostitute can turn into Maya Angelou. "Heresy!" I hear the poetry community and their fans screaming, but go ahead—read for yourself. In her 1974 memoir, *Gather Together in My Name*, Ms. Angelou reflects:

> I sat thinking about the spent day. The faces, bodies and smells of the tricks made an unending paisley pattern in my mind. Except for the Tamiroffish first customer, the others had no individual characteristics. The strong Lysol washing water stung my eyes and a film of vapor coated my adenoids. I had expected the loud screams of total orgasmic release and felt terribly inadequate when the men had finished with grunts and yanked up their pants without thanks.

The poet was born Marguerite Johnson, or "Rita," in 1928 in St. Louis. Maya Angelou is actually her stage name from her dancing days at the Purple Onion, a famous San Francisco cellar club. Her critically acclaimed, bestselling memoir, *I Know Why the Caged Bird Sings* (1969), provides an astonishing account of the first seventeen years of her life. She is raped as a child by her mother's boyfriend, goes mute for five years, accidentally becomes pregnant and carries the baby to term, finds redemption in great works of literature, and finally receives a scholarship to the California Labor School where she studies dance and drama.

With *I Know Why the Caged Bird Sings*, Ms. Angelou was finally able to "relieve the agony, the anguish, the *Sturm und Drang*." Now, when a person has to use German to tell how bad it was, you know the story is about to get really weird. And five years later, with the release of *Gather Together in My Name*, which chronicles Angelou's life from ages 17–19, the story does, indeed, get bizarre. Angelou pulls no punches describing her "first great slide down into the slimy world," and her grueling schedule working as a madam for two lesbian prostitutes. When the authorities discover what she is up to, they threaten to take her son away, and she hightails it to Arkansas. When the heat dies down, she moves back to San Francisco and offers herself to a married man for a small honorarium. Angelou rationalizes the decision to prostitute herself in the following way:

> There are married women who are more whorish than a street prostitute because they have sold their bodies for marriage licenses, and there are some women who sleep with men for money who have great integrity because they are doing it for a purpose.

Somewhere along the line, Angelou seems to have picked up a little Karl Marx and a touch of Adam Smith, and then put them together to pull off a strange philosophical trick.

From prostitute to poet, activist to actress, and playwright to professor, there seems to be nothing that Ms. Angelou can't do. In 2011, she was awarded the Presidential Medal of Freedom, and she is mentioned every year as a front-runner for the Nobel Prize, but make no mistake about it, Angelou is still capable of generating a juicy scandal. With the release of her controversial *Great Food, All Day Long*, Angelou outraged the health care community. Her allegedly "healthy" cookbook features recipes for such heart-stopping dishes as "Creamy Pork Hash," and even Angelou admits her recipe for pork tacos is so heavy it takes "three hours" before she's "almost ready for a second." Well, I guess we all know why the caged bird has high cholesterol.

PETE DOHERTY

PROFILE

DAY JOB: Dope fiend; itinerant musician

CLAIM TO FAME: Lead singer/songwriter for UK bands the Libertines and Babyshambles

THEATER OF OPERATIONS: England

Speaking of drug addiction, Pete Doherty is always a safe bet if you're looking to entertain yourself by watching someone act a donkey. His highly publicized rock-bottom(s), his arrests, rehabs, and relationships are constant fodder for tabloids, and despite making some damned good music in his early career with the Libertines and then later with Babyshambles, Pete Doherty is still a full-on ass. But this book isn't about asses, it's about hookers. And when you're a liberal lad from Northumberland with a guitar and a dream (and some hash, Special K, maybe a little crack, a spot of heroin, and ale), you'll do anything you can to get ahead, even give a little head.

In the rockography *Kids in the Riot: High and Low with the Libertines*, Doherty admits that before finding success with the Libertines, he moonlighted as a rent-boy:

I was working in a bar, selling drugs, working on a building site, writing poetry in the graveyard shift at The King's Head; and I was whacking off old queens for like £20. I remember once being taken back to this mews house in Chelsea, right old fucking badger he was. It was a bit daft actually. As he slept, I locked him in his room, tied a pair of trousers over his head and nicked all these American dollar bills out of his drawer. He's probably still there, with an erection, listening to classic FM radio.

Well, hell. What's rock and roll without a little love and some theft? Doherty could probably tell you, because when he engages in the aforementioned activities, which is more frequently than you might think, he often winds up in prison. It's getting old watching talented young musicians/songwriters turn into gurgling crapsimilies of their former selves, but part of the enjoyment in watching Pete Doherty self-destruct is this: He's a spoiled brat and a wastrel. His own mother wrote a book, appropriately titled, *Pete Doherty: My Prodigal Son.*

Pete was born into relative privilege, the son of a nurse and a military man, and he attended good schools. He even won a poetry competition and was on his way to a degree in English literature at the University of London, when in 1997 he dropped out and moved in with Libertines cofounder Carl Barât. By all accounts, Pete was a much more pleasant fellow to be around in the early days when whoring was his game. Later, the ravages of drug abuse took a terrible toll on the young Rimbaud wannabe. In addition to a roll call of criminal offenses, mostly drug-related, Doherty was charged with robbing Barât's flat while the Libertines were playing a gig without him; he hawked his bandmate's gear for dope. Then came the obligatory rock star's engagement to Kate Moss, who may be the very duchess of deep shit, or Circe, as men who fall in love with her seem to collapse under the weight of this waifish critter's increasingly vacant stare.

At the time of this writing Doherty is continuing his on-again off-again battle with drugs and fame and douchebaggery, but considering the 2011 death of Amy Winehouse, he should probably try to get a clue. In fact, Winehouse had this macabre tidbit to share on the subject of

Doherty before she died: "We're just friends. . . . I asked Pete to do a concept EP, and he looked at me like I'd pooed on the floor." Who knows what music magic would have emerged out of that relationship, but one thing remains clear: If you're going to collaborate with Doherty, it might make sense to poo on the floor first and *then* approach him about music. Well, at least he doesn't force his cats to smoke crack. Oh, wait. Photos published in British tabloid the *Sun* showed that he does. No kidding. Crack kittens.

STEVE MCQUEEN

PROFILE

DAY JOB: Actor

CLAIM TO FAME: "The King of Cool"

THEATER OF OPERATIONS: Hollywood

Born to an absent, barnstorming father and an alcoholic mother in Depression-era Indiana, Terrence Steven McQueen was dyslexic, partially deaf, and rebellious. His early years were a whirlwind of odd jobs—stints in gangs, the military, the circus, the merchant marine, and perhaps most notably as a masturbating stage performer in Havana, Cuba.

It takes some imagination to see the paragon of Hollywood "cool" sitting on a rickety stage near the *Malecon* in 1940s Havana, jacking off into a coffee cup three times a night to make a living. But in Darwin Porter's *Steve McQueen, King of Cool: Tales of a Lurid Life*, we are given a firsthand account of McQueen's stage act from a colleague:

> Steven's skit began its first show at 9:30 at night. The red curtain opened onto a scene in a cafe where [McQueen] was seated with a beautiful woman named Rosa. "I want some coffee," Rosa demanded of Steven. He briefly went off stage and returned with a cup of

coffee. . . . To the delight of the audience, Steven unbuttoned his trousers and produced his flaccid penis. Like the skilled fellatio artist she was, Rosa performed oral sex on him until he produced an erection. . . . He masturbated himself to climax, his "cream" shooting into her coffee. Rosa then proceeded to drink all of the coffee as the curtain went down to thunderous applause.

I've given this some thought, and I'd be willing to bet cash money that Steve McQueen is the only Oscar-nominated actor to get his start in show business in this particular way. Although Hollywood is a crazy place, and heaven only knows what kind of caffeinated ejaculate our screen stars have swallowed over the last century.

Before his move to Hollywood, McQueen also travelled to New York City, where he landed minor parts on stage along with plenty of places for his private parts in the orifices of various clients around town. According to Porter, McQueen once boasted that, "On those lean days I could usually pick up a bitch in the Village who would take me back to her apartment. I'd fuck her in exchange for a home-cooked meal." Steve was an equal opportunity rent-boy, hustling both sexes. Wearing a borrowed tuxedo he allegedly landed Lana Turner and Joan Crawford as early clients (not, unfortunately, at the same time), but Paul Newman and James Dean were also among the Who's Who of Hollywood heavyweights who were said to have hired McQueen. Even intergalactic sex symbols Natalie Wood and Marilyn Monroe supposedly availed themselves of his services. Now that's *range*, folks.

After his role on *Dead or Alive* made him a TV star, McQueen was soon cast in *The Magnificent Seven* (1960), a role that would launch his film career. *The Great Escape* (1963), *The Thomas Crown Affair* (1968), *Bullitt* (1968), *The Getaway* (1972), and *Papillon* (1973) followed, with McQueen becoming the highest-paid actor in Hollywood. In 1980 the King of Cool died a rather sudden and ignominious death in Mexico from sloppy surgery that was supposed to remove a cancerous tumor. He was only fifty years old.

EVA PERÓN

PROFILE

DAY JOB: First Lady of Argentina

CLAIM TO FAME: Deemed by Argentine congress as the "Spiritual Leader of the Nation"; immortalized in the musical, then the shitty Madonna movie, *Evita*

THEATER OF OPERATIONS: Argentina

Love her or hate her, you have to recognize the skills of Eva Perón (or Evita, of *Evita* fame). And, her sex appeal. Born in 1919 in Los Toldos, Argentina, a small town about 200 miles from Buenos Aires, Perón was one of four siblings born to Juana Ibarguren and Juan Duarte. The problem was, Duarte had a few other families happening on the side, and he was eventually forced to choose between them and stay put. Duarte did not choose the brood he sired with Ibarguren, so Juana took Evita and her four siblings to Junín, where they all lived together in a seedy, one-room apartment.

At the age of fifteen, seized with ambition and possessed of rather flexible moral boundaries, she left Junín for Buenos Aires, determined to make it. Such ill-advised moves to the big city on the part of very young folks rarely work out for the best. There are a few exceptions, like Rimbaud, or Beethoven, or Brad Pitt, but usually, the move involves getting robbed, drinking bad wine on a roof all day, explaining to your parents that artistic inspiration cannot be rushed, being unemployed, and living in a tent fashioned out of empty Franzia boxes. Trust me. And of course, there's the prostitution problem.

There is some ambiguity and/or disagreement about whether or not Evita was a bona fide prostitute. Some claim that story is a myth concocted by opponents to smear her name and that of her future husband Juan Perón, the president of Argentina from 1946 to 1955 and again (after Evita's death) from 1973 to 1974. But the jury is still out. It's pretty clear that Evita succumbed to the "casting couch," in order to further her career, but a streetwalker? It depends.

Here's the titan of Argentine letters, Jorge Luis Borges, on Evita:

> [Eva] was a common prostitute. She had a brothel near Junin. I mean,
> if a girl is a whore in a large city that doesn't mean too much, but in
> a small town in the pampas, everybody knows everybody else. And
> being one of the whores is like being the barber or the surgeon.

Of course, Borges's mother and sister were both jailed under the presidency of Juan Perón, so his version of events comes with echoes of axe grinding. Even so, Evita attained a level of success as an "actress," and at an artistic benefit for earthquake victims, she came alone and left with Perón, putting into motion one of the most controversial political alliances the world has ever known.

After his exile from Argentina and his move to Spain, Juan Perón was surprised when, after two decades, Evita's body turned up on his doorstep, a consolation from the generals who'd ousted him and buried Evita in an unmarked grave. Preserved to near-perfection (aside from being dead), the embalmed Evita lay in an open casket on the dining room table of his villa while Juan prepared a return to power. You would think Perón's new wife, Isabel, might have been a bit put out by this development, but you'd be wrong. Isabel is reported to have been loyal and caring toward her deceased predecessor. She lovingly combed Evita's long blond tresses every day in a wrong kind of crazy postmortem ritual.

To some Eva was a progressive feminist and friend to the poor, a supporter of laborers' rights and generous with her charity. To others, she was a selfish tit, a peroxided floozy who harbored fugitive Nazis and exploited her foundation for the poor to fill her and her husband's personal coffers. She was known constantly to suck on her ornate jewelry, a habit some saw as sexual and others viewed as an effort to flaunt her wealth in front of garden-variety arrivistes.

Evita's death in 1956 at thirty-three of uterine cancer unleashed an irrepressible crush of media attention that keeps her memory fresh in the public consciousness. The musical *Evita*, the movie *Evita*, dozens of books called *Evita* have together served to canonize her as some kind of a saint, but many folks in the know attribute her increasingly lofty status to the "miracle" of her haute Italian footwear.

Unfortunately, there is a darker, stinking underbelly to this story. The Peróns, as absolutists have a tendency to do, became intoxicated with power, eventually seizing control of the media, killing and torturing their opponents, and taking credit for all sorts of shit they didn't do like pave the way for women's suffrage in Argentina, something the socialists had been grinding away at for fifty years before Evita came along in her supple leather pumps, sucking on her gems.

THOMAS JANE

PROFILE

DAY JOB: Actor

CLAIM TO FAME: Star of HBO series *Hung*

THEATER OF OPERATIONS: Santa Monica Blvd., Los Angeles

"OMG, isn't it ironic that the star of a television show about prostitutes was once a prostitute?" you ask. No, it's merely a coincidence—put away the Alanis Morissette CDs. *Hung* revolves around defeated high school hoops coach, Ray Drecker. His house has burned down, he's lost custody of his twin daughter and son to the ever-excruciating Anne Heche, and he's heavily in debt. Lucky for Ray, he's also heavily in dick, a trait he puts to use as a male prostitute. It's a pretty cool idea for a show, and Thomas Jane is particularly convincing as the down-and-out, then up-and-in (as it were) Drecker.

Well, like many actors struggling to make it in Hollywood, Jane found himself living on "dreams," which unlike food stamps, will not provide even basic sustenance. So Jane girded up his loins and set out to supplement his income. Speaking with the *Los Angeles Times*, Jane explains:

> When I was a kid out here in L.A., I was homeless, I didn't have any money and I was living in my car. . . . I was 18. I wasn't averse to going down to Santa Monica Boulevard and letting a guy buy me a sandwich. Know what I mean? Hey, you grow up as an artist in a big city, as James Dean said, "you're going to have one arm tied behind your back if you don't accept people's sexual favors."

A couple of small problems with that: (A) Why are you going down to Santa Monica Boulevard if you're just whoring for sandwiches? This approach seems counterintuitive, as sandwiches are cheaper in East Los—more "bang for your buck," if you know what I mean; and (B) It doesn't appear that James Dean ever actually said that.

Look, if you're going to own being a prostitute, you can't go around hiding behind sandwiches and spurious James Dean quotations. It cheapens sandwiches, it cheapens prostitution, and it cheapens James Dean, although if made right, a muffuletta sandwich can be amazing. Jane also admits to busking, another shameful occupation. He admits, "I had two songs in my repertoire that I hammered to death—'Hey Joe' and 'Knockin' on Heaven's Door'. . . . People used to pelt me with change just to shut me up."

Hollywood finally discovered the struggling actor and put him to work standing up for once. Jane won cushy roles in *61★* (2001) and *The Punisher* (2004). His success on the silver/HD/plasma screens has made it possible for all of us to patronize sandwich shops in the Santa Monica Boulevard area without some asshole asking us where we're going with that gun in our hand. For now.

Oh, all right, Thomas—get your sweet cheeks over here, and let us buy you a sandwich.

Chapter V

WHORES
BEHAVING BADLY

"Something wicked this way comes," and with it a few satisfied customers and a trail of blood, greed, insanity, and murder. The "hooker with the heart of gold" is a myth we've seen smashed up against the depictions of the tart track in movies like *Midnight Cowboy* and lesser celluloid claptrap like *Pretty Woman*, where yes, she's a hooker and has a heart of gold, but in the end, we're all really hoping she electrocutes herself with that Walkman while making a mockery of Prince, the Revolution, and the industry.

Still and all, Julia Roberts's considerably obnoxious Vivian is no match for the following whores of terror. From serial-killing lunatics and felonious French Quarter floozies to a debased, coke-addled porn star whose most lethal weapon was his foot-long dong, these prostitutes stirred up a heap of trouble. Welcome to the dark side of the street.

ANDREW CUNANAN

PROFILE

DAY JOBS: C. S. Lewis enthusiast; serial killer

CLAIM TO FAME: Murdered Gianni Versace

THEATER OF OPERATIONS: South Beach, Miami

This depraved man-whore made headlines when, on the morning of July 15, 1997, he put two bullets into designer and fashion impresario Gianni Versace on the steps of Versace's South Beach, Miami, home. During a three-month crime spree leading up to his suicide in a wealthy john's houseboat, the dashing young Cunanan killed at least five people and became notorious as a member of the FBI's Most Wanted List.

Hailing from San Diego, Cunanan attended UCSD where he majored in history, but he found the butt beat more alluring than the ivory tower. After a brief stint slumming it—literally—in the Philippines, Cunanan had tricked up enough cash to make it back to San Francisco, where he set up shop in the Castro district and quickly became one of the more highly regarded prostitutes in town. He had myriad sugar daddies who supplied him with cash, credit, and fancy cars. Versions of Cunanan from past acquaintances, the media, and family members conjure up images of a veritable sex chameleon. One roommate asserts that he was super freakish; "heavy into the roughage and S&M, more the tying-up-and-whips type—just the degradation, not the asphyxiation." Meanwhile an exposé in *Vanity Fair* poo-pooed him as "just a gay gigolo down on his luck"; however, his mother offers clarification, telling us that her son was no sexual slumdog but was without a doubt a "high-class male prostitute." Whatever one's fetish or financial state, a stream of men and money does not always happiness make, especially when you are convinced you have AIDS (an autopsy proved he didn't), you have turned into a psychotic killer, and you have become oddly obsessed with the writings of C. S. Lewis.

A dark entry in the prostitution log, Andrew Cunanan is a disgrace to the profession, as his fame comes in exchange for innocent lives. Alas, he is in the sexicon and worth mention, if only to serve as a sinister reminder of what can happen if you mess with people who are greedy, deranged, and have access to your house boats.

VIRGINIA HILL

PROFILE

DAY JOB: "Bag lady" for the mafia

CLAIM TO FAME: Mob boss Bugsy Siegel's (along with other mafia big names) #1 gal

THEATER OF OPERATIONS: Chicago; Las Vegas

During the 1950s you didn't have squat for street cred unless you'd been with Virginia Hill, or "the Flamingo," as she was known. Virginia was born the sixth of ten children in the rustic shit-box that was Lipscomb, Alabama, where in 2011, enterprising citizens held a hot dog sale to retire the city's debts. That's country living, folks.

At seventeen Virginia left the confines of Alabama for the 1933 World's Fair in Chicago to try her hand at hooking. Young Ms. Hill turned out to be precocious in this regard, and she eventually attracted the likes and loins of big-time, old-school gang bangers ranging from the Franks (Nitti and Costello) to the Joes (Adonis and Epstein) to the infamous Ben "Bugsy" Siegel.

Hill served as a "bag lady" for the mafia, which contrary to how it may sound, did not involve her pushing a rusty grocery cart around downtown, screaming the theme song from *Fat Albert* at fire hydrants. No, in this case, our bag lady was an indispensible courier for the Chicago mob, moving dirty money and narcotics in her bag. Some argue her "bag" may have actually been a "suitcase," but that's a mystery for another day. What is clear is that the Chicago syndicate rewarded Hill

handsomely for her efforts on their behalf. Homegirl once even dropped
an $11,000 cold, hard gangster knot (the equivalent of about $150,000 in
2011 money) on a new house for the kinfolk back in Alabama.

When Hill arrived in California in the early 1940s and joined pel-
vises with Bugsy Siegel, her stock really began to rise, but Bugsy's
hotel (named, appropriately, the Flamingo) eventually floundered and
their relationship soured. Heat from the authorities and Bugsy's sinking business venture drove Hill to Paris, where she hung out long
enough for Siegel's enemies to track him down and shoot the shit
out of him. When she returned stateside and was given the news of
Siegel's murder, she fainted, then ran into the arms of an Austrian ex-
Nazi and ski instructor.

Virginia Hill may have been the best cocksucker in the United States,
but in 2009 "Sexy Cora," a German porn star, gave Ms. Hill a run for
her money. On bail for having sex in a public park, Sexy Cora set out
to break the world record for the most oral sex, with plans to service
200 men. Things went quickly awry for Sexy Cora when, according to
Britain's the *Sun,* "she was forced to call off the bid when she collapsed
after reaching her 75th man and was rushed to hospital with breathing dif-
ficulties." Sadly, Cora died before she could give the record another go.

Hey! What about that oral sex I mentioned earlier? Ah, yes. During
the 1950–1951 U.S. Senate Special Committee to Investigate Crime in
Interstate Commerce, known also as the Kefauver Committee, Hill was
hauled in to explain why she was so often seen dating known gangsters.
The committee also wanted to know why her dates with men using
uncreative though menacing nicknames, seemed to develop amnesia
whenever the question of taxes arose, specifically the matter of Virginia's
$161,000 in unpaid back taxes. When grilled by Senator Kefauver over
why she drew paychecks from so many dubious sources, Ms. Hill gave
it to him. The following is an excerpt from the interview transcript:

- **Sen. Kefauver**: How come that's the case, Miss Hill?
- **Virginia Hill**: Senator, are you *sure* you want to know why these men give me money?
- **Sen. Kefauver**: Of course I want to know, Miss Hill.
- **Virginia Hill**: Senator, they give me money because I'm the best damned cocksucker in the United States!

The response so shocked New Hampshire senator Charles W. Tobey, a notoriously pompous old fart, that UPI reporter Harold Conrad said, "Tobey all but swallowed his Bible."

Sadly, in 1966 at the age of forty-nine Virginia forced a handful of sleeping pills down her throat and dropped dead of an apparent suicide in a remote town in Austria. You will no doubt be happy to learn that she did divorce the Nazi before nodding off for good.

KHIONIYA GUSEVA

PROFILE

DAY JOB: Aging floozy

CLAIM TO FAME: Would-be assassin of the "Mad Monk," Rasputin

THEATER OF OPERATIONS: Tsaritsyn (today Volgograd), Russia

Losing one's nose isn't always the end of the world. In fact, for some people, it's a new beginning. And for Khioniya Guseva, a middling-to-effective prostitute in Romanov-run Russia, along with the abolishment of her nose came a revelation: She was born to be one of those people who embrace various religious zealots. This surely comes as no surprise and is a common U-turn among the naïve and/or noseless.

Guseva soon fell under the spell of Ilioder, a defrocked monk, radical anti-Semite, and former colleague of "The Mad Monk," Rasputin.

When Ilioder broke all ties to Rasputin, some assume he enlisted the
past-her-prime frosty prosty, Khioniya, to stick it to his old colleague.
Why? Rasputin's meteoric rise in influence and power within the
Romanov family had many embittered political and religious rivals out
to cut the wild-eyed mystic down to size. A kind of Tsarist Squeaky
Fromme, Khioniya was convinced by Ilioder that Rasputin was a false
prophet and a nun raper, so she set out—on Ilioder's orders—to send
Rasputin back to hell.

One day, Rasputin was hanging around, probably staring at people
with those penetrating eyes and making political and sports predictions, when, according to the deputy prosecutor of the Tobolsk district court, Khioniya, a woman "of repulsive ugliness, her nose was
crushed and misshapen" approached him, bowed politely, and begged
for a ruble. "You shouldn't bow," replied Rasputin, at which point
"Khioniya Guseva drew a sharp dagger out of her coat and struck
Rasputin in the stomach." Khioniya then ripped the knife up to
Rasputin's navel and his guts fell out, whereupon she screamed, "I
have killed the Antichrist!"

After the Mad Monk's death, his penis turned up in Paris around 1920.
In the 1970s the member found its way to a California antique dealer,
and it popped up again in London during the '90s, where an astute
observer noticed that the artifact was not a penis at all, but a dried-up
cucumber. But wait. In 2004, Dr. Igor Knyazkin opened the Museum
of Erotica in St. Petersburg, to showcase the 15,000-plus sex collectibles
he acquired over the years, including the Mad Monk's nearly foot-long
dong (11.8 inches) in all its original glory. Tests have yet to be run on
the *objet* to determine its authenticity, but let's hope this time it's at least
someone's penis and not a gourd.

Typically, this would be the end of things, but Rasputin didn't
go down easy. Entrails in hand, Rasputin picked up a stick and gave

Khioniya a wallop to her dome, followed by a near-mortal ass-kicking from incensed townspeople and assorted pro-Rasputin toughs.

Speculation remains that Khioniya may have been a spurned lover of the Mad Monk, or perhaps she was just an unsatisfied patient of the notorious mystic, soothsayer, and faith healer. Who wouldn't be furious if she went to some alleged "healer" and her nose fell off? However, it seems Khioniya's nose fell off independent of any quacky, quasi-salubrious mambo-jahambo on Rasputin's part; the problem was most likely the result of a powerful case of Bolshevik syphilis, or a knife fight.

In the end, it would take a few more stab wounds, a good clubbing, strangulation, a flurry of bullets, the removal of his penis, and an icy dip in the Neva River to kill Rasputin. As for Ms. Guseva, the authorities sent her up to the booby hatch in Tomsk, where she spent her days in what family members referred to as "exalted religiosity." She was released after the Bolshevik Revolution in 1917 and never heard from again. As for Ilioder, he fled to Finland after hearing of the abortive attempt on Rasputin's life, then moved to New York City and became a devout Baptist and a janitor at the Met Life building in Madison Square.

SADA ABE

PROFILE

DAY JOB: D-list geisha

CLAIM TO FAME: Hauling a penis around Shinigawa for a week

THEATER OF OPERATIONS: Japan

Geisha are supposed to operate on a separate plane of existence called "The Flower and Willow World," or *kary-kai*. And it is a geisha's residence in this farcical world of imagined flora and idyllic haiku that seems to make it okay for men to pretty much treat them as slaves or indentured servants. Sada Abe escaped all that. She was a risk taker who scoffed at convention. This was a geisha who would steal your heart *and* your penis.

In the late 1920s, Sada Abe was, by all accounts, a piss-poor geisha, a low-level drone in the Osaka geisha scene, spending most of her time just providing sex for money, which sounded suspiciously like straight-up prostitution. That being the case, Ms. Abe decided to muscle-up and join the ranks of the common streetwalkers. Abe proved to be wildly successful once she ditched the geisha routine and saw fit to hook down here with the rest of us. Abe eventually built up enough of a grubstake to—at the urging of one of her johns—begin an apprenticeship at a local restaurant. The owner of the restaurant was one Kichizo Ishida, who fell hard for Sada, despite his marriage to Mrs. Ishida. Sada fell for Kichizo too, and according to William Johnston's *Geisha, Harlot, Strangler, Star: A Woman, Sex, and Morality in Modern Japan*, the pair consummated their relationship in the middle of the restaurant, with a geisha who sang a love ballad as the two writhed around like a plate of *unagi-no-kabayaki*, popping and sweating on the grill. Well, that's all very romantic, but things were about to take a decidedly peculiar turn.

While prostitution is in no way unique to Japan, the Japanese do bring to the field at least one unique diversion, a culinary curiosity of the first order: the practices of *nyotaimori* and *nantaimori*, or, "eating sushi off of nude people." *Nyotaimori* (a buffet arrangement on top of a female) and *nantaimori* (male arrangement), consists of shelling out unfathomable amounts of money to pick cold sashimi off of a goose-bumped and presumably miserable model, or "plate." A relatively new phenomenon, scholars postulate that *nyotaimori* and *nantaimori* may have developed in response to the 1980s economic boom in Japan, when people were searching for new and ever more ridiculous ways to waste their plentiful yen.

Sada became upset because after their lovemaking Kichizo always insisted on returning home to his family, although "upset" doesn't really do justice to what happened next. During a four-day sex binge ending on May 18, 1936, Sada and Kichizo played out the usual fantasy: They played at strangling each other with Sada's obi before the ex-geisha brandished a huge knife and placed it on the tip of Kichizo's penis. Nothing new about that, right? Well, then Sada killed her lover and used her knife to separate him from his penis. She did have an explanation for this move, which she explained to one of her interrogating officers: "Since we were not husband and wife, as long as he lived he could be embraced by other women. I knew that if I killed him, no other woman could ever touch him again, so I killed him." When someone asked, "Okay, but why did you cut off his penis after you strangled him to death with that obi?" her answer was logical, "Because I couldn't take his head or body with me. I wanted to take the part of him that brought back to me the most vivid memories." Pretty touching stuff, but it gets better.

After carving her name on Kichizo's arm and writing "Sada, Kichi together" on his severed truncheon, Sada lay with the body awhile, then left with Kichi's dong in her handbag. She claims to have felt a strong sense of attachment "to his penis and thought that, only after taking leave from it quietly, could I then die. I unwrapped it and gazed at it. I put it in my mouth and even tried to insert it inside me. In the end, I intended to jump from a cliff on Mount Ikoma while holding on to his penis." Whoa. Luckily, the police finally tracked down Sada before her boner B.A.S.E. jump and she spent six years in prison.

Sada enjoyed a degree of celebrity after her release, writing a bestselling book and becoming a brief media sensation. Some people claim she is still alive, which would make her a whopping 106. As for Kichizo's penis, it was given to the Tokyo University Medical School, where someone once again absconded with it. And so it goes that Kichizo's unfortunate cock continues its "journey" today, perhaps as a paperweight or charm dangling helplessly from a keychain.

BARBARA HOFFMAN

PROFILE

DAY JOB: Biochemistry student

CLAIM TO FAME: Massage parlor murderess

THEATER OF OPERATIONS: Madison, Wisconsin

If you think that a happy ending is what happens at the finale of one of Hugh Grant's crimes against cinema, you've been missing out. And you must change your life. But before demanding your $15 back from the cineplex and heading downtown to the massage parlor for a "happy ending" you can get excited about, think twice. You could run into someone like Barbara Hoffman.

If you met Barbara Hoffman in Madison, Wisconsin, during the mid-to-late 1970s, you were probably either (A) looking for sex at Jan's Health Studio, one of the whorehouses-cum-massage parlors in town, or (B) in the biochemistry department at the University of Wisconsin–Madison, where Barbara maintained a 3.9 GPA, making the dean's list by day and turning tricks at the massage studio by night. Well, this kind of ambitious routine can lead to exhaustion, frustration, and, occasionally, murder.

Now, nobody here is going to judge anybody for rocking two disparate employment trajectories, especially if one of them is prostitution. I know how the landscape of contemporary biochemistry is changing by the nanosecond—or at least I imagine that it is—so it's clearly necessary to have a safety net to make sure your golden years are everything you dream they'll be. However, it's when you start to burden yourself with added responsibilities like taking out life insurance policies on your soon-to-be-dead client and your boyfriend that you start to get overextended. And that's exactly what happened to Ms. Hoffman.

In 1977, Barbara's boyfriend Gerald Davies walked into a police station and informed them that he'd helped Barbara dispose of a body at the nearby Blackhawk Ski Club. Sure enough, the police went out there and found a naked dead man. Police charged Hoffman with the murder of Harold Berge, one of her clients at Jan's. Davies was set to testify against Hoffman in court until he turned up dead in a bathtub. Unexplained bathtub death can be a game-changing snag for the wheels of justice, especially as Davies left a letter to the *Wisconsin State Journal* and his lawyer before his death, stating, "I was scared. I was jealous, Barb is innocent and I wrecked her life. All those stories I told about Barb were false." "Well, shit," thought everybody, "this changes everything." Our murderous masseuse has been cleared!

In Shakespeare's *Hamlet*, we are treated to a romantic description of poisoning from the character Lucianus,

> *Thoughts black, hands apt, drugs fit, and time agreeing;*
> *Confederate season, else no creature seeing;*
> *Thou mixture rank, of midnight weeds collected,*
> *With Hecate's ban thrice blasted, thrice infected,*
> *Thy natural magic and dire property,*
> *On wholesome life usurp immediately.*

Unfortunately, things aren't so poetic once the poison kicks in. Cyanide is a choker, halting your body's oxygen consumption. It goes down with an acrid burn, then you have to barf, and your head feels like it's been mounted by a jaguar. Your vision will soon blur; you'll do some "reeling"; and then, like an insouciant fart at the opera, you will collapse, and die, much to everyone's disgust (unless it's proven that you were murdered with cyanide, then they'll feel bad for leaving you dozing through *Tristan and Isolde* again).

Not so fast. The more the evidence changed, the more it stayed the same. Tests concluded that both Berge and Davies died from lethal doses of cyanide, and it was also discovered that Hoffman had enrolled in courses that included discussions about the toxic effects of cyanide on the human body (test results concluded that if you put lots of cyanide in a human body, the human body dies). Furthermore, Hoffman's boss at the massage parlor decided to come clean and related a conversation he'd had with Hoffman in which she expressed an interest in marrying Davies and killing him in Mexico on their honeymoon, then collecting on his life insurance policy. Davies had taken out three policies on himself worth $20,000 at the time of his death, and he listed Hoffman as his fiancée.

In the end, Hoffman was not charged in the death of her boyfriend Davies, whose death was ruled a suicide, but she was given a life sentence for killing Berge. The murder/suicide and its attendant tale of erotic massage and amino asses captivated the good people of Wisconsin, a folk normally preoccupied with binge drinking, cow-tipping, and mittens. But the collective memory of Barbara, the murders, and the media circus is decomposing like a corpse in the snow, while our ribald biochemist languishes in jail, no doubt wondering how her happy ending went all haywire.

JOHN HOLMES

PROFILE

DAY JOB: Porn star

CLAIM TO FAME: A good foot of coked-up, erotic dynamite

THEATER OF OPERATIONS: Los Angeles; wherever porno is made

Perhaps it's not fair to include Johnny "The Wad" Holmes in this infamous roll call. Indeed, most of John Holmes's evil deeds seem to have been perpetrated more out of stupidity than malice. And when you're walking around with an (allegedly) thirteen-inch dick, it's not inconceivable to presume much of the blood flow needed for proper mental functioning and advanced reasoning skills might be diverted away from one's brain during times of sexual activity, which, for John Holmes, were many and oft.

Have you ever wondered who has the biggest penis in the world? The biggest vagina? Maybe you were afraid your cache of Google searches would get you fired. Lucky for you, I've already been axed for that, but not before gathering some interesting data. The owner of the world's largest recorded penis is Mr. Jonah Falcon from Brooklyn, NY. Jonah's penis is nine and a half inches flaccid and thirteen and a half inches erect, and as he announced on *The Daily Show*, he can "envelop an entire door-knob" with his foreskin. Not to be outdone, the title "Woman with the Largest Vagina" goes to a Scottish giantess named Anna Swan. Anna (1846-1888) gave birth to a baby boy whose head was 19 inches in cir-cumference. And babies come from vaginas—so there it is.

Holmes was born John Estes in 1944 in Ashville, Ohio. His father abandoned the family when John was still a baby, and he was raised by his mother and stepfather, a violent alcoholic who John said would often arrive home after barhopping and throw up on him and the rest of the family. John eventually tired of this ceremony, and at age sixteen he drove a fist through his stepdad's face and headed out into the world, armed with a dream and a dong he once described as "bigger than a pay-phone, but smaller than a Cadillac." A photographer discovered John, or rather, John's miraculous penis in a public restroom and the young man was soon making 8 mm porn loops and modeling for *Swedish Erotica*, using a variety of stage names to keep his identity under wraps. Holmes eventually rose up through the ranks to become the most sought-after penis in the industry. But, with fame came drugs, and with drugs came some of the worst decision making the porn industry—or any industry—has ever seen.

As the Superfreak says, "Cocaine is a hell of a drug," and for Holmes it was no different. When the 1970s came to an end, John was drug-addled, broke, and limp but trying mightily to turn tricks in order to pay for his habit. In 1981, he even played a part—the extent of which is unknown—in the robbery of a Los Angeles drug dealer and club owner named Eddie Nash. Nash struck back with a vengeance, instructing his goons to pummel Holmes until he gave up his accomplices, which he did. The ensuing bloodbath was known as "The Wonderland Murders"; four people were bludgeoned to death at a rented house on Wonderland Avenue in Laurel Canyon. Nash may have forced Holmes to participate in the killings as an act of penance, although this was never proven.

"My choice early in life was either to be a piano-player in a whorehouse or a politician. And to tell the truth, there's hardly any difference."
—Harry S. Truman, thirty-third U.S. president

What is proven is that at some point during his pornographic exploits and whoring, Holmes contracted AIDS. In the mid-1980s, still broke, under constant investigation, and a mere shell of his former self, Holmes kept the disease from everyone but his manager, who forbade him to "act" in any more movies. Undaunted, Holmes made films in Italy, neglecting to tell his costars he'd been diagnosed with AIDS. He reasoned that everyone in the porn industry would eventually succumb to the disease anyway, but that was just a convenient excuse. Holmes's decision haunts the industry to this day. The Wad eventually died of complications from AIDS in 1988, assured a place in the hall of pornographers, prostitutes, and people with really poor judgment. Whether he was a murderer remains to be seen, but through porno reruns, long John and his lurid legacy continue to inspire, disgust, and intrigue to this day.

GERDA MUNSINGER

PROFILE

DAY JOB: Political *provocateur;* Russian spy

CLAIM TO FAME: At the head of Canada's first real sex scandal

THEATER OF OPERATIONS: Canada/East Berlin

With Canada, you never know what you're going to get. The country would be almost like a box of chocolates, were it not for the maple syrup lobby threatening to defenestrate anybody who dares mess with their sap. That statement wasn't even remotely true, but that you believed it for even a second indicates exactly the kind of weird behavior we can expect from Canucks.

On March 4, 1966, when John Diefenbaker, the House of Commons Tory Opposition Leader, chastised Justice Minister Lucien Cardin for botching Canada's National Security (from *what* or *whom*, one might ask), Cardin leapt up and snorted in that snooty French-Canadian argot that sounds a lot like a hedgehog reaching orgasm, "[Diefenbaker] is the very last person who can afford to give advice on the handling of security cases." Cardin then beseeched Diefenbaker to "tell about his participation in the Munsinger case when he was Prime Minister!" much to the amusement to those tuned in to the Canadian Broadcasting Corporation (CBC) and the continued consternation of Canadian politicians, too cold to really give a rat's ass in the first place.

For the love of back bacon, the House seemed to be thinking, *Okay, we give up—what's the Munsinger case?* The atmosphere in the chamber turned awkward and icy. So what *was* the Munsinger case that got JM Cardin in such an exasperated state and nearly brought down the sitting government? Well, gather around the fire, y'all. . . . It all started with a prostitute named Gerda Munsinger.

Gerda was born in Germany in 1929, where she was briefly married to an American serviceman. After immigrating to Canada in 1955, Munsinger slogged through a number of temporary jobs, eventually finding a more permanent position as a waitress and hostess at the Chez Paree nightclub. According to the CBC, it was at the Chez Paree that Gerda came into contact with, and then advanced to the bedrooms of, some of Canada's most prominent politicians, including members of parliament and Defense Minister Pierre Sévigny.

History is fraught with legendary cover-ups. But one cover-up they *don't* tell you about took place in New Guinea during the early 1970s: Operation Penis Gourd. Its mission? Covering up the Dani tribe with clothes. The Dani were a "Stone-Age" people, according to some members of the Indonesian government, and needed to be civilized. According to an article in *The Economist*:

> Jogging shorts and dresses were airlifted to the Baliem Valley in central Irian Jaya and distributed to the natives. An American missionary present at one distribution recalls that next day men were wearing the shorts on their heads and women were using the dresses as shoulder bags.

Operation Penis Gourd, as you may have divined, was a fantastic failure. The Dani remain mostly nude to this day, although in reality, it was the Indonesian government who were caught with their pants down.

Canada's first sex scandal was launched, but somewhere along the way, they lost Gerda. It turns out she was quietly deported back to East Berlin in 1961. But never mind that. In 1966, when the scandal broke, Cold War paranoia was still acute, so any mention of spying was enough to make even a silly government like the one Canadians mounted crumble and fall. Beware! Communists are coming for our comedians, our moose, and our hockey skills!

In fact, then prime minister Lester Pearson was so eager to close the books on the Munsinger "spying" case that he had a go at deflecting the issue by turning the discourse to Canada's death penalty. The debates on this perennial topic, unlike the discussions surrounding the Munsinger investigation, were heated but progressive, and would ultimately lead to Canada's abolition of the death penalty. Rumors circulated that Munsinger was dead, although she was eventually found by a reporter for the *Toronto Star* who claimed Gerda was very much alive, eager to clear her name, and hanging out in Munich. But, as these things go, Gerda's fifteen minutes were up, and in a truly postmodern Warholian twist, she wasn't even there to enjoy it. The Canadian government established a Royal Commission that ultimately found neither a security breach nor evidence of any crime committed.

In one of those brilliant Canadacentric instances where you're not sure if they're kidding, serious, or just French, Charles Lynch, Bureau Chief of the Southam News agency at the time of the scandal, held out hope that the "Munsinger Affair" might serve to ramp up Canada's "dull and unexciting" image and spur large numbers of tourists to attend Expo '67. And, by golly, it came to pass. Canada played host to the most widely attended World's Fair in history to date. Gerda died in Munich, for real this time, in 1998.

MATA HARI

PROFILE

DAY JOBS: Exotic dancer; ineffectual spy

CLAIM TO FAME: The original femme fatale; executed by firing squad for espionage

THEATER OF OPERATIONS: The Netherlands; France; Germany

Born in 1876 in the Netherlands, Mata Hari (née Margaretha Geertruida Zelle) is more famous for being executed as a German double agent during World War I than for anything else, but she is of particular interest as a whoretesan. After answering an ad placed in a Dutch newspaper by a man seeking a wife, an intrepid young Margaretha left home with her new husband and settled in Indonesia.

Her husband, a captain in the Dutch Colonial Army, turned out to be an alcoholic dolt who beat her brutally and often. He also kept a second wife, and he fooled around with various other women native to Java. When Margaretha had had enough, she again flung herself to the four winds, and one of those winds blew her into a dance company, where she adopted the stage name Mata Hari.

There may have been a small mix-up. Prior to her arrest in France, Mata Hari maintained that she *had* in fact been in the employ of France as a spy in German-occupied Belgium, where she met with a German consul to give him bogus documents—no harm, no foul, n'est-ce pas? It's curious, then, that Mata Hari, perhaps in a fit of confused allegiances and/or nudity, failed to inform her French spymasters of this bit of freelance espionage and double-agentry. I mean, come on. It's the cardinal rule of espionage and prostitution: Never double-book.

Mata Hari's reputation grew as a dancer and as one who wasn't afraid to take it off if the price was right. Her act eventually took Europe by storm, and she became the in-demand doxy to a number of famous politicians and to royalty, including, it's been rumored, the Crown Prince of Germany. As for her career choices, she is unapologetic, as quoted in *The True Life Fiction of Mata Hari*:

I took the train to Paris without money and without clothes. There, as a last resort and thanks to my female charms, I was able to survive. That I slept with other men is true; that I posed for sculptures is true; that I danced in the opera at Monte Carlo is true. It would be too far beneath me and too cowardly to defend myself against such actions I have taken.

Since the Netherlands was neutral during the Great War, Mata Hari was able to travel freely all over the world, shaking her equal opportunity moneymaker, much to the chagrin of Allied authorities, who suspected her of being a German spy. Eventually, Mata Hari found herself hoisted by her own leotard. In Paris, French and British intelligence intercepted a series of "secret" transmissions that resulted in the exotic dancer's arrest, as Mata Hari may have been a little too eager to please the epaulet-wearing military set. Always a sucker for a man in uniform, Mata Hari once quipped:

> I love officers. I have loved them all my life. I prefer to be the mistress of a poor officer than of a rich banker. It is my greatest pleasure to sleep with them without having to think of money. And, moreover, I like to make comparisons between the different nationalities.

French officers = People fit only to be farted on, decided Mata Hari when the stoic French authorities in uniform proved, for once, immune to her charms. They accused her of treason and espionage, and in 1917 they sentenced her to death by firing squad.

Facing her executioners, Mata Hari is said to have ripped open her Amazonian outfit and roared, "A harlot yes, but traitor never!" before the bullets pierced her chest, a femme fatale to the end. While a profound doubt still lingers as to her actual guilt, Mata Hari has attained the status of a mythical figure, the quintessential female spy: gorgeous, resourceful, courageous, loyal, and scantily clad to the end.

LA MALINCHE

PROFILE

DAY JOB: Turncoat (when wearing one)

CLAIM TO FAME: Confidant to conquistadores, specifically, Hernán Cortés

THEATER OF OPERATIONS: Aztec empire (modern-day Mexico)

Was La Malinche (also known as Doña Maria and Malintzin) a feminist prototype? The first Mexican-American? A traitor to her people? A vessel of modernity? Scholars have argued for all of these interpretations—but a prostitute? *¡Que escandaloso!* Some remain convinced that La Malinche was nothing more than a depraved strumpet. That she was forced into prostitution is not a mitigating factor for this tough crowd.

Born around 1502 in Coatzacoalcos, a pre-Columbian Mexican province, La Malinche was an indigenous beauty fortunate enough to be a part of the privileged, educated Aztec class under the emperor Moctezuma. Her father was an Aztec chief, although after he died, Malinche's ruthless mother sold her into prostitution to traders for some quick change and then held a mock funeral for the little girl, who was soon sold again to a *cacique* in Tabasco.

La Malinche's response was an oath along the lines of "To hell with this," and she wandered the streets of Tabasco until the Spanish *conquistadors*, led by Hernán Cortés, invaded the region in 1519 and took La Malinche, along with a few dozen other young women to serve as domestic labor for his travelling marauders. La Malinche eventually endeared herself to her captors, becoming the favorite of Cortés, translating, providing cultural insight into the Aztecs, advising him on tactical maneuvers, and even fighting by his side in battle.

Becoming a prostitute does not seem to have been her goal, although for those fans loyal to Team Tenochtitlan, what La Malinche did to her own people was a straight-up painted *puta* move.

La Malinche remains part of the indelible iconography of Mexico, although unfortunately not in sixteenth-century nudie books. Nobel Prize–winning author Octavio Paz, in his essay "The Sons of Malinche," writes of the "Chingada" (translated offensively as "The Fucked Mother"), an overwhelming whore character who encapsulates all manner of misfortune in Mexico:

> If the Chingada is a representation of the violated Mother, it is appropriate to associate her with the Conquest, which was also a violation, not only in the historical sense but also in the very flesh of Indian women. The symbol of this violation is doña Malinche, the mistress of Cortes. It is true that she gave herself voluntarily to the conquistador, but he forgot her as soon as her usefulness was over. Doña Marina becomes a figure representing the Indian women who were fascinated, violated or seduced by the Spaniards. And as a small boy will not forgive his mother if she abandons him to search for his father, the Mexican people have not forgiven La Malinche for her betrayal.

That's an awfully big grudge for just one little Latina.

LAS GOTERAS

PROFILE

DAY JOB: Gangbangers

CLAIM TO FAME: "The Mexican Dwarf Wrestler Killers"

THEATER OF OPERATIONS: Mexico City (DF), Mexico

When news broke that "Lucha Mini" stars, *La Parkita* ("The Little Ghost") and *El Espectrito Jr.* ("Mini-Death"), were seen with prostitutes in Mexico City before a match, nobody was surprised. The legendary whoremongering, dwarf-wrestling twins were always up to party

serious. What *was* surprising was that the two favorites of the Lucha
Mini circuit were found dead—drugged and robbed—in room 52 at
the Hotel Moderna in Mexico City, apparently killed by *Las Goteras*,
or "The Drops," a ruthless gang of streetwalking *rameras* who'd rather
"pick your pocket than pleasure your pecker." (*Author's quotation marks;
author thinks this would be a good slogan for* Las Goteras *if they are looking for
internal and external advertising and branding services. Contact author directly
for rates.*) But really, who are *Las Goteras*, and what the hell do these
streetwalking gangs of murderous prosties want? Love, just like the
rest of us, probably.

Pequeño Olímpico is the Barry Bonds of Lucha Mini, or "Mini-estrella,"
the art of Mexican dwarf wrestling. Why not the Hank Aaron or the
Willie Mays? Because Aaron and Mays played the game with honesty
and fundamentals and without the aid of performance-enhancing drugs,
which, in the case of Pequeño Olímpico, are, in an ingenious physiologi-
cal coup, administered through his pituitary glands. You see, Pequeño
Olímpico is not a "little person," but merely a little person, standing
five feet six and a half inches *tall*. I'm no expert, but that's no dwarf.
That's a short guy in a mask and tights trying to get a head up on the
competition. Five foot six and a half? That's not much shorter than I
am, and you don't see me—like Señor Olímpico—defending my crown as
two-time champion of the *Campeonato Mundial Mini-Estrella*, the World
Series of mini-estrellas, try as I might.

Let's not be naive, though. Money can't buy love, but it can sure as
hell buy a lot of drugs, food, sex, and other essentials that may or may
not be featured on Maslow's Hierarchy of Needs. These wily and ruthless Goteras were all about satisfying those needs that can be satisfied
with a pocket full of plata.

The *modus operandi* of Las Goteras was to find a Juan or two,
spike their drinks with a quantity of Mexican eyedrops and hork the
unsuspecting clients' money and clothes. In the case of La Parkita

and El Espectrito, the two Goteras got a bit too heavy handed with the eyedrops, and the result was *la muerte* for our hapless Mexican minis. Apparently, the two floozies failed to calculate the difference in molarity required to poison a four-foot tall *guerrerito* as opposed to a typical-sized *luchador*. But, come on. Just maybe there's a little bit of La Gotera in everyone. Who among us hasn't thought about drugging a dwarf-wrestler, dragging him to a dingy Mexican no-tell motel, and taking his money?

The tale of Las Goteras is shrouded in both mystery and Spanish, but stories like these are valuable. They remind us that no matter what kind of raunchy, Byzantine fictions we dream up, things are happening in hotel rooms across the planet that are simply beyond a normal citizen's ability to imagine. Could this prove that Heisenberg was right about uncertainty and that Einstein was wrong about God not playing dice with the universe? If God *is* playing dice with the universe, I'm thinking those dice are loaded and weighted in such a way that chaos and absurdity carry the day. For evidence of this, one need look no further than TV Azteca footage showing the funeral procession in which hordes of mourners are wearing Mexican Lucha Libre masks in honor of the diminutive departed.

On May 23, 2011, a criminal judge sentenced three members of Las Goteras for their roles in the Lucha Mini murders. Two, a man and a woman, were sentenced to twenty-four years in prison, while another Gotera got twelve years.

VALERIE SOLANAS

PROFILE

DAY JOB: Writing manifestos

CLAIM TO FAME: She shot Andy Warhol

THEATER OF OPERATIONS: New York

Remember *The Little Rascals* TV episode where the boys in "Our Gang" inaugurate "The He-Man Woman Hater's Club" because not one of them has been invited to the Valentine's Day party? What, you may ask, does this episode of *The Little Rascals* have to do with the lady who shot Andy Warhol?

Well, Valerie Solanas started her own club that served as a kind of "She-Woman Man-Haters Club," but she called it the "Society for Cutting Up Men," or SCUM. Spanky's He-Man Woman Haters Club may have been the inspiration for SCUM, but Valerie's platform was considerably more sinister. The Little Rascals' goal was simply to exclude women, while Solanas's purpose leaned more toward the extermination of men altogether. Perhaps Valerie should be applauded for her breadth of vision, but SCUM's charter contains some hard-to-swallow rhetoric. Here's an excerpt from Valerie's "SCUM Manifesto":

> Life in this society being, at best, an utter bore and no aspect of society being at all relevant to women, there remains to civic-minded, responsible, thrill-seeking females only to overthrow the government, eliminate the money system, institute complete automation and destroy the male sex. . . . The male is a biological accident.

Damn, Valerie.

But let's start at the beginning. Solanas was born in 1936 in Ventnor, New Jersey, which ipso facto provides a good excuse for acting like a lunatic. She was, however, smart, impulsive, and ambitious. The problem was that her father sexually abused her and then abandoned the family while Solanas was still very young, so maybe we need to cut her some slack for the extreme ideology she later adopted. While exhibiting increasing lunacy, Ms. Solanas managed to secure a psychology degree from the University of Maryland. That would be a "good looking out" to the Terrapin's Psychology Dept.

Prostitution helped Solanas pay for college, where she engaged in lab work that she believed offered proof positive that the existence of men was accidental and wholly unnecessary. After her stint in graduate school, Solanas sat down in earnest to write the "SCUM Manifesto," and in 1960 she found her way to Andy Warhol in New York City. Still making her way as a prostitute in the Big Apple, Ms. Solanas attained a kind of hanger-on status at the Factory, the home of Warhol's art studio and the place to go for a good old-fashioned orgy.

In 1967 Valerie Solanas was determined to make her mark as a writer, and she thrust her theatrical opus, *Up Your Ass* upon Warhol. She was under the impression he would eventually produce this play in which the main character is a fast-talking, man-loathing prostitute. The play was so graphic even Warhol was grossed out, and he tossed it, much to the dismay of the fragile scribe.

The sad truth is that Solanas was, by now, deeply disturbed as evidenced by her decision to off Andy Warhol. After putting a bullet in the artist, she was sent to prison and passed around to various mental institutions.

As for *Up Your Ass*, after Warhol died, the play finally turned up in a mountain of the artist's literary detritus, which was about to be tossed into the trash bin. Solanas's main character is her alter ego, Bongi, a street-smart lesbian panhandler, and the play itself is "garbage-mouthed, dykey," and " anti-male," by the playwright's own account. In spite of Solanas's apparent low opinion of her own work, when the play finally opened in 1999, an audience actually showed up at the George Coates Performance Works Theatre in San Francisco, and after the premiere a critic published a review in *The Spectator Magazine*:

No small part of the enjoyment to myself and other freaks is the attention paid to pussy, cock and balls . . . and of course, turds. Scatologists will feel right at home with the parts about cooking and dining on shit. (With chopsticks, no less!)

I hate how you can never get a reviewer to state whether or not he or she actually *liked* or *disliked* a performance. A ticket to the theater is just too damn expensive to purchase on the promise of turds, cocks, and balls alone, usually.

After stints at numerous state institutions, Solanas was released crazier than ever and spent the rest of her days harassing everyone around her and whoring. She died a lonely death in a welfare hotel in San Francisco in 1988, a bewildering little rascal to the end.

AILEEN WUORNOS

PROFILE

DAY JOB: You're looking at it

CLAIM TO FAME: America's most famous female serial killer

THEATER OF OPERATIONS: Florida highways and byways

It's hard not to fall in love with Aileen Wuornos, especially when you see her disrobe in *The Devil's Advocate*, starring fellow prostitute Al Pacino. Incorrect. I'm thinking of Charlize Theron, who played Wuornos in the movie *Monster*. It's significantly harder to love the actual Wuornos, a woman who was probably nothing like Charlize Theron, and who was definitely not afraid to shoot you. Although it's hard, probably impossible, to fall in love with Aileen, sometimes it's easy to sympathize with her.

Aileen Wuornos (née Pittman) was born in 1956, raised in Troy, Michigan, and it just got worse from there. She never had the pleasure of meeting her father, a schizophrenic pederast serving a life sentence (until he hung himself in his cell) for the rape and attempted murder of an eight-year-old boy. When Aileen was six, her mother abandoned her and her brother, leaving the two shit-out-of-luck siblings with their grandmother, who died soon thereafter of liver failure, and their grandfather, who sexually abused and beat her.

According to numerous sources, around the time she turned eleven, Aileen began to prostitute herself for cigarettes and spare change, and she also began to have sex with her brother who was a year older. Even a dime-store psychologist can see that early on her concepts of sex and sexuality were outré, to put it mildly. Already Aileen's life seemed to be testing the limits of crappy cosmic card dealing. Yet, killing folks is no way to behave; you can't just go around shooting every asshole you meet. If you could, Karl Rove would probably not have lived long enough to go so bald.

Remember that breakfast cereal you invented called "Cereal Killers" that featured images of famous serial killers on the box? And did you receive a dismissive response from General Mills, too? Well, Aileen's old watering hole, the Last Resort Bar, in Port Orange, Florida, actually did manage to capitalize on mealtime murderabilia, selling "Aileen Wuornos Crazed Killer Hot Sauce." "Warning!" reads the label, "This Hot Sauce could drive you insane, or at least off on some murderous rampage. Aileen liked it and look what it did to her. . . . Not to be used by women with PMS." I know, our idea was better, and it was not so sexist. I'll let you know what the folk at Kellogg's say, but it doesn't look promising.

By 1989, Aileen the hooker had climbed the criminal ladder to Aileen the "Damsel of Death." Aileen was a self-described "exit-to-exit" hooker who earned around $1,000/week working I-75 in Florida. Her average workweek consisted of fifty tricks, give or take a few. Who knows why or when she went completely bonkers, but by the time of her capture in 1991, Wuornos had killed seven men.

Initially Aileen claimed that her first "victim," a man named Richard Mallory, had violently raped her, a mistake that prompted her to do him in. She claimed the same about the other six murders, although no indisputable proof could be found to substantiate her claims. When she was convicted at trial, she howled, "I'm innocent. I was raped! I hope you get raped! Scumbags of America!" a claim that might strike a more sympathetic nerve if she hadn't stated quite cavalierly shortly before her execution, "I robbed [the men], and I killed them as cold as ice, and I would do it again."

In 2002 when asked if she had any last words before her execution by lethal injection, Wuornos clarified everything: "I would just like to say I'm sailing with the rock, and I'll be back, like Independence Day with Jesus. June 6, like the movie. Big mother ship and all, I'll be back, I'll be back." Mother ship? Where did she get that New Age bombast? Did Tom Cruise slip the prison chaplain a copy of *Dianetics*? It would be just Aileen's luck.

AMANDA LOGUE AND JASON ANDREWS

PROFILE

DAY JOBS: Modeling; acting in porn; Tweeting

CLAIM TO FAME: Natural-born idiots

THEATER OF OPERATIONS: Florida

How many times have you screwed yourself by thoughtlessly shooting off a text, talking about how you're horny and about to murder somebody? If you're anything like prostitutes/porn stars Amanda Logue and her boyfriend Jason Andrews, you are going to encounter real trouble.

Like many a doomed relationship, this one was about sex and greed. Jason was a Brit, an aspiring DJ with a penchant for techno and gay-for-pay. Amanda was a toothy fetish model, aspiring escort, and Southern belligerent. Together, they made porno movies, marketed themselves to both sexes and dreamed of a future together doing basically the same things, but with more money.

In 2010, a few weeks before they planned to commit the grisly murder of a tattoo artist who'd hired Amanda for a kinky sex party in St. Petersburg, Florida, the prosty pair posted pornographic videos of themselves grunting, shopping at a local flea market, and Tweeting bad puns about murder: "we're killing time waiting for a party to find us"; and "something exciting surprises in store for here tonight." One wonders, were they just trying to remove any lingering doubt about the depths of their stupidity? Regarding their deadly itinerary, the two went on to have a grammarian's nightmare of an exchange on their Blackberries, illustrated by court transcripts released to the media:

- **Andrews**: I'm so glad you're really commited to this take. Keep eyes for a knife, etc for me!"
- **Logue**: They are pakn up. I'm FUCKING exited. To fuck up someone God damnit I want to fiuck after we kill hum
- **Andrews**: Ok. Front door or bna9k? Front not yet though
- **Logue**: K I'm horny! 1'm getting him to play music be quit wen come im Sorry not ready. Fixing get on tablke
- **Andrews**: I will bring the bottle too! Oops, its empty! Yay sweating on a stakeout! . . . Shit. I OMG, I feel like I'm never gonna leave this bloody loo! You ok?"

Records from the court proceedings confirm that Andrews waited outside while the sex party was in full swing. After the guests left, Andrews apparently entered the victim's home with a bottle of something and Amanda was, indeed, horny, although we are left to speculate on what kind of moral and/or physical evacuation of the bowels Andrews was referring to while in the loo.

If Jason and Amanda's texts provide any insight as to their performance that night, we can probably use our imagination with some accuracy to reconstruct the scene and their tense conversation in the moments leading up to the murder.

A man lies naked on a massage table. Amanda dances around to something soulful and mellow to provide irony, probably Lionel Richie. Jason comes in complaining of cooties in his stomach and holds an empty bottle of Kaopectate.

- **AMANDA**: Ooh. U luuk lik shit. I'm not horny anymre.
- **JASON**: R U speekung Dutch? Srry. Had 2 pööp.
- **AMANDA**: Lts kill this guay and go shuppin'
- **JASON**: LOL cant' understand a word ur saying! Jst txt me and tell ,e what to do.
- **AMANDA**: K
- **GREEK CHORUS:** Euripides is rolling over in his fucking grave.

Returning to a more fact-checkable reality, the next day a relative found the victim's body in a scene of absolute carnage, while Logue Tweeted that she and Jason were "laying around eating popcorn and watching movies." You know, throw them off the scent. Jason (code name Addison) and Amanda (code name Sunny Dae) were soon caught and charged with murder, dizzying as that prospect may seem.

MARY "BRICKTOP" JACKSON

PROFILE

DAY JOB: Jacking you up (and off)

CLAIM TO FAME: "The meanest woman in New Orleans"

THEATER OF OPERATIONS: The Big Easy, Louisiana

Mary Jane Jackson didn't suffer fools—or anybody, really—and what's more, she often kicked or stabbed the mortal shit out of anyone who got in her way. She was born in New Orleans in 1836, and at the age of thirteen she began a life of prostitution. By fourteen, she had established herself as the mistress of a local bartender. When the bartender decided that Mary, now seventeen years old, had become too much to handle, he locked her out of his establishment, leaving her to fend for herself alone in the Big Easy. Mistake. Mary, in a roaring fit of pique, rhino-charged back into the saloon and walloped the man, taking with her most of his nose and an ear in the fracas. The wrath of the redhead they called "Bricktop" was now a legitimate cause for concern.

Prosthetics have come a long way since John Miller fumbled around every morning, trying to attach his ball and chain arm, get breakfast ready, make the bed, and so on before doling out his daily ass whuppings. In fact, in 2011 a British man became the world's first person to have a Smartphone docking system built into his prosthetic arm. But fear not. Even this incredible innovation will not be much help to Captain Hook. You get shit service on the high seas, and he probably doesn't have many buccaneers with whom to play "Words with Friends," anyway, considering his ornery disposition.

Bricktop soon moved on to a bordello on Dauphine St., where she was popular with the boys; she was beautiful, even glamorous, once you cleaned all the blood, nose parts, and other gory morsels off of her. Her presence made for a rambunctious house, however, and she was hard-pressed to find a respectable bagnio that would have her. Bricktop finally landed a steady gig at Archie's Dance-House, and for the next year and a half, she terrorized the freak out of folks.on Gallatin St. and surrounding areas.

While on the job, Bricktop committed two gruesome murders using her signature weapon: two five-inch blades attached by a center grip made of German silver. Talk about "a thing of beauty." Imagine a perpetually agitated, prowling, hobgoblin-whore with long red hair and hands like the business end of a Cuisinart. As per usual, she was given the heave-ho from Archie's, where they frowned on employees eviscerating their clientele.

Miss Jackson decided to go total freelance, and complete dementoid, eventually teaming up with Bridget Fury and one or two other Louisiana coquettes. The local papers had a ball. Here are some gems from an article describing Bricktop after another murder arrest in 1861:

> In 1859, "Bricktop" and two other women knifed a man who objected to their foul language. In her short prison term for that offence, "Bricktop" encountered John Miller, temporarily serving as a jailer. Usually on the other side of the law, Miller had lost an arm and replaced it with an iron ball and chain attached to his stump; it constituted a horrifying weapon. The pair worked the old trick known as "buttock and twang."
>
> This year, Miller took a whip to "Bricktop" to give her a trashing. It was a mistake: "Bricktop" flogged him! She started by dragging him around the room by his own ball and chain. She bit his hand when he pulled a knife, then used the weapon to kill him.

Ah, the buttock and twang. *That* old gag. The buttock and twang would typically involve Bricktop removing a man's pants, while Miller snatched the victim's wallet and using his bowling ball hand smashed the guy's head in. Bricktop was sentenced to ten years, but nine months into her sentence, the governor let loose most of the prison population, including Bricktop, who was never seen again. For this reason, some people in cineaste circles consider her the Keyser Söze of strumpets.

DELIA SWIFT (BRIDGET FURY)

PROFILE

DAY JOB: Mentee of Bricktop Jackson; pickpocket; thug

CLAIM TO FAME: Being furious

THEATER OF OPERATIONS: Late nineteenth-century New Orleans

Unlike her friend, mentor, and partner in crime, Mary Bricktop Jackson, Delia Swift wasn't a local girl. She found her way to New Orleans via Ohio. But make no mistake about it, shortly after her arrival this violent vixen became a major figure in the seedy New Orleans underworld of gangs, brothels, and bedlam. Swift, like Bricktop, began her career as a prostitute around the age of twelve, selling her body while her father served as the whorehouse fiddler, until he killed a girl, leaving Delia with nothing.

Luckily, Delia was a skilled pickpocket, attractive, and completely demented, so she fared better on the street than most. Delia, who by now had been aptly renamed "Bridget Fury," was also absolutely in love with knifing people. Convicted for shanking one fellow, the Fury escaped from a penitentiary in Cincinnati and made her way to New Orleans. Arrested in New Orleans, the state of Louisiana tried to send her back to Ohio, but the Ohio governor was no fool. He was content to let the New Orleans Police Department (an explosive oxymoron if there ever was one) deal with that troublesome redhead. Yes, along with a pair of sisters and sundry stragglers, one of the most feared gangs in all of New Orleans—a town known for ferocious gangs—was led by two wild and crazy hookers who looked a lot like a cross between Little Orphan Annie and early drafts of Botticelli's Venus, where she was painted to look drunk and violent. It's really not fair or accurate, though, to mention Annie in the same breath as Bricktop and Bridget Fury. Annie's tween gaucheries look like child's play next to those two.

The fuzz finally caught up with Bridget Fury and threw the book at her: life imprisonment. She had dozens of collars ranging from murder to throwing eggs at other hookers. An open and shut case? No. What followed is part of a continuing pattern to this day, but with somewhat less press coverage. It turned out that so many of the city's top politicians, johns with political clout, were impressed by whatever Bridget Fury had going on that they granted her a general amnesty after she served just four years—a shady deal that was also afforded Mary Bricktop.

Can a girl really be guilty if she was born with a short fuse? The answer is yes, especially if after that fuse burns down, she traipses around town, carving up passersby on the street. Court transcripts from the period examine the issue:

> We have seen her several times before the Recorder, and always wondered at the wildness and good-humor expressed by her face, and the politeness of her demeanor in Court. Though so smooth and smiling outside, it appears that she is in reality another Lucretia Borgia; that is a fiend incarnate when insulted.

So the message here is don't judge a trick by his or her cover. And watch your back, especially in Louisiana.

Chapter VI

THE MAGICAL MYSTERY WHORES

Like any storied tradition, prostitution is fraught with its share of hearsay, fables, false Gods, magical beasts, and bogeymen. Most Western religious texts are rife with whore stories; ancient Asian lore abounds with tales of mystical courtesans and debauched deities; and in some cultures they just invent harlots to serve as foci for annoying ditties. Were any of these elusive sexpots real? Depending on your level of gullibility, you might find the following stories of this randy gang useful for understanding where many of our most debased notions about sex have their genesis. To understand the phenomenon better, it helps to take a closer look at our myths, where the imagination runs rampant and truth and booty are often not what they seem.

THE WHORE OF BABYLON

PROFILE

DAY JOB: Reigning over the kings of the Earth

CLAIM TO FAME: Satan's main squeeze

THEATER OF OPERATIONS: Babylon

The Whore of Babylon (*neé* Mystery) had it rough. Hell, she *still* has it rough. For over two millennia this poor creature has put a real fright into unsuspecting Sunday school students and sundry other readers of Revelation. Sometimes thought of as Satan's "Pretty Woman," this whore pops up in the Bible wearing an outrageous purple ensemble with gold accoutrements, and she is holding up a cocktail featuring the "abominations and filthiness of her fornication." If that means what I think it means, the Whore of Babylon should feel lucky she ever got a date at all. It's amazing, really, how disorganized and (to be quite honest) unattractive many of these early/mythological prostitutes were. Thank goodness for progress in both fashion and prostitution, because the Whore of Babylon sounds a lot like a garden-variety monster, as opposed to a sultry, swinging lady of the night.

> *"Being a hooker does not mean being evil. The same with a pick-pocket, or even a thief. You do what you do out of necessity."*
> —Samuel Fuller, American director, screenwriter

With a large tattoo on her forehead that reads, "MYSTERY, BABYLON THE GREAT, THE MOTHER OF HARLOTS AND ABOMINATIONS OF THE EARTH" one is left marveling at (A) what lengths some people will go to for attention, and (B) how big her forehead must have been.

A close reading of the text suggests that not only was "Mystery" a tattooed ghoul, she was also as big as a house. Actually, she's even bigger than a house: "And the woman which thou sawest is [a] great city, which reigns over the kings of the earth." That's *thick*. The Whore of Babylon might be just a metaphor, but in any case, if you're the devil, you've got to take pretty much any piece of ass that comes your way.

Fat, faithless, freaky streetwalking fiends drunk "with the blood of saints" aren't for everybody, but the Bible tells us: "Judge not, lest ye be judged." Does this admonition apply to the Antichrist, one wonders? Even a fiend needs a friend once in a while.

SHAMHAT

PROFILE

DAY JOBS: Resident skeezer; temple harlot

CLAIM TO FAME: Civilizing mankind

THEATER OF OPERATIONS: Mesopotamia

It's 2500 B.C. in Mesopotamia, and Gilgamesh, the king of Uruk, is sitting pretty in Sumer. He's two parts God and one part man, and he's running around acting like a damned fool. Meathead that he is, Gilgamesh challenges every man he sees to a heavy-lifting competition, which he knows he will inevitably win, as do the men he challenges. It is nowhere near sporting, and the men of Uruk are getting fed up. Aggravating the situation further, after Gilgamesh exhausts the men of Uruk, he moves from house to house having sex with their wives.

Luckily for the male population of Uruk, the goddess Aruru, who created mankind, took note of Gilgamesh's habit of taking unfair advantage, and she sought to create a foil, a rival of sorts, for Gilgamesh. The ancient poem *The Epic of Gilgamesh* explains what followed:

Aruru washed her hands, she pinched off some clay, and threw it into
    the wilderness.
In the wild she created valiant Enkidu,
born of Silence, endowed with strength by Ninurta.
His whole body was shaggy with hair,
he had a full head of hair like a woman,
his locks billowed in profusion like Ashnan.
He knew neither people nor settled living,
but wore a garment like Sumukan.
He ate grasses with the gazelles,
and jostled at the watering hole with the animals;
as with animals, his thirst was slaked with water.

Aruru must have been a little disappointed in her creation, because
a dude who eats grass and jostles animals is probably no improvement
over Gilgamesh. Where is his wit, his tact, and his ability to engage in
airy persiflage? Is he even a grown ass man?

This is where Shamhat, the Mesopotamian streetwalker, steps into
the jam:

Shamhat unclutched her bosom, exposed her sex, and he took in her
    voluptuousness.
She was not restrained, but took his energy.
She spread out her robe and he lay upon her,
she performed for the primitive the task of womankind.
His lust groaned over her;
for six days and seven nights Enkidu stayed aroused,
and had intercourse with the harlot
until he was sated with her charms.

Having taken all the starch out of Enkidu, Shamhat convinces him
to go into town and give Gilgamesh a run for his money; man up a little,
you know? A bunch of shepherds clean him up, give him a nice hair-
cut and send him off to the city of Uruk, where folks think he looks a

lot like Gilgamesh, the guy he is supposed to stop from cock-blocking
every man in town.

Shamhat encourages Enkidu to relax, try to fit in with the locals. She
urges him, "Eat the food, Enkidu, it is the way one lives. / Drink the beer,
as is the custom of the land." Enkidu gets a little carried away. He "ate the
food until he was sated, he drank the beer—seven jugs!" Uh-oh.

Drinking seven jugs of beer in one sitting is a pretty solid showing, but
do you ever wonder who among us has been the *most* hooched-up, like,
ever? Though you won't find it in any reputable book of records, in
2004, Pyotr Petrov, a sixty-seven-year-old Bulgarian national's blood
alcohol content (BAC) was measured at an astonishing .91 percent, the
highest BAC on record. The *lethal* limit usually kicks in around .40 percent. According to doctors, Mr. Petrov was not only not dead, but he
chatted amicably with his doctors. Petrov's curriculum vitae is presumably
under review by the League of Extraordinary Alcoholics and the Blind
Drunk Avengers.   ,

Enkidu heads out to ambush Gilgamesh, but Gilgamesh puts the
over-served new guy on his prat. Alas, after the first two tablets of
The Epic of Gilgamesh, Shamhat doesn't figure, and so like some shitty
Sumerian buddy movie, Gilgamesh and his foil, the now calm, relatively collected, and sober Enkidu, take off on a juvenile camping trip
around Mesopotamia playing grab-ass and "slaying monsters." So in
spite of Shamhat's best efforts, *The Epic of Gilgamesh*, a seminal work
from one of the world's most formidable empires, ends up reading a lot
like *Tango & Cash*.

MOLLY
MALONE

PROFILE

DAY JOB: Food cart proprietor

CLAIM TO FAME: Ireland's favorite moll

THEATER OF OPERATIONS: Dublin

Molly Malone is not just the name of a seedy Irish bar; it's also the name of an iconic figure in the annals of whoredom. The eponymous Molly may or may not have been an actual streetwalker in Ireland during the closing years of the seventeenth century. Legend and lyrics, however, have it that one Molly Malone, a down-on-her-luck fishmonger-cum-part-time hussy was found dead on the corner of what are now Grafton and Suffolk streets in Dublin. A woman of unsurpassed beauty and infected with any number of venereal diseases, Molly was said to have plied her trade from Grafton Street and St. Stephen's Green to the ivory tower at Trinity College. University environments are notorious havens for cockles, mussels, and assorted deviants.

How and why did sweet Molly die? Some claim VD; the more naive presume food poisoning (cockles and mussels can go bad before you know it). But more importantly, how did Molly live? What was she like? The truth is, nobody is really certain. Some historians claim that she was the mistress of King Charles II, while others stick closer to the script, arguing that she was just an omnipresent nuisance to most of Dublin who went up and down the streets screaming about crustaceans. Still others aver that she was simply the personification of your every-day Irish harlot.

Whatever your gullibility quotient, you can travel to Dublin today and behold the statue of Molly Malone erected at Grafton and Suffolk. In what is assuredly a warped interpretation of how a destitute seventeenth-century Irish prostitute might actually look, the Molly in the statue appears vigorous and free of cooties, though she is pushing a wheelbarrow full of dead fish and wearing a revealing dress out of which her breasts are jockeying for egress.

In many ways, the Irish are much like us, creating their own peculiar religions, mythologies, superheroes, and saints to explain away another society gone maniac. Take the story of St. Brigid, Ireland's unofficial patron saint of the open bar. As one legend goes, Brigid was doing community service in a leper colony when the lepers ran out of beer, so Brigid stepped up and changed the lepers' bath water into brew.

And if you're looking to say the official Irish prayer in honor of St. Brigid, here it is:

> *"I'd like a great lake of beer for the King of Kings.*
> *I would like to be watching Heaven's family drinking it through*
> *all eternity."*

Amen.

Nobody can say for sure if Molly was indeed real, although the Dublin Millennium Commission proclaimed June 13, the alleged date of her death, as "Molly Malone Day," which the Irish celebrate by getting trashed and having messy sex. This is pretty much like all other days in the land of Erin, but at least on Molly Malone Day they have a somewhat legitimate excuse.

TIRESIAS

PROFILE

DAY JOBS: Largely ignored advice columnist/prophet

CLAIM TO FAME: Lived as both a man and a woman

THEATER OF OPERATIONS: Ancient Greece

Zeus and Hera, as you know from *Clash of the Titans* (the old, good, bad version, not the new, bad, bad version) or maybe from school, were always fussing at each other. One argument they couldn't settle was the one about whether men or women get more enjoyment out of sex. You could make the argument that it only makes sense to discuss this issue on a case-by-case basis. However, if you are one of the gods living high on Mount Olympus, you can manipulate mortals any old way you want. You can even set up an experiment in which the control variable is also the dependent variable, and thereby get a definitive answer about who gets more pleasure out of a roll in the hay.

Tiresias, the blind prophet of Thebes, was the subject of just such an experiment. You may recognize Tiresias from *The Odyssey*, *Antigone*, or Ovid's *Metamorphoses*, stories in which he gives people excellent advice that they rarely take. Indeed, Tiresias was the Rodney Dangerfield of the Aegean: He got no respect.

As if he didn't have enough to worry about, Hera punished Tiresias severely when he killed two snakes with a stick while the snakes were making sweet, serpentine love. Outraged, the goddess sentenced Tiresias to spend a period of seven years as a woman. If you're wrestling with the question of whether this punishment fits the crime, just give it up—the Greeks had a dizzying system of torts.

As a woman, Lady Tiresias totally thrived, finding that (s)he really cottoned to the idea of prostitution. (S)he, accumulated all sorts of wealth and valuable experiences from the other side of the gender fence, too. One has a finite amount of energy of course, sexual or otherwise, and toward the end of his tenure as a woman, Tiresias ran out of steam and had to eventually settle down, marry a nice man, and give birth to a son. One wonders how family reunions, locker room hijinks, and bachelor/bachelorette parties were handled during—and after—Tiresias's "transformation."

Has anybody ever told you to "go fuck yourself"? It's called "autocopulation." But if you're thinking of making a superpower clone warrior baby, you're out of luck, says my narrow-minded therapist, Dr. Guerrero. Even if you have both sets of parts, you can't reproduce, unless you are a species of hermaphroditic worm, like *C. elegans*. And for your XXX files, there is also something called "autopederasty," and it's not as felonious as it sounds, but it's a doozy. Defined as an "uncommon occurrence of a man, one with an unusually long penis, inserting his penis into his own anus. Due to the position and detumescence of the penis, ejaculation is not considered possible." Nothing is impossible, you cynical dictionary.

As for the blindness, there are two possibilities. One, Tiresias may have seen Athena naked—something that drives Athena *crazy*—thus incurring her wrath and in a fit of furor, she poked his eyes out. The other, much more plausible explanation is that eventually, Zeus and Hera got around to querying Tiresias about what he had learned in his time as a woman. They asked her/him, "Which sex enjoys greater pleasure in the act of lovemaking?" Now, Hera was still pissed at her/him for the snakes thing, and she was increasingly furious with Zeus for being such a philandering oaf. In fact, the couple almost came to thunderbolts, when Zeus claimed he had a right to sleep around, because women derived more pleasure from sex than men. When posed with the question, Tiresias answered,

If the sum of love's pleasures adds up to ten,
nine parts go to women, only one to men.

Hera wasn't pleased with this response, and promptly had Tiresias's eyeballs removed from their sockets. Zeus, feeling bad about his wife's poor sportsmanship, gave her/him the gift of foresight, which was nice, but still doesn't explain why the old galoot didn't duck out of the way when one of Apollo's arrows sailed across a lake and ran Tiresias through a few years later.

OSHUN

PROFILE

DAY JOB: Creationist

CLAIM TO FAME: African river goddess

THEATER OF OPERATIONS: Nigeria

Oshun has seen it all, literally. She was (and is) said to be present at all functions and family gatherings as a kind of mother/spirit to look over the proceedings. But if you're thinking this goddess is some matronly old crone who spends her days baking bundt cakes, you've got another think coming. And as far as mothers go, they don't get much tougher than Oshun.

> *"Madaming is the sort of thing that happens to you—
> like getting a battlefield commission or becoming the dean of
> women at Stanford University."*
> —Sally Stanford

In African Yoruba legend, Oshun was one of seventeen deities, or *orisha*, whose charge was to civilize the untamed Earth. Sixteen of these deities were male, and only one—Oshun—was female. As you may have guessed, all sixteen male deities misspent their time on Earth.

They may have thrown some rocks around and played in the mud, but they did nothing to improve the world. The Earth remained a bone-dry wasteland, uncivilized, thirsty, and howling for happy hour. Oshun tried mightily to convince these obstinate ogres that she was holding some pharmaceutical grade water and that a little H_2O could make a big difference, but she was unsuccessful. The world began to rot. Finally, at a loss, the guys went to consult an oracle, which rightfully gave them what for. There is absolutely no record of the following exchange:

- **Oracle**: (*impatiently mashing up a bunch of yams*) What's up, bitches?
- **Ted**, one of the sixteen *orisha*: (*to colleagues*) I got this, fellas. Uh . . . yeah, hi there, oracle. We're in a bit of a jam.
- **Oracle**: Why am I not surprised?
- **Ted**: Hey, why all this attitude? We said we were sorry—we'll never ask for Lotto numbers again. So, anyway, this Earth thing is turning into a real turkey. The land looks good, but sort of arid, and we've got all these beach chairs and cocktail umbrellas with nowhere to put 'em.
- **Oracle**: Have you asked Oshun over there for help?
- **Ted**: Oh, come *on*! She's a chick. She's going to invent rom-coms or *Us Weekly* or some other damned shit.
- **Oshun**: Ted, if you say one more word, I'm going to rip off that eerie excuse for a child's penis of yours and throw it into the North Atlantic Desert.
- **Oracle**: She's not kidding, Ted. Look, I've seen her do it. Why don't you just let her do her thing with the water?
- **Ted**: What in the *fuck* is water? Why do we come here?

The Oracle nods at Oshun, who snaps her fingers, inundating the Earth with rivers, lakes, oceans, rum runners, and piña coladas. Ted and the other orisha fellows roll their eyes contemptuously and storm out of the Oracle's studio, a schooner in the (as of a few moments ago) North Atlantic Ocean. The cries of orisha echo

*in the distance, as they float out to sea, until one of them invents kickboards, saving
the deities from certain doom.*

But let's not get all hung up on this mythical twaddle. According
to *documented* legend, the oracle explained to the *orisha* that if they had
only bothered to satisfy the needs of women (read Oshun) they would
not have run into problems in the first place. Not being complete fools,
the men all begged forgiveness from Oshun and urged her to let them
please her in the sack. *Oh, hell no*, thought Oshun, making sure that
none of her male consorts gave her pleasure until they paid up and paid
early. And they did. Perhaps not coincidentally, Oshun is also the goddess of the marketplace and of driving hard bargains. Sorry, fellas.

MARY MAGDALENE

PROFILE

DAY JOB: Sinner

CLAIM TO FAME: Palled around with Jesus

THEATER OF OPERATIONS: Galilee

It's curious how hackles rise when someone goes and mentions that
Mary Magdalene, Jesus's BFF with whom he hoofed it around Galilee,
was a flatbacker. The problem is that a lady looking a lot like Ms.
Magdalene betrays a foot fetish and anoints Jesus's funky bunions with
her tears and a variety of ointments. Luke 7:36–50:

> And behold, a woman in the city who was a sinner, when she knew
> that Jesus sat at the table in the Pharisee's house, brought an alabaster
> flask of fragrant oil, and stood at His feet behind Him weeping; and
> she began to wash His feet with her tears, and wiped them with the
> hair of her head; and she kissed His feet and anointed them with the
> fragrant oil. Now when the Pharisee who had invited Him saw this,

he spoke to himself, saying, "This Man, if He were a prophet, would know who and what manner of woman this is who is touching Him, for she is a sinner.

You'll admit there is some sexy ambiguity during this exchange. Also, when it comes down to it, everybody likes a foot rub, and what's more, when is a foot rub just a foot rub? Never. To quote John Travolta's character Vincent Vega in *Pulp Fiction*:

I ain't saying it's right. But you're saying a foot massage don't mean nothing, and I'm saying it does. Now, look, I've given a million ladies a million foot massages, and they all meant something. We act like they don't, but they do, and that's what's so fucking cool about them.

He does have a point. Well, a little later on down the line, we learn that there were "certain women who had been healed of evil spirits and infirmities." One was "Mary, called Magdalene, out of whom went seven devils." This passage has led some to conflate the godless prosty grooving on Jesus's toes and the woman who is at Jesus's side during his crucifixion and his burial, the one who first discovers the empty tomb after Jesus hits the road. A fierce debate continues to rage about whether or not Mary Magdalene was in fact a prostitute. Some of the faithful just don't want to hear it. A typical exchange:

- "She was."
- "Was not."
- "Was too."
- "Was not."
- " . . . "
- " . . . "
- "Was."

Of course, the Mary Magdalene dispute is a mere squabble compared to the correlation-causation brawls concerning Jesus screaming at a fig tree in chapter 11 of Mark. Why the tree wilts overnight after Jesus gives it a hollering is the source of a quarrel that has split theologians and arborists into two snarling camps, creating a powder keg environment and a rift that may never heal.

After the fig tree goes down, Jesus offers a challenge to Peter (and anyone else who cared to listen):

> For verily I say unto you, That whosoever shall say unto this mountain, Be thou removed, and be thou cast into the sea; and shall not doubt in his heart, but shall believe that those things which he saith shall come to pass; he shall have whatsoever he saith.

One of the great biblical mysteries is why nobody takes Jesus up on this offer. I, for one, would relish shouting, "be thou removed, and be thou cast into the sea!" at various inanimate objects, even if nothing happened.

PHRYNE

PROFILE

DAY JOBS: Model; blasphemer

CLAIM TO FAME: Pulling a "Kanye" at the Festival of Poseidon

THEATER OF OPERATIONS: Ancient Greece

"Hey there, I'm Mnesarete—looking for some company?"

"You're *who*?"

"Mnesarete!"

"How do you spell it?"

"You don't spell it honey, you take it out on the town. Maybe a little conversation, a little night life; you know, some *companionship.*"

"This seems like a sting. I'm going down to the agora, where the *real* whores are," the insensitive ancient Greek frat boy would say, and Mnesarete would walk back to her crib, broke, incensed, and cursing her name.

Luckily, Mnesarete possessed a beauty rivaled by few mortals, which is still impressive even if you acknowledge there were far fewer mortals back then. She was also possessed of enough business savvy to recognize that changing her name to "Phryne" (literally, *toad*) would arouse much more interest among members of the local john population of Athens. The name-change worked wonders for Phryne, and her beauty is celebrated to this day in works of prose, paint, and plaster all over the world.

The Greek cynic, Diogenes, was an extraordinarily far-out individual. He lived in a bathtub in an Athens marketplace, where he made a lot of noise about the "simple life" being the virtuous life. He claimed to be emulating the virtues of Hercules, who would never have slept in a bathtub and must have been embarrassed to death by this patchouli-oiled hothead wannabe. After seeing a man drink water with his hands, Diogenes even gave away his last bit of crockery, a cup, and spent the rest of his days lapping up drink like a be-togaed baboon and subsisting primarily on a diet of rancid onions. That's not all. Most Athenians saw as obnoxious his desultory daylight treks through the city while carrying a lit lantern and claiming to be searching for "one honest man." Nobody was devastated when pirates finally captured Diogenes and sold him into slavery.

Phryne knew it was important to make an eye-catching entrance when she re-entered the market and set out to court new clients. After some career-counseling and real-time training on the island of Lesbos— the alleged training ground for up-and-coming prostitutes—Phryne announced her presence with authority at the Festival of Poseidon in Eleusis, where she took it all off "in sight of the whole Greek world."

As you can imagine, the calls came roaring in. Not only did Phryne serve as the model for Praxiteles's statues of Venus, she became courtesan to the Greek elite: the philosopher Diogenes (for whom she gave it up for free), the King of Lydia, and the Athenian leader Demosthenes, among other notables, were among her clients and confidants.

When the beautiful blasphemer finally roiled up enough jealousy and scandal in Athens, it was decided that her little nudie shuffle into the Aegean foam was a profanity against Poseidon, and folks demanded she face prosecution. Her case was taken up by the Johnnie Cochran of the day, a famous orator named Hypereides—another of Phryne's celebrity clients.

Plutarch describes a circus trial:

> When she was on trial for impiety he became her advocate; for he makes this plain himself at the beginning of his speech. And when she was likely to be found guilty, he led the woman out into the middle of the court and, tearing off her clothes, displayed her breasts. When the judges saw her beauty, she was acquitted.

If she shows a tit, you must acquit. Now that's both working it *and* owning it. After the trial, much of Phryne's life was the subject of speculation, which is good, because it's titillating to speculate on Phryne easing into an even steamier existence, away from the prohibitions of Athens and deep into the drug-fueled rave/courtesan scene gaining traction on the island of Ibiza.

RAHAB

PROFILE

DAY JOB: Doing the best she can

CLAIM TO FAME: Mention her name twice in a row and see . . .

THEATER OF OPERATIONS: Jericho

Another of the Bible's more popular whores is Rahab, a wily minx from Jericho, the city featured prominently in the Book of Joshua. Note: She is not to be confused with Rahab, the teeth-gnashing sea leviathan that haunts Isaiah. That is an entirely different Rahab whose livelihood depends on a more biblically acceptable occupation of eating (as in consuming) her fellow human beings.

Our Rahab is equally ferocious, however, in her horizontal way. We first encounter the hooker, Rahab, managing a brothel in downtown Jericho, where two Hebrew spies who need to lay low and maybe party a little, approach her. Rahab is sympathetic to the spies, and is kind enough to hide them in some flax when local soldiers arrive at her place to arrest the operatives.

"Rahab! There's a rumor going around that you're harboring a couple of Jewish spies. Is that true?" the uppity Egyptian cadre want to know.

"What would ever give you that idea?" the coquette replies.

"Well, if I'm not mistaken, I see a couple of circumcised fellows hiding under that pile of barley oats behind you," says the head of the search party.

"Any society that can't distinguish between flax and barley deserves to fall," says Rahab portentously. The soldier murmurs his annoyance, but local custom prevents men from entering Rahab's whorehouse uninvited, so they eventually disperse. In Joshua 2:9–13, Rahab then explains her end of the bargain to the spies with a kind of entrepreneurial spirit that inspires prospective MBAs to this day:

Now then, please swear to me by the LORD that you will show kindness to my family, because I have shown kindness to you. Give me a sure sign that you will spare the lives of my father and mother, my brothers and sisters, and all who belong to them, and that you will save us from death.

Looking to satisfy your wildest desires, or just browse around, visiting live sex shows, sex museums, and night freaks on display in the windows? Here is a quick roll call of some of the world's top red-light districts:

BOY'S TOWN, NUEVO LAREDO, MEXICO: Here, prostitution is controlled by the state, which is odd, considering the many available activities that just couldn't be legal.

DE WALLEN, AMSTERDAM, NETHERLANDS: The grand dame of red light districts, this area is an unforgiving maze of alleyways where you can get really, really lost.

REEPERBAHN, HAMBURG, GERMANY: Once home to the Beatles, the Reeperbahn area today contains more pictures in shop windows of people eating literal shit than you could ever imagine.

KAMATHIPURA, MUMBAI, INDIA: This red light district is Asia's largest, and was originally imagined as a refuge for British soldiers during the Raj.

SOI COWBOY, BANGKOK, THAILAND: The district is named after T. G. "Cowboy" Edwards, who opened one of the first bars there in 1977. Because you go there for the history.

The spies agree, telling her to hang a piece of red cloth outside of her house, so they'll know not to butcher her and her family along with the rest of the city. On a side note, this instance of hanging something red outside one's window is said to be the genesis of the idea behind today's "red-light districts," the low hum of the bulb now replacing the flutter of the fabric.

In one of the more lopsided victories in history, the Jews walked around the perimeter of Jericho for a week, playing little trumpets and waiting. Then, at the end of the week, Joshua tells everyone to either shout really loud, or start blowing on his or her trumpet. It works and the walls of Jericho fall, leaving the city to be sacked and every man, woman, and child killed except for Rahab and her peeps.

All Biblical savagery aside, perhaps the most compelling fact about Rahab is that, according to the Babylonian Talmud, one only needs to mention her name twice in a row to inspire paroxysms of lust, and instant ejaculation. This goes *way* beyond the pedestrian positions employed by your average prostitute, and it goes a long way toward explaining the inevitable approach/avoidance conflict a young boy suffers when reading the *Shlach Lecha* at his bar mitzvah.

THE YELLOW ROSE OF TEXAS

PROFILE

DAY JOB: Indentured servant

CLAIM TO FAME: Texas hero, maybe

THEATER OF OPERATIONS: The Lone Star State

The Yellow Rose of Texas is one of the truly enigmatic figures in whoredom. Some folk claim that the most famous (or infamous) whore in Texas was indeed no whore at all. If we are to believe the legend, Emily West, a "freed woman of color," was integral to the Texans' defeat of Santa Anna's army at San Jacinto.

While travelling to Texas from the north, Ms. West runs into Captain James Morgan, who offers her a bright future as an indentured servant and prostitute on his Texas ranch. She weighs her options, recognizes that as an African American woman she has few, if any; and becomes the captain's concubine. When Santa Anna's army comes charging through in 1836, West literally charms the pants off the opium-addled general himself. Santa Anna kills everybody else on the ranch and picks up West as a replacement for his stay-at-home wife in Mexico City, along with his "travelling wife" who had to turn back when her ornate and unwieldy carriage was unable to cross a particularly treacherous puddle.

One of the really compelling myths out there is that "The Yellow Rose of Texas" is a tune written by none other than the recluse of Amherst and one of America's greatest poets, Emily Dickinson. How the hell did this rumor get started? Perhaps because Dickinson often uses a form called "running (or common) meter." Former U.S. Poet Laureate Billy Collins explains:

> This is the meter of a lot of ballads. It's the meter of Protestant hymns. It's the rhythm of many nursery rhymes . . . almost every one of [Dickinson's] poems can be sung whether you like it or not to the tune of "The Yellow Rose of Texas."

Like it? We love it.

Then, just before the Battle of San Jacinto, West seizes the moment: she entices Santa Anna to blow a little opium and get naked before the Texans' attack. Things take a turn for the worse for the Mexicans, who are forced to flee over shouts of "Remember the Alamo" from the Texans and "¡Pinche mierda! Somebody grab my *pantalones*," from Santa Anna. The order was apparently ignored, as the general was captured the next day in nothing but a linen shirt and his undies. Emily West is then celebrated as a hero of the Texas Republic, and even today, patriotic, potbellied Texans gather around campfires to sing about the Yellow Rose of Texas.

What the hell does that anachronistic claptrap have to do with Emily West? Not much, really. Her actual life was one of unbelievable hardship and oppression, void of the romantic notion that she somehow sacrificed her body for the good of the Texas Republic. But, we love our myths, and so the Yellow Rose of Texas endures as a symbol of Texas independence and whoredom across the ages, while the song that bears her name also remains in circulation, serving as an inspiration for besotted yokels who see nothing wrong in uttering the word "darky."

JOROGUMO

PROFILE

DAY JOB: Spinster

CLAIM TO FAME: Infamous samurai groupie

THEATER OF OPERATIONS: Ancient Japan

Everybody knows that when a spider turns 400 years old, it is granted special powers. Specifically, the spider can shape-shift into a super-hot hussy, lure busters into her trailer, and rock a lute solo that so entrances her audience that they sit there grooving to her licks while she spins a spider web around them, eventually devouring her captive clients whenever she's feeling a little peckish. Sounds familiar, right? No? Well it would, if you were a three-centuries-old half-digested samurai, or perhaps a historian.

Jorogumo (literally "prostitute spider") was an alleged hustler during Japan's Edo period, and she's not for amateurs. Y'all just ain't ready. As legend has it, the Jorogumos' (there are a few scurrying about in the literature) primary concern is to marry a samurai, or at least eat one. If you were fortunate enough to possess samurai characteristics (loyalty, obedience, and perhaps a letter of recommendation) you were, unfortunately, fair game for Jorogumos. Here's how it would typically go down:

A samurai, fresh from some battle, comes upon a lake fed by a silver waterfall and squats to wash all the blood and crap off himself, take a drink of water, etc.

SAMURAI: All this killing. And for what? A stratospheric bill from Takeuchi's cleaners, that's what. Ah, me.

Jorogumo, in spider mode, creeps up on the samurai, showing an octet of thin naked legs. As described in legend, she "has a long, slender back, and a pointed rear end with long black limbs. Its thread is sticky like bird-lime and is tinged with yellow."

SAMURAI: Eek! A spider! Beat it!

The samurai flutters his hands wildly at Jorogumo, and then falls into the lake. The samurai's awkward attempt to right himself and regain his composure causes his metallic armor to clang. He sees Jorogumo, now in smoking super-model form.

SAMURAI: Oh my! Hi there. How un-bushido of me. Jesus, I feel like I could just die. In fact . . .

The samurai readies himself for *seppuku*, or ritual suicide.

JOROGUMO: Hey, not so fast, sweet cheeks. No need to go overboard.

SAMURAI: You don't think so?

JOROGUMO: Nah. C'mon, come over here and kick off your boots and armor. Let's party at my place. Get you out of that wet steel.

SAMURAI: (*pumps fist*) Yes!

JOROGUMO: (*rolls her eyes*) Dipshit.

Then it's back to Jorogumo's place for some heavy petting and lute playing. They make love for a few minutes, the samurai collapses in amorous exhaustion and in the morning, there's Jorogumo, back in spider mode, tying up loose ends in the web she's made to contain the samurai. The samurai tries to move, but he's stuck in the brilliant, gossamer thread.

SAMURAI: Damnit! You're that whore-spider everybody's been talking about.

JOROGUMO: (*laughs deviously*) Indeed.

SAMURAI: Perhaps we could compromise? Like you can spider out during the day, but then you whore-out again at night? What say?

In this moment, Jorogumo spits hot acid on the face of the samurai, sucking away his skin with a staccato, arachnoid slurp.

JOROGUMO: Eat your heart out, Peter Parker.

Jorogumo lets loose a happy belch, then plops down on her futon, fondling her throbbing lung slits and rearranging her epigastric plates, slick with love and digestive fluid.

Myths often feature grains of truth about nature, and the legend of Jorogumo is no different. Researchers at the Zoological Institute in Hamburg, Germany, performed experiments at a kind of spider orgy, discovering that a female spider normally enforces a "ten-second rule," which ensures her mate makes things snappy and gets the hell out before she loses patience and devours the boys, Jorogumo style.

NAAMAH

PROFILE

DAY JOB: Succubus

CLAIM TO FAME: Sacred angel of prostitution

THEATER OF OPERATIONS: Eden and surrounding area

The Zohar is the chief text of the Jewish Kabbalah, and it's typically seen as an allegorical or mystical interpretation of the Torah. Since the Torah has most of the good action (the Bible is more Merchant/Ivory, the Torah is all Michael Bay), you can imagine the Zohar gets pretty radical. And it is in the Zohar that we encounter Naamah, although to be fair, like most religions, there's cross-pollination all over the place, so the Zoharistas can't totally claim her, nor can anyone else (even the Satanists have tried to bring her in). That said, apologies if your religion claims Naamah as the queen of Tupperware or the wife of Criss Angel or some other damned thing. The point is, she's all over the place and she's coming to bonk your brains out, then take your soul, if not your bankroll.

First of all, Naamah is the daughter of Cain, whom you may remember from such holy episodes as "Killing My Brother with Agricultural Tongs" and "Wandering around East of Eden with a Note on My Head." And yes, Naamah was probably another fiery redhead, like her pops. You don't hear much about her, though, which is surprising, since she was, according to many sources, the most beautiful woman in the world, although we've heard that one enough to know better by now. And, she was a demon, which everyone can get bullish about.

In the Zohar, Naamah is portrayed as the wily witch of fuck—a little demon who creep into a man's room while the moon is waning, has sex with him in order to become pregnant so she can spawn more demons. No money changes hands, nothing tangible anyway like ducats or shekels, and it doesn't really seem like rape, so why is she considered a prostitute? Because ancient religious texts tells us so, that's why. This logic will frustrate a historian every time.

> *"To call a man an animal is to flatter him;*
> *he's a machine, a walking dildo."*
> —Valerie Solanas

In the Bible (Genesis 4:22), Naamah is the daughter of Lamech and Zillah. In the Talmud (Genesis Rabba 27), she's Noah's wife. What? Did you think Noah's wife was Emzara, the daughter of Rake'el? Complicating matters further, some scholars claim that Naamah was a male. An issue like this calls for primary sources, but the quest to locate the genesis of the Naamah prostitution myth in the holy texts is a fool's errand. She (or he, or it) is a vital virago in the racy retinue of sex workers, but like a succubus, it's there, you just can't feel the damage until the cock crows.

BIBLIOGRAPHY

BORN TO WHORE

Lao Ai

Sima, Qian, and Burton Watson. *Records of the Grand Historian*. Hong Kong: Columbia University Press, 1993.

Valeria Messalina

Juvenal. Satire VI. In *The Internet Ancient History Sourcebook*. Fordham University. *www.fordham.edu/halsall/ancient/juvenal-satvi.asp*

Shai Shahar

"Jessie." "Just a Gigolo." *Heeb* magazine, February 8, 2010.
"BIO." *ShaiShahar Homepage. www.shaishahar .com/bio.html*

Blanche Dumas

Gould, George M., and Walter L. Pyle. *Anomalies and Curiosities of Medicine: Being an Encyclopedic Collection of Rare and Extraordinary Cases, and of the Most Striking Instances of Abnormality in All Branches of Medicine and Surgery*. New York: Kaplan, 2009.

Xaviera Hollander

Hollander, Xaviera. *The Happy Hooker*. New York: HarperCollins World, 2002.

Madame de Pompadour

Mitford, Nancy. *Madame de Pompadour*. New York: New York Review of Books, 2001.
Darnton, Robert. "An Early Information Society: News and the Media in Eighteenth-Century Paris." *American Historical Review*, 105, no. 1. *www .historycooperative.org/journals/ahr/105.1/ ah000001.html*
Sidebar:
Smythe, Lillian C., and D'Argenteau Florimund Mercy. *The Guardian of Marie Antoinette: Letters from the Comte De Mercy-Argenteau, Austrian Ambassador to the Court of Versailles, to Marie Thérêse, Empress of Austria, 1770–1780*. London: Hutchinson, 1902.

The Spanish Barbara

Burchard, Johann, and F. L. Glaser. *Pope Alexander VI and His Court: Extracts from the Latin Diary of Johannes Burchardus*. New York: N.L. Brown, 1921.

Milly Cooper

"Milly Cooper, 96, Makes £50k a Year as an Escort" *Mail Online*, February 23, 2011. *www.dailymail.co.uk/news/article-1359769/ Milly-Cooper-96-makes-50k-year-escort.html*

The Painted Women

Berger, John. *The Success and Failure of Picasso*. New York: Vintage International, 1993.

Aspasia

Aristophanes. *Acharnians*. Perseus Digital
Library. *www.perseus.tufts.edu/hopper/text?do
c=Perseus:abo:tlg,0019,001:502*

Febo Di Poggio

Norton, Rictor. *My Dear Boy: Gay Love Letters
through the Centuries*. San Francisco:
Leyland Publications, 1998.
Squires, Nick. "Michelangelo's Last Judgment
Figures 'based on Male Prostitutes.'"
Telegraph, November 12, 2010. *www
.telegraph.co.uk/culture/art/art-news/8129566/
Michelangelos-Last-Judgment-figures-based-
on-male-prostitutes.html*

Bagoas

Chugg, Andrew. *Alexander's Lovers*. Raleigh,
NC: Lulu, 2006.
Plutarch. *The Age of Alexander*. London:
Penguin, 2010.
Rolfe, John C. (trans.). *Quintus Curtius: History
of Alexander*. Loeb Classical Library, 2
volumes. Cambridge, MA: Harvard
University Press, 1971.

Carol "The Scarlot Harlot" Leigh

Leigh, Carol, and Annie Sprinkle. *Unrepentant
Whore: The Collected Work of Scarlet Harlot*.
Long Beach, CA: Streamline, 2003.

Jeff Gannon

Aravosis, John. "A Man Called Jeff."
AMERICAblog News, February 14, 2005.
*http://www.americablog.com/2005/02/man-
called-jeff.html*
Kurtz, Howard. "Jeff Gannon Admits Past
'Mistakes,' Berates Critics." *Washington
Post* February 19, 2005.

Liu Rushi

Chang, Kang-i Sun, Haun Saussy, and
Charles Yim-tze Kwong. *Women Writers
of Traditional China: An Anthology of Poetry
and Criticism*. Stanford, CA: Stanford
University Press, 1999.
Stefanowska, A. D., Lily Xiao Hong Lee,
Sue Wiles, and Clara Wing-chung Ho.
*Biographical Dictionary of Chinese Women:
The Qing Period, 1644–1911*. Armonk,
NY: M.E. Sharpe, 1998.

Sally Salisbury

Walpole, Horace. *The Letters of Horace Walpole,
Fourth Earl of Orford*. Edited by Helen
Wrigley Toynbee and Paget Jackson
Toynbee. Oxford: Clarendon, 1903.
Linnane, Fergus. *London's Underworld: Three
Centuries of Vice and Crime*. London:
Robson Books, 2005.

Markus Bestin

Canning, Andrea, and Cole Kazdin. "Just a
Gigolo? Or the Rosa Parks of Sex Work?"
Nightline. ABC. Airdate: February 1,
2010.
Stadtmiller, Mandy. "My Night with a Prosti-
dude." *New York Post*, February 2, 2010.

Mineko Iwasaki

Kolsky, Alyssa. "Real Geisha, Real Story." *Time*,
November 25, 2002.
Sima, Calvin. "A Geisha, a Successful Novel
and a Lawsuit." *New York Times*, June 19,
2001.
Iwasaki, Mineko, with Rande Brown. *Geisha,
a Life*. New York: Washington Square,
2003.

Etta (Ethel) Place

Reeve, W. Paul. "Just Who Was the Outlaw Queen Etta Place?" Utah History to Go, *History Blazer*, May 1995. *www.historytogo. utah.gov/utah_chapters/pioneers_and_cowboys/ justwhowastheoutlawqueenettaplace.html*

Van Gelder, Lawrence. "Butch and Sundance, Maybe. But Etta?" *New York Times*, January 19, 1992.

Browne, Malcolm W. "Hunting 2 Outlaws, They Find Skeletons." *New York Times*, January 17, 1992.

Porfirio "Rubi" Rubirosa

Levy, Shawn. *The Last Playboy: The High Life of Porfirio Rubirosa*. New York: Fourth Estate, 2005.

Cohen, Gary. "The Legend of Rubirosa." *Vanity Fair*, November 2002.

Xue Susu

Berg, Daria. "Cultural Discourse On Xue Susu, A Courtesan in Late Ming China." *International Journal of Asian Studies* 6, no. 2 (2009): 171.

Cass, Victoria Baldwin. *Dangerous Women: Warriors, Grannies, and Geishas of the Ming*. Lanham, MD: Rowman & Littlefield, 1999.

Nell Gwyn

Anonymous. *The Life, Amours and Exploits of Nell Gwyn, The Fortunate Orange Girl*. London: Fairburn, 1820.

Pepys, Samuel. *The Diary of Samuel Pepys, from 1659 to 1669*. Edited by Richard Griffin Braybrooke. Whitefish, MT: Kessinger, 2004.

Beauclerk, Charles. *Nell Gwynn: A Biography*. London: Macmillan, 2005.

La Belle Otero

Castle, Charles. *La Belle Otero: The Last Great Courtesan*. London: M. Joseph, 1981.

"Suivez-Moi, Jeune Homme." *Time*, April 23, 1965.

Casanova

Casanova, Giacomo, and Gilberto Pizzamiglio. *The Story of My Life*. New York: Penguin, 2001.

PROMINENT PIMPS AND MANDARIN MADAMS

Jessie Williams and Edna Milton

McComb, David G. *Spare Time in Texas: Recreation and History in the Lone Star State*. Austin: University of Texas Press, 2008.

Cannon, Bill. *Texas: Land of Legend and Lore*. Dallas: Republic of Texas, 2004.

Watts, Marie W. *La Grange*. Charleston, SC: Arcadia, 2008.

Snoop Dogg

Touré. "Snoop Dogg: America's Most Loveable Pimp." *Rolling Stone*, November 28, 2006).

Sarracino, Carmine, and Kevin M. Scott. *The Porning of America: The Rise of Porn Culture, What It Means, and Where We Go from Here*. Boston, MA: Beacon, 2008.

Lulu White

Madden, Annette. *In Her Footsteps: 101
    Remarkable Black Women from the Queen
    of Sheba to Queen Latifah.* Berkeley, CA:
    Conari, 2000.

Scott, Andy. "Like Paris and London, Storyville
    District Had Its Own Unique Blue
    Book." *Storyville District. www
    .storyvilledistrictnola.com/bluebook.html*

Landau, Emily. "Lulu White." *Encyclopedia
    of Louisiana History, Culture and
    Community—KnowLA. www.knowla.org/
    entry.php?rec=856*

Heidi Fleiss

Heidi Fleiss: Hollywood Madam. Directed by
    Nick Broomfield. Metrodome, 2005,
    DVD.

Lalama, Pat. "Heidi Fleiss Opens 'Dirty'
    Laundromat." *FoxNews.com*, July 2, 2007.

Madame Gourdan

Bloch, Iwan, and James Bruce. *Marquis De
    Sade: His Life and Works.* New York:
    Castle, 1948.

Zacks, Richard. *History Laid Bare: Love, Sex,
    and Perversity from the Ancient Etruscans
    to Warren G. Harding.* London: Michael
    O'Mara, 1995.

Isaiah and Carol Reed

Isaiah Reed website. *www.isaiahreed.com*

James Lipton

Lipton, James. *Inside Inside.* New York: Dutton,
    2007.

"James Lipton Reveals He Once Worked
    as a Pimp in Paris." *Huffington Post.*

*www.huffingtonpost.com/2007/10/22/james-
    lipton-reveals-he-o_n_69443.html*

Wyatt Earp

"Wyatt Earp Was a Pimp in Peoria!"
    *TombstoneArizona.com www.clantongang
    .com/oldwest/pimpinpeoria.html*

McMurtry, Larry. "Back to the O.K. Corral."
    New York Review of Books, March 24,
    2005.

*Wyatt Earp History Page. www.wyattearp.net/
    peoria.html*

Sabrina Aset

Aset, Sabrina. "What Do You Call a Female
    Stud?" *Church of The Most High Goddess—
    Religion of the Goddesses. www.goddess.org/
    sabrina/index.html.*

Tamaki, Julie. "Santa Clarita / Antelope Valley:
    Attempt to Overturn Prostitution
    Laws Denied." *Los Angeles Times. http://
    articles.latimes.com/1994-03-16/local/
    me-34763_1_santa-clarita*

Alexander, Jack. "Church Uses Sex to Save
    Sinners." *Weekly World News*, March 16,
    1994: 17.

Kristin Davis

Kristin Davis website. *www.manhattanmadam
    .com/bio.*

Davis, Kristin. *The Manhattan Madam: Sex,
    Drugs, Scandal and Greed inside America's
    Most Successful Prostitution Ring.* Beverly,
    MA: Hollan, 2009.

Vyadro, Michelle. "Madam Kristin Davis
    on the Anniversary Eve of Spitzer's
    Downfall." *New York. http://nymag.com/
    daily/intel/2009/03/madam_kristen_davis_
    on_the_ann.html*

Dennis Hof

Rita Cosby Live and Direct. ABC. November 2005. Television transcript.

Mead, Rebecca. "American Pimp." *New Yorker*, April 23, 2001.

"Party Favors: An Interview with Cathouse's Dennis Hof." *FRED Entertainment*. www.asitecalledfred.com/2007/02/20/party-favors-an-interview-with-cathouses-dennis-hof/

Fillmore Slim

Fillmore Slim website. *www.fillmoreslimmusic.com*

American Pimp. Directed by Allen and Albert Hughes. Underworld Entertainment, 1999. DVD.

Chase, Colby. *A Place for Me: International Street Life to Spiritual Insight*. Bloomington, IN: Iuniverse Inc, 2010.

Polly Adler

Adler, Polly. *A House Is Not a Home*. Amherst: University of Massachusetts Press, 2006.

"Polly Adler's Brothel." *Dorothy Parker Society*. www.dorothyparker.com/dot32.htm

Rosebudd Bitterdose

Bitterdose, Rosebudd, *Rosebudd: The American Pimp*. Vallejo, CA: Real Fly Publishing, 2000.

Lemons, Stephen. "American Pimp." *Salon.com*, July 26, 2000. www.salon.com/2000/07/26/rosebudd/

"Pimptuition." *Suck*, October 25, 1999.

Jason Itzler

Italiano, Laura. "'King of All Pimps' Drops Trou, Cries, in Kooky Court Appearance." *New York Post*, September 9, 2011. www.nypost.com/p/news/local/manhattan/king_appearance_all_pimps_drops_YUAdkPqQB9ilQIX1L9I5nL

HUSTLING FOR A HIGHER CAUSE

Theodora

Procopius. *Secret History* (chapter 9). Translated by Richard Atwater. Ann Arbor: University of Michigan Press, 1961.

Herbert Huncke

Huncke, Herbert. *Guilty of Everything: The Autobiography of Herbert Huncke*. New York: Paragon House, 1990.

Kaufman, Alan. *The Outlaw Bible of American Poetry*. New York: Thunder's Mouth, 1999.

"Herbert Huncke." *American Museum of Beat Art*. www.beatmuseum.org/huncke/HerbertHuncke.html

Ginsberg, Allen. *The Book of Martyrdom and Artifice: First Journals and Poems, 1937–1952*. Edited by Juanita Lieberman-Plimpton, and Bill Morgan. Cambridge, MA: Da Capo, 2006.

Jean Genet

Genet, Jean. *Prisoner of Love*. Translated by Barbara Bray. New York: New York Review of Books, 2003.

Barber, Stephen. *Jean Genet*. London: Reaktion, 2004.

Ditmore, Melissa Hope. *Encyclopedia of Prostitution and Sex Work*. Westport, CT: Greenwood, 2006.

Annie Sprinkle

Annie Sprinkle website. *www.anniesprinkle.org*
Vitzthum, Virginia. "Annie Sprinkle Springs
    Forward." *Salon,* February 8, 2000.

Calamity Jane

McLaird, James D. *Calamity Jane: The Woman
    and the Legend.* Norman: University of
    Oklahoma, 2005.
DeArment, Robert K. *Deadly Dozen: Twelve
    Forgotten Gunfighters of the Old West, Volume
    2.* Norman: University of Oklahoma,
    2007.

Sally Stanford

Montanarelli, Lisa, and Ann Harrison. *Strange
    but True San Francisco: Tales of the City by
    the Bay.* Guilford, CT: Globe Pequot,
    2005.
"Sally Standford: San Francisco's Most
    Famous Madam." *Woman Around Town.*
    *www.womanaroundtown.com/sections/living-
    around/sally-standford-san-franciscos-most-
    famous-madam*
Stanford, Sally. *The Lady of the House.* New
    York: G. P. Putnam's Sons, 1966.

Debra Murphree

Harris, Art, and Berry, Jason, "Jimmy
    Swaggart's Secret Sex Life," *Penthouse,*
    July 1988.
Henneberger, Melinda. "Debra Murphree
    Joins Hall of Fleeting Fame." *Dallas
    Morning News,* June 12, 1988.

Raven O

Baker, Jonathan. "One Night with Raven O."
    OutinJersey.net. June 4, 2010. *www
    .outinjersey.net/index.php?option=com_*
content&view=article&id=743:one-
    night-with-raven-o&catid=41:special-
    features&Itemid=66
"Catching Up With Raven O." *New York Press,*
    February 18, 2010. *www.nypress.com*

Neal Cassady

Kaufman, Alan. *The Outlaw Bible of American
    Poetry.* New York: Thunder's Mouth,
    1999.
Ginsberg, Allen. *Collected Poems, 1947–1997.*
    New York: HarperPerennial, 2007.
Cochrane, Lauren. "Neal Cassady: Drug-
    taker. Bigamist. Family Man."
    Guardian, January 16, 2011. *www
    .guardian.co.uk/books/2011/jan/18/
    beat-poets-cassady-kerouac-ginsberg*
Plummer, William. *The Holy Goof: A Biography
    of Neal Cassady.* New York: Paragon
    House, 1990.

Belle De Jour

"Belle De Jour Drops Her Anonymity." *BBC
    News,* July 12, 2011.

Lupe Vélez

Jenkins, Henry. *The Wow Climax: Tracing the
    Emotional Impact of Popular Culture.* New
    York: New York University Press, 2007.
Anger, Kenneth. *Hollywood Babylon.* San
    Francisco: Straight Arrow, 1975.
Conner, Floyd. *Lupe Vélez and Her Lovers.* New
    York: Barricade, 1993.

Denham Fouts

Leddick, David. *Intimate Companions: A
    Triography of George Platt Lynes, Paul
    Cadmus, Lincoln Kirstein, and Their Circle.*
    New York: St. Martin's, 2000.

Trout, Christopher. "An Introduction
to Denham Fouts." *BUTT
Magazine*, February 23, 2010. *www
.buttmagazine.com/uncategorized/
an-introduction-to-denham-fouts/*

Scotty Bowers

Bowers, Scotty, and Lionel Friedberg. *Full
Service: My Adventures in Hollywood and
the Secret Sex Lives of the Stars.* New York:
Grove/Atlantic, 2012.
Debruge, Peter. "Bartender to Babylon."
Variety, June 22, 2006. *www.variety.com/
article/VR1117945748*

Quentin Crisp

"Crisp: The Naked Civil Servant." *BBC News*,
November 21, 1999.
Crisp, Quentin. *The Naked Civil Servant.* New
York: Holt, Rinehart and Winston, 1977.

Regina Savitskaya

Brokhin, Yuri. *Hustling on Gorky Street: Sex and
Crime in Russia Today.* New York: Dial,
1975.

Natalie "Natalia" McLennan

McLennan, Natalie. *The Price: My Rise and Fall
as Natalia, New York's #1 Escort.* Beverly
Hills, CA: Phoenix, 2008.
Jacobson, Mark. "The $2000 an-Hour
Woman." *New York*, July 10, 2005.
*www.nymag.com/nymetro/nightlife/sex/
features/12193/*

Ashley Dupré

Launier, Kimberly, and Katie Escherich.
"Ashley Dupré Exclusive: 'My Side of the
Story.'" ABC News. April 19, 2008.

Kovaleski, Serge F., and Ian Urbina. "For an
Aspiring Singer, a Harsher Spotlight."
New York Times, March 13, 2008.
Ashley Dupré website. *www.myspace.com/
ashleydupre*

Mike Jones

Jones, Mike, and Sam Gallegos. *I Had to Say
Something: The Art of Ted Haggard's Fall.*
New York: Seven Stories, 2007.
Harris, Dan. "Haggard Admits Buying Meth."
ABC News. *http://abcnews.go.com/GMA/
story?id=2626067*
Ted Haggard website. *www.tedhaggard.com/*

Ninon de L'Enclos

"Ninon De Lenclos." *Internet Encyclopedia of
Philosophy. www.iep.utm.edu/lenclos/*
Ditmore, Melissa Hope. *Encyclopedia of
Prostitution and Sex Work.* Westport, CT:
Greenwood, 2006.

Queen Semiramis

Ringdal, Nils Johan. *Love for Sale: A World
History of Prostitution.* New York: Grove,
2004.
Stronk, Jan P., and Ctesias. *Ctesias's Persian
History.* Düsseldorf: Wellem, 2010.
Brien, Harriet. *Queen Emma and the Vikings:
Power, Love, and Greed in Eleventh-Century
England.* New York: Bloomsbury, 2005.

Hawk Kincaid

Sterry, David Henry. "Hawk Kincaid, Ex-Rent
Boy, Spits Fierce @ Sex Worker Literati."
*www.davidhenrysterry.com/hawk-kincaid-ex-
rent-boy-spits-fierce-sex-worker-literati-2/*
Sterry, David, and R. J. Martin. *Hos, Hookers,
Call Girls, and Rent Boys: Professionals*

Writing on Life, Love, Money and Sex.
Brooklyn: Soft Skull, 2009.

SURPRISE STREETWALKERS

Al Pacino

"Al Pacino: Daily Dish." *SFGate*, October 12,
    2009.

Nancy Reagan

Kelley, Kitty. *Nancy Reagan: The Unauthorized
    Biography.* New York: Simon & Schuster,
    1991.
"As Not Seen on TV: The Rest of the Reagan
    Story." *New York Press*, December 9,
    2003.

Bob Dylan

Green, Andy. "Questions about Bob Dylan's
    Claim That He Was Once a Heroin
    Addict." *Rolling Stone*, May 23, 2011.

Cary Grant

Eliot, Marc. *Cary Grant: A Biography.* London:
    Aurum, 2008.

Malcolm X

Marable, Manning. *Malcolm X: A Life of
    Reinvention.* New York: Viking, 2011.
Tatchell, Peter. "Malcolm X—Gay Black
    Hero?" *Guardian* (London), May 19,
    2005, G2.

Marilyn Monroe

Churchwell, Sarah Bartlett. *The Many Lives of
    Marilyn Monroe.* New York: Henry Holt,
    2005.
Bell, Rachael. "Struggle to Stardom." Crime
    Library on TruTV.com. *TruTV.com*

Barbara Payton

Payton, Barbara. *I Am Not Ashamed.* Los
    Angeles: Holloway House, 1963.
Porter, Darwin. *Howard Hughes: Hell's Angel.*
    New York: Blood Moon, 2005.
O'Dowd, John. *Kiss Tomorrow Goodbye: The
    Barbara Payton Story.* Albany, GA: Bear
    Manor Media, 2006.

Clark Gable

Simcha. "Clark Gable: Gayer Than Gone with
    the Wind." *The Frisky*, April 1, 2008.
Bret, David. *Clark Gable: Tormented Star.* New
    York: Carroll & Graf, 2007.

Kurt Cobain

Sandford, Christopher. *Kurt Cobain.* London:
    Gollancz, 1995.
Norris, Chris. "The Ghost of Kurt Cobain."
    Spin, April 2, 2009.

Maureen McCormick

McCormick, Maureen. *Here's the Story:
    Surviving Marcia Brady and Finding My
    True Voice.* New York: William Morrow,
    2008.
Martinez, Jose. "'Brady Bunch' Star Maureen
    McCormick Admits to Swapping Sex
    for Cocaine in New Memoir." *New York
    Daily News*, October 13, 2008.

Roseanne Barr

Plotz, David. "Domestic Goddess Dethroned." *Slate*, May 18, 1997.

Sessums, Kevin. "Really Roseanne." *Vanity Fair*, February 1994.

Dee Dee Ramone

Keeley, Christopher. *Addict Out of the Dark and into the Light*. Bloomington, IN: Xlibris, 2007.

Ramone, Dee Dee. *Legend of a Rock Star: A Memoir*. New York: Thunder's Mouth Press, 2002.

Rupert Everett

Moir, Jan. "Rupert—Unleashed and Unloved." *Telegraph* (London), October 2, 2006.

Witchel, Alex. "Rupert Everett Is Not Having a Midlife Crisis." *New York Times Magazine*, February 18, 2009.

Maya Angelou

Lupton, Mary J. *Maya Angelou: A Critical Companion*. Westport, CT: Greenwood, 1998.

Angelou, Maya. *Gather Together in My Name*. New York: Random House, 1974.

Pete Doherty

"Doherty 'Forced Cat to Smoke Crack.'" *San Francisco Chronicle*, September 7, 2007.

Welsh, Pete. *Kids in the Riot: High and Low with The Libertines*. London: Omnibus, 2005.

Steve McQueen

Porter, Darwin. *Steve McQueen, King of Cool: Tales of a Lurid Life*. Staten Island, NY: Blood Moon Productions, 2009.

Eva Perón

Borges, Jorge. *Jorge Luis Borges: Conversations*. Jackson: University Press of Mississippi, 1998.

Thomas Jane

Schreffler, Laura. "'Hung' Star Thomas Jane Reveals He Was a Gay Prostitute." *Daily Mail* (London).

LaCapria, Kim. "Thomas Jane of 'Hung' Admits He Was a Real-Life Male Hooker." *Inquisitor*.

WHORES BEHAVING BADLY

Andrew Cunanan

Indiana, Gary. *Three Month Fever: The Andrew Cunanan Story*. New York: HarperCollinsPublishers, 1999.

Virginia Hill

Longrigg, Clare. *No Questions Asked: The Secret Life of Women in the Mob*. New York: Hyperion, 2004.

Edmonds, Andy. *Bugsy's Baby: The Secret Life of Mob Queen Virginia Hill*. Secaucus, NJ: Carol Publishing Group, 1993.

Khioniya Guseva

Moynahan, Brian. *Rasputin: The Saint Who Sinned*. New York: Da Capo Press, 1999.

Sada Abe

Johnston, William. *Geisha, Harlot, Strangler, Star: A Woman, Sex, and Morality in*

Modern Japan. New York: Columbia University Press, 2005.

Barbara Hoffman

Balousek, Marv. *50 Wisconsin Crimes of the Century*. Oregon, WI: Badger Books, 1997.

John Holmes

Sugar, Jennifer, and Jill C. Nelson. *John Holmes: A Life Measured in Inches*. Albany, GA: BearManor Media, 2008.

Sager, Mike. *Scary Monsters and Super Freaks: Stories of Sex, Drugs, Rock 'n' Roll, and Murder*. New York: Thunder's Mouth, 2003.

Gerda Munsinger

"Canada: The Munsinger Affair." *Time*, March 18, 1966.

"Politics, Sex and Gerda Munsinger." *CBC Archives*. http://archives.cbc.ca/politics/national_security/topics/69/

Mata Hari

Samuels, Diane. *The True Life Fiction of Mata Hari*. London: Nick Hern Books, 2002.

Coulson, Thomas. *Mata Hari: Courtesan and Spy*. New York: Harper & Brothers, 1930.

Crofton, Ian. *Traitors and Turncoats: Twenty Tales of Treason from Benedict Arnold to Ezra Pound*. London: Quercus, 2010.

La Malinche

Candelaria, Cordelia. "La Malinche, Feminist Prototype." *Frontiers: A Journal of Women Studies* 5, no. 2 (1980).

Las Goteras

Hilton, Perez. "Two Mexican Luchador Little People Wrestlers Murdered By Hookers!" *PerezHilton.com*

Associated Press. "Two Mexican Midget Wrestlers Killed by Fake Prostitutes." *Fox News*.

Valerie Solanas

"Valerie Jean Solanas (1936–88)" *Guardian* (London). www.guardian.co.uk/books/2005/mar/08/news4

"Original Review of Valerie Solanas' Long Lost Play 'Up Your Ass,' by Red Jordan Arobateau, from *The Spectator* Magazine, circa 2000." *Scribd.com*

Aileeen Wuornos

Vronsky, Peter. *Female Serial Killers*. New York: Berkley Books, 2007.

Philbin, Tom. *The Killer Book of Serial Killers*. Naperville, IL: Sourcebooks Trade, 2009.

Amanda Logue and Jason Andrews

Alfano, Sean. "Porn Actors Amanda Logue, Jason Andrews indicted for murder of Florida Tattoo Artist." *New York Daily News*, July 16, 2010.

Harwell, Drew. "Porn Stars Accused of Sex-Party Murder Shared Exploits on Twitter, Text Messages." *Tampa Bay Times/St. Pete Times*, June 27, 2010.

Yuen, Pat. "Web exclusive: Text msg between Amanda Logue and Jason Andrews prior to killing Dennis Abrahamsen." *Pat Yuen Blog*.

Mary "Bricktop" Jackson

Asbury, Herbert. *The French Quarter: An Informal History of the New Orleans Underworld*. New York: Knopf, 1936.

Fido, Martin. *The Chronicle of Crime: The Infamous Felons of Modern History and Their Hideous Crimes*. New York: Carroll & Graf, 1993.

Delia Swift (Bridget Fury)

Fido, Martin. *The Chronicle of Crime: The Infamous Felons of Modern History and Their Hideous Crimes*. New York: Carroll & Graf, 1993.

Asbury, Herbert. *The French Quarter: An Informal History of the New Orleans Underworld*. New York: Knopf, 1936.

Schafer, Judith Kelleher. *Brothels, Depravity, and Abandoned Women: Illegal Sex in Antebellum New Orleans*. Baton Rouge: Louisiana State University Press, 2009.

THE MAGICAL MYSTERY WHORES

The Whore of Babylon

The Bible. Authorized King James Version; (Revelation 17:5).

Shamhat

Sandars, N. K., (trans.). *The Epic of Gilgamesh*. New York: Penguin Books, 1972.

Dalley, Stephanie. *Myths from Mesopotamia: Creation, the Flood, Gilgamesh and Others*. Revised edition. Oxford: Oxford University Press, 2000.

Shoham, Giora. *The Mytho-Empiricism of Gnosticism*. Brighton, UK: Sussex Academic Press, 2003.

Molly Malone

Kilfeather, Siobhán Marie. *Dublin: A Cultural History*. New York: Oxford University Press, 2005.

Yorkston, James. "*Cockles and Mussels, or Molly Malone*" (comic song [1884]).

Tiresias

Mann, Eles. *The Image in the Mirror*. Bloomington, IN: AuthorHouse, 2005.

Warner, Marina. *Monuments and Maidens*. Berkeley: University of California Press, 1985.

Hathaway, Nancy. *The Friendly Guide to Mythology*. New York: Penguin Books, 2002.

Oshun

Glazier, Stephen. *The Encyclopedia of African and African-American Religions*. New York: Routledge, 2001.

Mary Magdalene

The Bible. Authorized King James Version (Luke 7–8).

Phryne

Cooper, Craig. "Hyperides and the Trial of Phryne." *Phoenix* 49, no. 4 (Winter, 1995): 303–18.

Naiden, F. S. *Ancient Supplication*. Oxford: Oxford University Press, 2009.

Athenaeus. *The Deipnosophists*. Cambridge, MA: Harvard University Press, 1928.

Rahab
The Bible. Authorized King James Version (Joshua 2:9–13).

The Yellow Rose of Texas
Harris, Trudier, "The Yellow Rose of Texas": A Different Cultural View. *Callaloo* 20, no. 1 (Winter, 1997): 8–19.

Jorogumo
"Jorogumo." *Wikipedia. http://en.wikipedia.org/wiki/Jor%C5%8Dgumo*
Tada, Katsumi, and Natsuhiko Kyōgoku. *Deciphering the Hundred Demons.* Tokyo: Kodansha, 2006.

Naamah
Zohar. *Zohar: The Book of Enlightenment.* New York: Paulist Press, 1983.

SIDEBARS

www.sexworldrecords.com
www.oddee.com/item_97082.aspx
www.thedailyshow.com/watch/tue-march-2-2010/jonah-falcon-needs-a-job
www.womenintheancientworld.com/medicine%20in%20ancient%20egypt.htm
www.martinfrost.ws/htmlfiles/oct2008/banquet-chestnuts.html
www.theregister.co.uk/2007/10/11/autopsy_controversy/
www.universitypressclub.com/archive/2010/02/oxford-english-dictionary-outs-gay-princeton/
www.nytimes.com/1996/02/20/movies/play-a-hooker-and-win-an-oscar.html
www.guardian.co.uk/music/2006/nov/12/popandrock8
www.artichoke-festival.org/
www.permanentrevolution.net/entry/1556
www.babble.com/pregnancy/giving-birth/pelvic-floor-muscles-exercise-vaginal-birth/?page=6
www.intimatemedicine.com/sex-in-society/sexy-language/
www.ex-designz.net/encyclopedia.asp
www.autopederasty.blogspot.com/2011/03/yes-its-posibleand-its-fantastic.html#comment-form
http://en.wikipedia.org/wiki/Diogenes_of_Sinope
www.airlinecreditcards.com/travelhacker/embracing-the-taboo-worlds-top-red-light-districts/
www.gaylife.about.com/cs/mentalhealth1/p/roy.htm
www.esquire.com/features/what-ive-learned/learned-siegfriend-roy-0800
listverse.com/2009/05/10/10-incredibly-bizarre-sexual-practices/
www.nytimes.com/2007/04/18/dining/18nake.html
www.amazon.com/Mondo-Lucha-Go-Go-Honorable-Wrestling/dp/0060855835
www.telegraph.co.uk/culture/art/art-news/8129566/Michelangelos-Last-Judgment-figures-based-on-male-prostitutes.html
www.thisislondon.co.uk/standard/article-23781038-91-blunders-by-secret-service.do
www.dailykos.com/story/2005/05/16/114393/-White-House,-Secret-Service-Stories-on-Gannon-Guckert-Passes-Dont-Match
www.abcnews.go.com/blogs/politics/2007/04/white_house_sec/
www.nybooks.com/articles/archives/2002/sep/26/the-secret-intelligence-wars/?pagination=false
www.wedding.theknot.com/wedding-planning/wedding-customs/articles/50-wedding-traditions-superstitions-facts-trivia.aspx
www.starpulse.com/news/index.php/2010/02/26/courtney_love_used_hookers_to_get_drug

www.theatlantic.com/magazine/archive/2009/06/
    what-makes-us-happy/7439/
www.telegraph.co.uk/technology/news/8848476/
    Man-gets-smartphone-dock-built-into-
    prosthetic-arm.html
www.cianmolloy.ie/cian_book.html
www.thepint.ie/historyofdrinking.aspx
www.musingsoverapint.com/2008/02/st-brigid-of-
    ireland.html
www.newadvent.org/cathen/02784b.htm
www.papuaweb.org/dlib/irian/index.html
www.thecrimereport.org/news/inside-criminal-
    justice/you-say-loitering-for-sex-i-say-just-
    hanging-out
www.enotes.com/topic/Storyville

ACKNOWLEDGMENTS

I would like first to offer my profound gratitude to my agent, Jon Sternfeld, whose prodding, cynical, impatient, and touchy nature is matched only by his kindness, loyalty, and unyielding support. I wish you all the best in your new career with the red pen—you've already proven to be a tremendous editor of this book. Many thanks to the gang at Adams Media: Meredith O'Hayre, for the bunnies, rainbows, and brilliant suggestions and to Brendan O'Neill for believing in me—twice—and helping *Whore Stories* take flight. Thanks also to my parents, whose wonderful suggestions, constant whore jokes/puns/innuendo, and source material were invaluable, and a little weird. Thanks in particular to my mother, bless her, for her tireless, thoughtful, and stoic reading of this raucous thing, along with her unequaled editing expertise and invaluable insights. And finally, my love, thanks and respect to the magnificent MHS, forever.

INDEX

ABOUT THE AUTHOR

Tyler Stoddard Smith's writing has been featured in *UTNE Reader, McSweeney's, Esquire, Best American Fantasy*, and *The Morning News*, among others. He is also a regular contributor at *The Nervous Breakdown* and an associate editor at *The Big Jewel*. He lives in Austin, Texas. Visit his website: *tylerstoddardsmith.wordpress.com* and follow him on Twitter: *@Tyler_stoddard*.